FRANK SINATRA

JOHN HOWLETT

COURAGE BOOKS

Philadelphia, Pennsylvania

This edition published by arrangement with Plexus Publishing Limited, London. Text Copyright © 1980 by John Howlett. Copyright © 1980 by Plexus Publishing Limited. Quotation from *The Moon's A Balloon* by David Niven, © 1975 by David Niven, Hamish Hamilton Limited, London.

Canadian representatives: General Publishing Co. Ltd., 30 Lesmill Road, Don Mills, Ontario M3B 2T6. International representatives: Kaiman & Polon, Inc., 2175 Lemoine Avenue, Fort Lee, New Jersey 07024.

9   8   7   6   5   4   3   2   1
The digit on the right indicates the number of this printing.

Library of Congress Cataloging in Publication Data:
Howlett, John, 1940-   , Frank Sinatra. Originally published: New York: Simon & Schuster, ©1979. Includes index. 1. Sinatra, Frank, 1915-   , 2. Singers — United States — Biography. 3. Moving-picture actors and actresses — United States — Biography. I. Title.
ML420.S565H7 1985 784.5'0092'4 [B] 85-30886

ISBN 0-89471-433-3 (Cloth)

Book designed by Chris Lower. Jacket design by Chris Lower, painting by Bill Prosser.

This book can be ordered by mail from the publisher. Please include $1.00 postage and handling for each copy. *But try your bookstore first!*

an imprint of
Running Press Book Publishers, 125 South 22nd Street, Philadelphia, Pennsylvania 19103.

CONTENTS

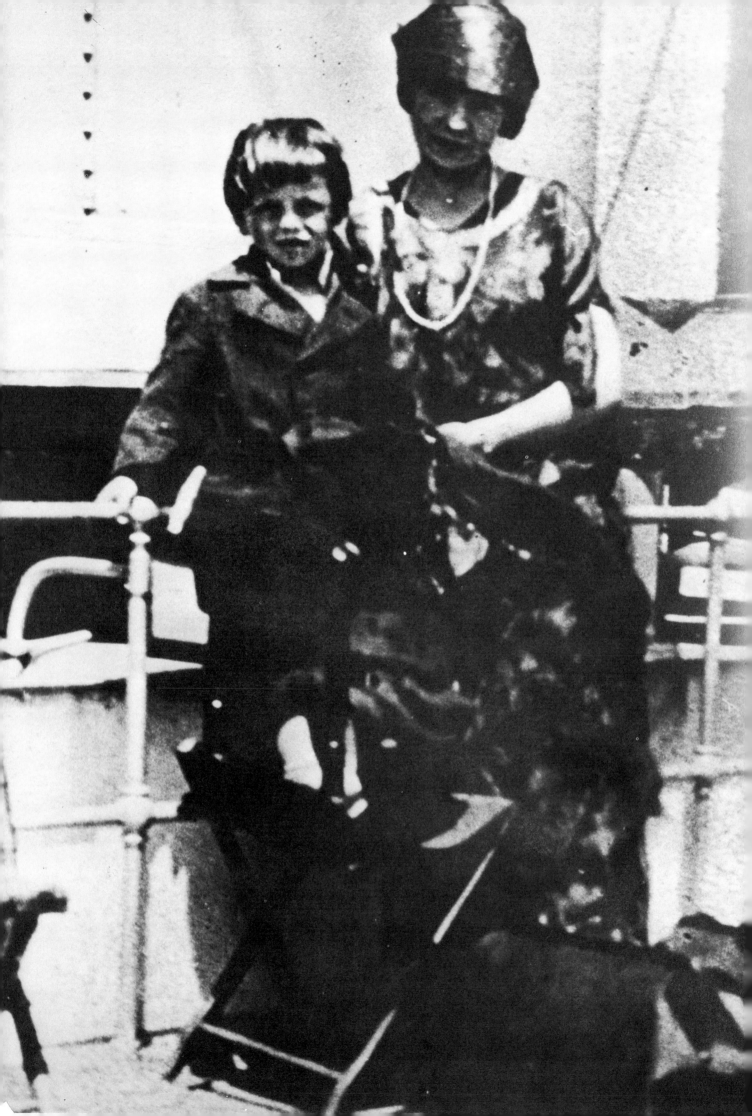

1 THE EARLY YEARS 1915-1939

Frank Sinatra was born into an Italian Family in the seaport community of Hoboken, with its sprawl of docks and rail yards along the Hudson river on the outskirts of Jersey City. The families of both his parents had come originally from other urban waterfronts, Natalie Garavanti from Genoa, in North Italy, and Antony Martin Sinatra from Catania, under the shadow of Mount Etna on the east coast of Sicily. They had been married six years when their eldest, and, as it turned out, only child was born on a snowy December day in 1915.

The baby was huge and the birth difficult. The thirteen pound monster was dragged out with clumsy forceps, one side of his face bleeding and an ear all but torn off. The doctor gave him up for lost and concentrated on trying to save the mother's life. It was Frank Sinatra's grandmother, Rosa Garavanti, who picked up the infant and held it under a cold tap until it choked, yelled and breathed.

The physical scars of that birth remain to this day and the emotional trauma may have influenced the insecurities of what was to become a solitary childhood. The circumstances of birth were strangely consistent with a life and career that were to fluctuate between the extremes of vulnerability and survival. Apparently the story of his 'miracle' birth was often repeated to the young boy. The incentive already existed for him to go out and do something special with himself, and from the very beginning he was set apart from the rough and tumble kids up and down the street. 'I wanted a girl,' Dolly Sinatra was to say many years later. 'I bought a lot of pink clothes when Frank was born. I didn't care. I dressed him in pink anyway. Later, I got my mother to make him Lord Fauntleroy suits.'

The Sinatras lived modestly in a frame-house neighbourhood. Martin Sinatra had been a professional boxer, a bantam-weight fighting under the, necessarily, Irish name of Marty O'Brien, usually a support billing on the fight programmes of New Jersey or Manhattan. Dolly Sinatra had trained as a nurse, working for public organizations in her neighbourhood where she was already known as an organizer of petition and protest.

By the time of Frank Sinatra's birth the First World War was beginning to impinge on American industrial life. While Europe was bleeding away a generation of

The young Frank with his mother Dolly. Dolly was to have a lasting influence on her only son until her death in 1977.

young men at Verdun and on the Somme, the Hoboken shipbuilders began to gear up for war contracts, replacing losses from the U-boat campaign in the Atlantic. Dolly Sinatra used her local contacts to find work for her husband as a boilermaker in the shipyards.

When war work ended and the yards began to shed their extra men, the Sinatras used family money to buy one of the many local taverns. Prohibition was on its way and, whether he was aware of it or not at the time, Frank Sinatra spent some of his childhood in the atmosphere of the early speakeasies, the small-time mobster operations that were to become the foundation of so much of American organized crime and corruption. The gangster years were beginning and Sinatra was to know them from their small-café, small-town origins, long before his teenage adulation of the 'Scarface' image, as portrayed by Paul Muni or Edward G. Robinson.

If the prohibition laws conditioned one part of his childhood world, the Ratification of Article XIX at the end of the war governed the pattern of his family life. American women had won themselves the right to vote and Dolly Sinatra's political activities became an almost full-time concern. She had already been involved with the local Democrat Party and was now given an official ward post at the head of the Italian community in Hoboken. Young Frank Albert began to see less and less of his mother and spent most of his time either with his maternal grandmother, Rosa Garavanti, in her local grocery store, or later, with an elderly Jewish neighbour, Mrs Goldberg.

Dolly Sinatra's political activities advanced the family. Martin Sinatra was given a post in the fire station (where he eventually worked his way up to the rank of captain) and the family moved into better class housing. In fact the traditional poverty and hardship with which publicists later tried to colour Sinatra's childhood were never strictly true. In the context of the time and the place, the Sinatras lived well enough. If the boy suffered, it was from an emotional rather than material deprivation and, indeed, psychiatrists have often enough traced his chronic insecurities to the ambitious but absentee mother of his childhood and adolescence, his single-minded ambition to the street corner dreaming of an only and lonely child. 'I never had any brothers or sisters,' Sinatra later explained. 'In my neighbourhood every family had twelve kids and they fought constantly. But whenever there was a beef or a party, you never saw such closeness.' The Italian and Jewish families living around him in Hoboken were large dynasties not only

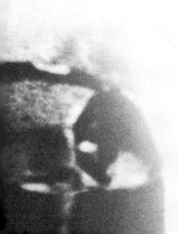

of brothers and sisters, but of uncles and aunts, cousins and nephews. He may have watched them with envy, for in later years he would build and carefully tend his own families: his family of first wife and children that was to survive thirty years of 'broads' and three further marriages; and his families of 'buddies', the 'Varsity', the 'rat-packs' and the 'clans', ever changing, but as essential to him as his public and his performing.

Childhood friendships never seemed to last long in the street-gang atmosphere of Hoboken and even in those early days Sinatra was something of a figure apart to his contemporaries. For one thing he was better dressed than the others, encouraged or obliged by an image-conscious mother. *La bella figura* is important to any Italian, but in those years of economic uncertainty, dress and cleanliness were the boundary lines between respectability and destitution. They would remain life-long obsessions for Sinatra.

The Hoboken school-kid enjoyed other privileges over his friends. He would often have money in his pocket, or a pass to a local swimming pool. He always shared his luck and was more often than not disappointed in the feedback from his generosity. He learned early on that there are limits to friendship bought with money or favours. One day he let a group of friends into the swimming pool by smuggling his pass over the fence. But when they were caught, the friends ran off and left Frank to take the rap. 'I was hurt,' Sinatra said, 'but I was hurting from something more. All those times I got those guys into the pool! When I am getting clobbered, not one of them comes to help me. They just—scramsville.' That was not behaviour consistent with the young Sinatra's ideas of friendship and loyalty. His quiet-spoken father had passed down to him the Sicilian ethic of friendship, the code of the *galant'uomo* and it was to that code that the young Sinatra began to adjust his expectations. The code teaches generosity in friendships and patronage, but demands in return loyalty and, above all, respect. As a boy on the streets Frank Sinatra often had to fight for that respect in a context that was

usually racial. Irish, Italian, Jewish and Negro working class eyed each other with envy or suspicion, and the angry hurt pride of a skinny kid who had been called 'wop' or 'dirty guinea' led Sinatra into his first and usually unsuccessful fist-fights. The Italians were on the defensive. Working their way up from the bottom of the pile, they had been tarred or scarred by the first of the anti-Red witch hunts that had put a lot of Italian anarchists and communists behind bars in a Federal campaign that was to climax in the executions of Sacco and Vanzetti. An early brush with the cops of Jersey City gave Sinatra an instinctive suspicion and dislike of authority, and the street fights in Hoboken left him with a hatred of racial prejudice that would govern his later political activity. Perhaps too much of the beaten, angry 'skinny guinea' survived in the show-biz King who always surrounded himself with heavy body-guards—strange needs for the boy who might himself have become a bantam-weight pro. Father and Uncle Domenico 'Babe Sieger' Garavanti had both been boxers and Sinatra was taught the basics of self-defence from an early age. Later, as a teenager, he trained in gyms. The fight game was the one traditional

if precarious way to climb out of those East Coast backstreets. No one believed the skinny kid could actually sing his way to fame and fortune.

Sinatra's schooldays at the David E. Rue Junior High were undistinguished and unspectacular. He won no prizes either in the classroom or as a sportsman. He was not expelled, as has sometimes been claimed, but graduated at fifteen years of age into the Demarest High School. Notwithstanding the ambitions of his mother, he left high school in his sophomore year, bored with schooling, impatient to move on. His mother had hoped he would go on to the Stevens Institute of Technology and, indeed, he did enrol briefly in the Drake Business School. But he was by then already singing, his wilder ambitions beginning to form. Though he worked for a time loading delivery trucks at the *Jersey Journal*, most of his time was spent learning songs off the radio. The skyline of Manhattan across the Hudson river was giving him big ideas.

Dolly Sinatra's brother, Uncle Domenico Garavanti, was the first to encourage the boy in a musical direction. 'All the talent Frank got, he got from my father,' Dom Garavanti later said. 'Pop had a tremendous voice, he was a great singer. I remember when Frank was just a kid, all the relatives used to come out from Brooklyn and New York on a Sunday. There'd be lots of food and wine and Pop would sing. Dolly, too, used to sing at weddings and other family affairs. Like in most Italian families in those days, Frank just grew up with a lot of music around him, good music, real music.' Uncle Dom Garavanti bought Frank a ukelele for the boy's fifteenth birthday and to everyone's surprise the young Sinatra mastered enough chord technique to strum an accompaniment to the Italian songs he heard at family gatherings. He may not have persuaded friends or relatives, but he was convincing himself that he had a voice, singing on the sidewalks in the evenings, or at beach parties on summer holidays with relatives. He was ready for the radio when it arrived in the Sinatra home, picking up the popular songs and learning them well enough to sing at his first 'concerts'.

The boy's singing was for the moment tolerated in the family as a hobby. His early public performances were even arranged by his mother, one or two dollar gigs at the weekly gatherings of the Hoboken Sicilian Cultural League, or at the Democrat Party meetings. At high school Sinatra had made himself responsible for the hiring of musicians for school dances and it was there that he had his first limited experience of singing with a band. His status as paymaster gave him the privilege of standing up in front of the band a couple of

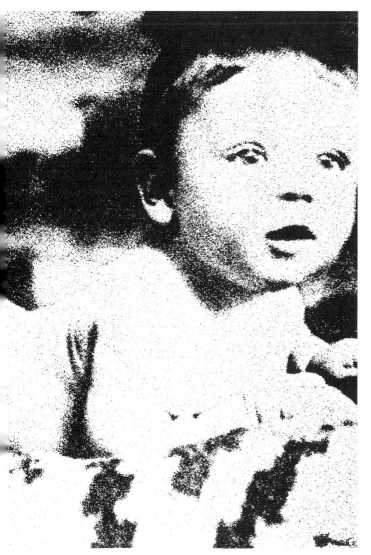

Far left: Frank Sinatra's parents.
Left: An early photograph of Francis Albert Sinatra.

7

times during the evening to sing a number with them.

A schoolfriend recalls: 'He didn't seem nothing more than a bag of bones in a padded jacket, but he was already making the girls turn round and watch him when he was up there on the platform. He had a kind of style.'

Formative years indeed—and in a sense Frank Sinatra belonged to a generation of pioneers. Live, non-electronic music in the dance halls was the be-all and end-all for the kids in the late 1920s and popular music was predominantly instrumental. There were few vocalists who could dominate large theatres or clubs without the benefits of amplification. Al Jolson, Joe Howard, Fanny Brice, Eddie Leonard, Arthur Tracy, Belle Baker, were the voices Sinatra might have heard on record. But he was only just into his teens when the scene began to change. In 1927 the first of the radio networks, NBC, opened coast-to-coast broadcasting. CBS followed a year later and the national, as opposed to state or city, audience was created, giving vocalists the exposure and the intimate listening conditions denied them by the big theatre halls. Gene Austin was the first to celebrate this new world, selling a million records of his 'My Blue Heaven'. Vying with him were Russ Colombo and Will Osborne and, above all, Rudy Vallee who was the first male vocalist to complement his singing with a 'stage' presence. He became the first resident host of a network variety show and, as a personality—'Heigh ho everybody!'—must have influenced not only the young Sinatra, but more immediately, the prince-elect of the 1930s, Bing Crosby. Vocalists were on their way and although the big bands continued to dominate popular music until the end of the Second World War, the best known tunes were usually vocal numbers with catch lines—'Just One More Chance', 'I've Found a Million Dollar Baby'—and the bands were having to focus more attention on their vocalist solos or groups.

One March evening in 1933 the eighteen-year-old Sinatra took his girfriend, Nancy Barbato, to hear Bing Crosby in a Jersey City vaudeville. He left the Loews Journal Square Theatre, turned to Nancy and told her, 'I'm going to be a singer.' And back home that evening he made the same statement of intent to his parents. 'I saw Bing Crosby tonight and I've got to be a singer.' The performance had excited, but not overawed him. He was confident he could hold his own with the best of them. His girlfriend, and wife-to-be, agreed with him.

It was new territory for the hopeful and the unknown. There were no demo discs or tapes in those days; no company talent scouts or ambitious young managers. Initial recognition might come from an amateur talent contest, exposure from local radio station, income from the dance halls or roadhouses. The pop singer with his own group was unknown. At any level the vocalist needed musicians, and the ultimate ambition was a contract with one of the big bands. It was a long, hard road the eighteen-year-old had decided to follow, and there were no lucky breaks to make those early years any easier.

'My old man thought that anyone who wanted to go into the music business must be a bum,' Sinatra said many years later. 'So I picked up and left home for New York.' Nor was Frank's mother ever convinced. She had already objected to the pictures of Bing Crosby on her son's bedroom wall and it was another two or three years before she gave up trying to persuade him back into higher education, or into a job she might have considered respectable. But at least she helped out with the $65 needed for a secondhand portable public address system. For most of the next six years of his life, Frank Sinatra was dragging the rhinestone studded case of microphone and loudspeaker round from ballrooms to clubs, playing as many dates as he could muster for the three or four dollar fee he claimed.

First recognition, as such, came from a local talent contest in a Jersey City theatre. Amateur contests were a regular feature of vaudeville and many of the theatres interlinked their competitions. Thus Sinatra's win in Jersey City qualified him for another contest over the river on Manhattan. This first New York concert was one of the more frightening of his early

Below: Frank at ten years. Right: Ten years later, 'Frankie Boy' had polished up his image.

appearances. The audience controlled the duration of the performances, yelling for the 'hook' if someone's singing or clowning did not come up to their expected standards. The 'hook' was a long, curved pole used to pull the failures off stage. Many years later Sinatra remembered the moment of his first New York stage appearance. 'I'm standing there shaking, figuring that the moment they announce a guy from Hoboken, he's dead!' But Sinatra survived his allotted time without cat-calls or 'hook'—though he failed to pick up any of the prizes which might have led him to a radio contest or into the more important theatres.

Broadway was already becoming familiar to the emaciated, bright-eyed kid from Hoboken. One of his regular chores was the trudge from music publisher to music publisher, trying to talk the free music sheets and orchestrations out of them. It was his success at this game that led him to some of his better dates with local bands, for his 'library' of music soon had a reputation among less well-endowed musicians. Professionals or amateurs, good or bad, he would sing with them all and if they did nothing to advance his career he was at least accumulating experience. The variety of gigs with a variety of orchestras was teaching the

young Sinatra the tricks of voice survival against the big band noise—not much finesse in those early days, but at least the knowledge of which phrases and notes to hit hard and how to draw attention away from the dance floor or the band leader. The 'mike' technique was there from the beginning, that particular stance of a slight and vulnerable young man holding onto the microphone stand as though it was the only prop keeping him up on his feet.

The P.A. system and the music sheets kept him going through eighteen months. Then the parental gift of a car made him mobile and gave him another 'plus' as far as the other musicians were concerned. He had become friendly with one of the local singing groups, a trio of Italian truck-drivers who called themselves 'The Three Flashes'—Jimmy Petrozelli, Patty Principe and Fred Tamburro. The trio had a regular gig at a local roadhouse and Sinatra hung around them like a camp follower. Once or twice he sang with them. Mostly he just chauffeured them in his car. But they were Italian and they were from Hoboken. When they were given a break, 'Frankie Boy' as they called him, knew how to apply a bit of pressure. The Three Flashes had been asked by a local promoter to make some tests for one of the more popular and influential talent-shows—the Major Bowes Amateur Hour. The young Sinatra was formally auditioned by the trio and taken on as a fourth member just before the tests and Fred Tamburro admitted later that the audition had been arranged after pressure applied by influential local figures—in particular Dolly Sinatra and the boss of the local Democrat Party. Not that the graft did anything but improve the Three Flashes. As fourth Flash, Sinatra made lead singer inside a week and by the time they gathered to rehearse the Major Bowes show it was clear to them all that the skinny kid was their number one attraction.

Bowes renamed the quartet 'The Hoboken Four' and their first public performance took place at the Capitol Theatre in New York on 8 September, 1935. The show was wired into one of the local radio stations and the performance was well enough received by both theatre and radio audiences for the Major to sign them up as part of his travelling circus. Two months short of his twentieth birthday Frank Sinatra went on the road for the first time—his salary, $50 a week plus meals.

It was not a happy time—in a sense a formatively negative experience. The tight schedules were normal enough, inescapable if the company was to make good profits for the Major. But expenses were low and the *esprit de corps* accordingly muted. The skinny kid singer was an easy fall-guy for two of the three trucker co-stars who resented his talent on stage or his easy ways with the ladies. Often he was abused; sometimes beaten up. And at other times he would manage to take the mickey himself in his own particular way. Even in those early days he was never specially tolerant of the mediocre or the lazy.

But as a singing personality he did not disappoint either his sponsor or himself. Backstage after any of the shows in any of the cities he was the centre of attraction for the girls who wanted autographs—or something more. Even on the company bus he could create his magic in the wee, small hours. One of the instrumentalists later remembered: 'When people were fed up with eating or drinking or necking or reading or whatever, then Frankie Boy would start singing from somewhere down the back and everyone would shut up like someone turned the volume down. He wouldn't even need a guitar or a harmonica. He'd just cut clean into a song. No ribbing. No harmonizing. Just everyone listening. Even then he had the magic, whether the bums liked it or not.'

The bums didn't like it. Especially, it seems, those two of the original Three Flashes. Once, halfway across the continent, a weary Sinatra leaned down the counter at a roadhouse and stage-whispered to the third of the Flashes: 'Why don't you hit me too, and make it unanimous?'

Another survivor of that troupe recalls the night when the tensions found their way onto the stage: 'They were singing and one guy in the group—the one who didn't lean on Frank—started to giggle. He caught himself after a while and got back into the harmony but then Frank started it. Pretty soon they were all giggling and the curtain had to be rung down. They went back to their dressing-room and waited for Major Bowes to come and bawl them out. One of the group began yelling at Frank: "What are you, crazy?" Frank was still smiling about it all and he said, "I can't help it, that's my sense of humour." I'll never forget it. Frank was sitting on an old wardrobe trunk, one leg crossed over the other. One of the guys who always beat him rushed over, screaming "Well, here's my sense of humour," and he let Frank have a solid right that sent him flying off his trunk and onto the floor in a heap. Frank picked himself up, looked at the guy, then just turned and walked out. He went back to Hoboken a few days later.'

But it wasn't the abuse or the beatings that finally made the skinny kid give up the tour. He put up with it all while he could see it leading somewhere—west to the coast, Burbank and Hollywood, dropping big enough splashes in little ponds on the way across. It was only when the troupe arrived in California that Sinatra lost heart. Set up against the big-time of the night clubs and cinema, he could see only too clearly the nowhere he was heading for with the amateurs of the Major Bowes troupe. He gave up the $50 rip-off and set off back home to pick up the trudge where he left off, in the clubs and local radio stations of New Jersey and Manhattan.

In fact he dropped only $10 on his first salary back

home. The Union was a club much patronized by the Hoboken Sicilian Cultural League. They took on Dolly Sinatra's son for $40 a week while he found his feet again in the rough and tumble of clubs, dance halls and above all, local radio and night club hustlers on 52nd Street.

Sinatra had seen Crosby and Vallee make their nationwide names on the radio networks and he had experienced the dead-end of small-time theatre touring. The way up was clear enough to him, graduation from the local radios to the networks and a nationwide audience, with vaudeville and the big theatres as the cream on top of the cake.

He started courting the radio offices, plugging himself, offering to sing for free whenever they had a vacant spot. Most of his early radio breaks were on WNEW, though he went on steadily increasing his coverage until his voice could be heard almost any time of night and day on one or other of the local stations. And singing for free it turned out to be. Only WAAT of Newark ever paid him a fee—the 70 cents bus fare from home to studio.

It was the lack of radio facilities that prompted him to give up his job at the Union Club. The club had refused to wire up for a radio link and having issued them with an ultimatum, Sinatra walked out on his weekly salary into the most difficult months of his slow climb. Every day he was hustling the radio stations, pushing for auditions with any band looking for a vocalist. Had he been less convinced of his own talent, this was the time he might have given up hope. Girlfriend Nancy helped him out, not only with encouragement, but sometimes, said later publicists, with money from her secretary's pay packet. The two of them had already been courting for years, though for Dolly Sinatra the Barbato family did not come up to her hopes of a 'good' marriage. The daughter of a plasterer in Jersey City, Nancy Barbato was both Italian and Catholic, but not outstanding enough for Mrs Sinatra Snr. The brown-eyed, dark haired girl was

too quiet, apparently unambitious, unsophisticated. Notwithstanding the opinions of her future mother-in-law, this quiet girl gave Frank and emotional security he had never previously known. 'In Nancy,' he said 'I found beauty, warmth and understanding. Being with her was my only escape from what seemed a grim world. All I knew up to that time were tough kids on street corners, gang-fights, and parents who were always busy trying to make money. . .'

But it was a busy parent who may well have helped manoeuvre Sinatra's next break. For all her lack of enthusiasm about Frank's singing, Dolly Sinatra made sure that every good Democrat in the New Jersey party was aware of her son's ambitions. When a vacancy occurred in a local roadhouse—the Rustic Cabin on Route 9W near Alpine, N.J., Sinatra was offered a regular evening job as compere and singer. His work at the Cabin was hard at $15 a week, but at least he had something of a band to sing with and, even more important, a wire into local radio stations. He may not yet have built up a regular audience of any importance, but his name and his face were becoming familiar around the radio offices and the publishing houses on Broadway and 52nd Street. The ever-important collection of songs and music—the 'orks' and 'freebies'—had to be kept up to date and with fifteen or so local radio spots each week, the song-pluggers were beginning to take him seriously. One such front man who took a liking to the 'wild-eyed bag-of-bones' was Sinatra's manager-to-be, Hank Sanicola. A tough

Top left: Frank begins to make his mark. Top: With Major Bowes (centre) and the Hoboken Four. Above: Sinatra and the Andrews Sisters.

compaesano, Sanicola was bred in the hurly-burly of the Bronx, a mail clerk at Warners when he first started smuggling 'freebies' to the kid from Hoboken. He followed Sinatra for four hard years, pushing, encouraging, passing on the gossip of the music world, writing his name for auditions, and coaching Sinatra in enough of the new releases to get the wire at the Rustic Cabin hooked up as a regular feature on local radio.

Air time was also good publicity for the roadhouse and after a few months the management were persuaded to raise Sinatra to $25 per week. A couple

11

Sinatra probably learned all there was to know about microphone technique in his early years as M.C. and entertainer at Hoboken's Union Club and the Rustic Cabin near Alpine, N.J. Inset: Sinatra married his first wife, the beautiful brown-eyed Nancy Barbato, in February 1939, while working at the Rustic Cabin.

of weeks later, at a Catholic church in Jersey City, Our Lady of Sorrows, he married Nancy Barbato (on 4 February, 1939). 'I'm going places,' Frank had often warned her. 'I don't want anyone dragging on my neck.' Nancy had always replied: 'I'll never get in your way'—a promise she was to keep to the bitter end. There were not many people at the wedding who could have foreseen the extraordinary changes of life-style and ambience that this unpretentious young girl would have to cope with in the next ten years. Frank Sinatra was twenty-four and still an unknown. The wedding rated a small picture and paragraph in the Hudson County social news column of the *Jersey Observer*. According to the column, the couple were to live in Garfield Avenue, Jersey City. The Rustic Cabin had given Frank a five-day furlough and the first Sinatra honeymoon was a hurried four-and-a-half day car tour into North Carolina. On their return home the new couple moved into an apartment on Garfield Avenue and Sinatra resumed commuting between his days spent hustling up and down Manhattan and his nights working at the Rustic Cabin.

It was boring enough work but good experience nonetheless. The combination of compere and usher helped Sinatra develop an easy-go-lucky banter with his clients which he was never to lose throughout his thirty-five years of night club dates. He had absorbed comedy routines—especially the new, audience-insult techniques—from New York clubs like the 18, or Tony's Place. He toned them down for the New Jersey audiences but the intimate style remained. On his own, as a stand-up performer, Sinatra would never be a great comic—he needed the quick wit of a Dean Martin or a Sammy Davis Jnr to shine as an act, but at least the confidence and ease were always there. After the early, less comfortable days at the Rustic Cabin, there were not to be many audiences that could throw him off his stride.

Good experience or not, work at the Rustic Cabin was hardly demanding of much talent. Apart from the $25 a week, the only reason Sinatra persisted there was the magic radio wire that gave him air time. It finally paid off in that summer of 1939. Benny Goodman's former trumpeter, Harry James, had started a new band and was looking for a vocalist. One night he heard Sinatra on the radio from the Rustic Cabin. He started asking around about the kid from Hoboken. Hank Sanicola picked up the gossip and sent Frank to see James, then playing a fill-in date at the New York Paramount. The two men, almost contemporaries, made friends and a couple of evenings later, the band leader appeared in person at the Rustic Cabin. He heard Sinatra through a couple of numbers: 'I liked Frank's way of talking a lyric,' said James. 'I went back the following night with Gerard Barrett, my manager, and we signed him for $75 a week.' A couple of days later Sinatra met the other members of the band at the theatre which more than any other was to mark the early milestones in his career, the Paramount, on 44th and Broadway. On 30 June, 1939, he appeared with the band on their first tour stop at the Hippodrome Theatre in Baltimore.

2 THE SLOW WAY UP 1939-1942

By the end of the thirties the frenzy of swing had relaxed into the more tuneful and orchestrated music fashionable on the dance floors. The new style and sophistication offered more scope to those also-rans of the band world, the featured vocalists—Ray Eberle with Glen Miller, Peggy Lee with Benny Goodman, Bing Crosby with Paul Whiteman, Ella Fitzgerald with Chick Webb, Perry Como with Ted Weems. Radio audiences were demanding time for the vocalists and good songs were beginning to appear. The early band years of Sinatra's career could not have been better timed.

Harry James had played trumpet with Benny Goodman and it was with Goodman's encouragement and financial support that the Harry James band had been formed early in 1939. They had begun unspectacularly, the fill-in appearance at the New York Paramount where Sinatra first met them being their most prestigious date so far.

After Sinatra's first concert with them out in Baltimore, the band moved back onto Manhattan, playing at the Roseland Ballroom on Broadway through the hot summer weeks of the World Fair. *Metronome* magazine wrote at the time of Sinatra's 'pleasing vocals' and 'easy phrasing', though George Simon, who wrote the article, later revealed that his special mention of the vocalist had been as good as dragged out of him by the band manager, who knew how badly the young singer needed recognition and publicity.

There had been no problems, musical or otherwise, when Sinatra joined the band. He fitted in well and was generally liked and admired by the musicians as a good voice and a hard worker. When the band moved west in the autumn, Nancy Sinatra went on the road with them and remembers those days as perhaps the happiest of her married life.

In Chicago the Harry James band played at the Hotel Sherman, where one reviewer commented that Sinatra's passionate interpretations were not always very convincing. Another article, in *Down Beat*, reported a conversation between a journalist and Harry James: 'Who's that skinny little singer? He sings a great song.' 'Not so loud,' replies James. 'The kid's name is Sinatra. He considers himself the greatest vocalist in the business. Get that! No one ever heard of him. He's never had a hit record. He looks like a wet rag. But he says he is the greatest. If he hears you complement him he'll demand a raise tonight. . . .'

On 13 July that summer of 1939 Frank Sinatra entered the recording studios for the first time as a professional vocalist with a band. There was neither recognition nor publicity for Harry James' young vocalist, not even a credit on the record label—he was for the moment just another of the performers in an up-and-coming band. But it turned out to be, nonetheless, a significant date in Sinatra's career. Twenty years later he told Robin Douglas-Home: 'You can never do anything in life quite on your own, you don't live on your own little island. I suppose you might be able to write a poem or paint a picture entirely on your own, but I doubt it. I don't think you can ever sing a song that

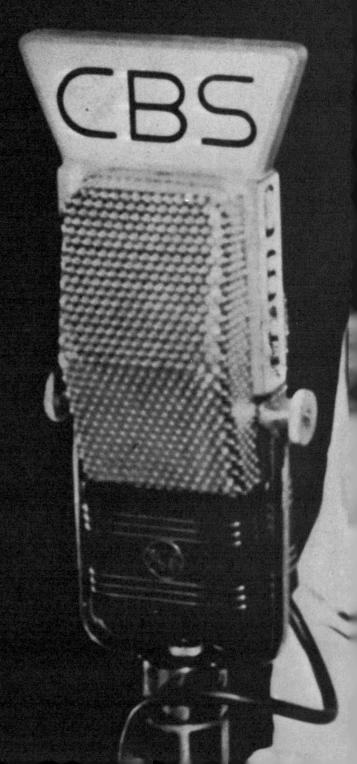

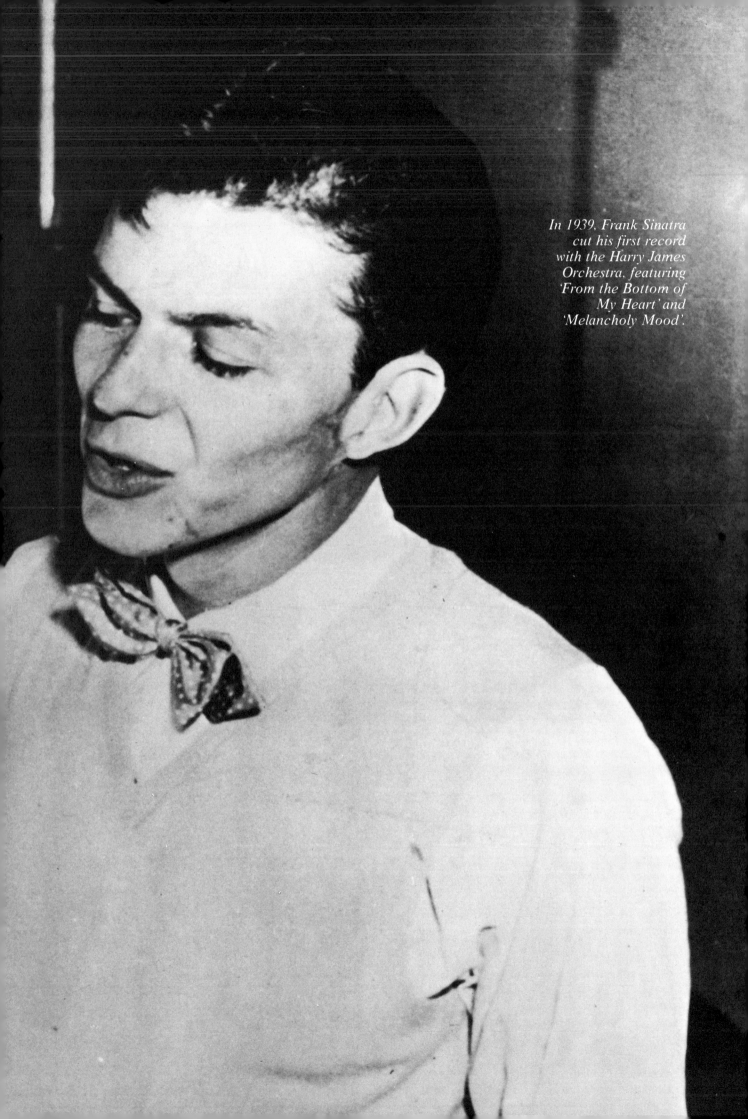

In 1939, Frank Sinatra cut his first record with the Harry James Orchestra, featuring 'From the Bottom of My Heart' and 'Melancholy Mood'.

way, anyhow. Yet, in a sort of paradoxical way, making a record is as near as you can get to it—although of course, the arranger and orchestra play an enormous part. But once you're on that record singing, it's you and you alone. If it's bad and gets criticized, it's you who's to blame—no one else. If it's good, it's also you.'

On that July afternoon the Harry James band had recorded 'From The Bottom Of My Heart' and 'Melancholy Mood', and though the reviews for the ensuing single were hardly flattering, the young band vocalist heard himself on disc for the first time, as it were, leading the music. The review in *Variety* had found 'little appeal' in either side of that first single and in fact none of the songs that came out of Sinatra's five recording sessions with the James band made any great impact at the time of their original release. 'From The Bottom Of My Heart', 'Melancholy Mood', 'My Buddy' and 'These Are The Things I Love' still survive on a CBS album, 'The Essential Frank Sinatra, Volume One'. But one of the Harry James songs did become a Sinatra classic—the Altman/Lawrence song 'All Or Nothing At All'. Recorded in August 1939, it sold an insignificant 8,000 copies on original release, and the magazine *Down Beat* commented, 'the band still has a long way to go'. Four years later that same recording, re-released, would become an instant best-seller.

The sad truth was that with only nine months' playing behind them, the band had not yet made its name, and the further west they trekked that summer and autumn of 1939 the more difficult the gigs became. A final piece of bad luck ruined even the partial success of the tour. Just prior to their booking there, the Palomar Ballroom in Los Angeles burnt down and James was forced to take a substitute date in the sophisticated clubland atmosphere of Victor Hugo's in Beverly Hills. 'The chichi crowd didn't dig our loud kind of music', Harry James recalled. 'The help out-numbered the customers. After days of complaints and an empty dance floor, the management cancelled us. To make matters worse they refused to pay us.' It was the second time Frank Sinatra had arrived on the West Coast to experience failure. After one recording session in a Burbank studio ('Ciribiribin' and 'Everyday Of My Life') the band headed back east all but bankrupt. In the annual *Down Beat* poll that December, Harry James only made number twelve in the Swing Band list and the nervy, impatient 'skinny little singer' was wondering where the next break was coming from. He had heard that Tommy Dorsey's vocalist, Jack Leonard, was about to take the plunge and go it alone and the twenty-four-year-old Sinatra was wildly apprehensive of Leonard's possible success as a solo singer. Top solo singer was the spot he was aiming for and he didn't want anyone arriving there before him.

In fact Jack Leonard's break with the Dorsey band opened up a short cut to the top of the band ladder.

Gossip and trade press speculation had already given Alan DeWitt the vacant vocalist spot in the Dorsey set-up, but in fact Tommy Dorsey had been listening to and watching the young Frank Sinatra ever since Hank Sanicola had sent him a demo disc of 'All Or Nothing At All'. Jimmy Hilliard of CBS had also advised Dorsey to listen to the Harry James vocalist. Hilliard had heard Sinatra when the James band was playing at the Sherman Hotel in Chicago. Hilliard remembers Harry James' opening session in the Panther Room: 'My back was to the bandstand, but when the kid started talking a chorus, I had to turn around. I couldn't resist going back to the next night to hear him again.'

It was in Chicago again, after Christmas, that Dorsey finally caught up with the young Hoboken singer. 'He's got something besides problems with acne,' Hilliard told Dorsey. 'Harry can't be paying him much. Maybe you can take him away.'

Harry James had originally signed Sinatra on a two-year contract, seventeen months of which were still to run. But although in difficulties himself, James made no fuss. 'Nancy was expecting a baby and Frank needed the money and I wasn't going to stand in his way.' The two men parted on a nod and a handshake and Sinatra, not without regret, said goodbye to the band he had been touring with for the last six months.

Sinatra has his own recollection of that farewell. 'When I told Harry about Tommy's offer and said I wanted to leave, he just tore up my contract there and then and wished me luck. That night the bus pulled out with the rest of the boys at about half-past midnight. I'd said goodbye to them all and it was snowing, I remember. There was nobody around and I stood alone with my suitcase in the snow and watched the tail-lights disappear. Then the tears started and I tried to run after the bus. There was such spirit and enthusiasm in that band, I hated leaving it.'

The lonesome feeling would last some time. It was not easy to move into a set-up so full of talent as the Dorsey band and the songs and audiences were still tuned into the Jack Leonard sound. 'For maybe the first five months with Dorsey I missed the James band,' Sinatra recalls. 'There was a group of Jack Leonard's fans in the band and they sort of resented a newcomer in his place. So I kept to myself. But then I've always been a loner—all my life. Eventually I shared a room with another loner, Buddy Rich, who was drummer with the band.'

At least the Dorsey band was the right spot for a vocalist. Unlike the Glen Miller sound, Dorsey numbers were usually built round a vocal subject and gave adequate musical and stage space to the singers. Not that Sinatra's first contact with Dorsey had been anything less than total disaster: 'I'd sung in front of Dorsey once a few years before I'd joined him. Or rather I *hadn't* sung! It was an audition and I had the words on the paper there in front of me and was just going to sing when the door opened and someone near me said, "Hey, that's Tommy Dorsey." He was like a god, you know. We were all in awe of him in the music business. Anyway, I just cut out completely— dead. The words were there in front of me but I could only mouth air. Not a sound came out. It was terrible. When he eventually did send for me and ask me to join his band, the first thing he said was "Yes, I remember that day when you couldn't get out those words".'

Sinatra's first concert appearance with the Dorsey band was in Rockford, Illinois, during the last week of January, 1940. There was plenty of vocal competition for him to contend with. Connie Haines had moved with him from the Harry James band and the Pied Pipers were already well established as part of the Dorsey sound. Jo Stafford was the girl member of this vocal quartet and she remembers the first appearances of Sinatra with the band, at times singing on his own, at times with the group. 'There was no upstaging when he sang with us. I have never seen anyone try so hard to blend in. He really worked at it and it was the same when he was adapting himself solo with the band.'

Apart from musicians of the quality of Ziggy Elman, Buddy Rich, Joe Bushkin and Bunny Berigan, the Dorsey set-up also included a major plus for Sinatra in the person of former trumpet player and arranger, Axel Stordahl. Introduced to the Dorsey band by Jack Leonard, Stordahl was principally a vocalist's arranger. He would play a major part in creating the Sinatra sound and was one of the first members of the Tommy Dorsey troupe to encourage the newcomer to settle down.

Two events in the summer of 1940 helped that process of settling for Sinatra. Already by the end of May he had shared eight recording sessions with the band and in that eighth session on 23 May they had cut 'I'll Never Smile Again'—the band's second attempt at the song after Dorsey had discarded an earlier version recorded in April. Two months later the song was top of the hit parade, where it stayed for a record seven week run. Frank Sinatra was still anonymous as part of the band 'vocals' when he made this first impact on the record buying public, but it was a clear indication to the young singer that the big time with Dorsey was not limited to the theatres and dance halls. The second event in a happy midsummer was the arrival of the Sinatras' first child, Nancy Sandra Sinatra, on the night of 7 June. It was perhaps significant that Sinatra's work schedule meant he was woken with the news in his room at the Astor Hotel in New York. Even on Manhattan the late night band dates prevented him from returning home and the eighteen-

Sinatra's poise developed as he settled in as vocalist with the Tommy Dorsey Band.

month-old marriage had been often enough strained and uneasy. With the birth of Nancy Sandra, friends and family hoped the situation would improve.

Impatient for recognition and success, there were many distractions and not a few disappointments for Frank Sinatra during those early months with Dorsey. A mid-season *Billboard* poll on male vocalists placed him way down the list at number 22 and he had to content himself for the moment with occasional mentions or reviews in the music and show-biz papers. 'Sock all the way,' *Variety* had written of the new Dorsey vocalist that spring. 'He's sure of himself and it shows in his work.' *Billboard* was more guarded in a May review: 'Sinatra, a good ballad singer, is nil on showmanship.'

And showmanship was one of the many fast lessons Sinatra learnt in this first year with the Dorsey band. It turned out to be the most formative and instructive period of his whole singing life. Touring with Harry James had been hard work but good fun, touring with Major Bowes uncomfortable and no fun at all. Touring with Tommy Dorsey was just plain hard work. The band was one of the busiest in the country, always filling the gaps between the major engagements with lucrative one-night gigs on the road. That first Sinatra year they played bookings at the New York Paramount, at the Meadowbrook, Cedar Grove, New Jersey, the Hollywood Palladium and the Astor Roof. They took part in a film, *Las Vegas Nights*—an appropriate enough title for Sinatra's first Hollywood appearance. And in between major dates the band trecked twice across the continent in the team bus, often travelling eighteen hours between evening engagements at colleges and provincial theatres, or daytime sessions in recording studios. The routine demanded a discipline that was good training for any young entertainer and Dorsey was a hard ring-master. A distant, rather detached man, he did not offer the same companionship or intimacy that Sinatra had found with Harry James. In his biography, Robin Douglas-Home quoted Sinatra recollecting impressions of his former band leader. 'Tommy was a very lonely man. He was a strict disciplinarian with the band—we'd get fined if we were late—yet he craved company after the shows and never really got it. The relationship between a leader and the sidemen, you see, was rather like a general and privates. We all *knew* he was lonely but we couldn't ask him to eat and drink with us because it looked too much like shining teacher's apple.

'Anyway, one night two of us decided to hell with it, we'd ask him out to dinner. He came along and really appreciated it. After that he became almost like a father towards me—and this in spite of the fact that, being a John Rebel, I was always the guy who had to pass on the beefs of the boys in the band.

'One time there was a lot of unrest in the band because of travelling all night in Greyhound buses without any refreshments. So I went to Tommy and said: "Look, the boys are unhappy—hard seats, no air, no refreshments. When they come on the stand they're *out*. . . ." After that there were always twelve cases of Coke on every bus—till Joey Bushkin introduced the band to Pernod and all the Coke suddenly went green. . . .'

Sometimes they were playing nine 45-minute shows a day and the young singer up to twelve songs in each show. 'No problems,' Sinatra said. 'No warm-up even; I had real strong pipes in those days.'

But it wasn't just discipline and endurance that Sinatra learned from Dorsey. The keys to his singing success, his breathing, his phrasing and his presentation, were all picked up in those early months with the band.

Presentation—showmanship—was an all important part of a Dorsey show, the planning and staging of the concert from beginning to end, the progression from number to number and the highlighting of each of the major musicians and vocalists. 'A beginning, a middle and an end,' Sinatra figured and he was to demonstrate that same detailed planning of themes and atmosphere in all his future club dates and concerts and, above all, on his record albums.

Dorsey played a 'singing trombone' in long, lyrical, drawn-out phrases. As vocalist with the band Frank Sinatra had to follow the same musical pattern and it was a style that appealed to the young singer. His reputation had been built on expressive phrasing, the deliberate attempt to project both the meaning and

mood of the lyrics. Dorsey's phrasing now taught him to convey with the same clarity and precision the musical structure of a piece, contrasting or complementing it with the lyrics and the mood.

Expressive phrasing meant the ability to hold the flow of a song without the mechanical interruptions of breathing. Secret number three learned from Dorsey —perhaps the most important single technical development in Sinatra's singing—was the breathing trick that Dorsey employed in the middle of long notes, whereby he could keep the note sounding while snatching an extra few seconds of air through the side of his mouth.

Professionally and technically, Sinatra made enormous advances during that first year with Tommy Dorsey. He was also getting the kind of exposure he had hitherto only dreamed of—continual radio spots, discs released every month, reviews in all the top show-biz papers and a second film apperance with the band in *Ship Ahoy*. Slowly, imperceptibly at first, the Tommy Dorsey vocalist began to be recognized and named. The records still came out under Dorsey's name with 'vocal chorus', the general credit to cover Sinatra, Connie Haines and the Pied Pipers. But on radio the skinny young singer was being openly named and during the dance floor shows it was becoming increasingly obvious that a large section of the audience had come not to dance, but to hear the songs. Each time the band moved into a vocal number and Sinatra stepped forward, the crowd would begin to gather round the stand. Sinatra was now challenging the favourite band vocalists, Ray Eberle, Dick Haymes, Bob Eberly and the 'loner', Bing Crosby.

Victor Records began to slip in Sinatra's name as a subsidiary credit on the Dorsey discs.

By May 1941 Sinatra had climbed from twenty-second to top of the *Billboard's* annual College Music Survey. At the end of the year, one month after Pearl Harbour, Sinatra displaced his idol Bing Crosby at the top of the *Down Beat* poll, dominated by Crosby since the mid-thirties. Tommy Dorsey had mixed feelings about the runaway success of his vocalist. The band had only managed second spot in both 'Swing' and 'Sweet' band polls, headed respectively by Benny Goodman and Glenn Miller. As a soloist Dorsey had slipped to fourth place behind Artie Shaw, Harry James and Benny Goodman.

Now Frank Walker of Victor Records had asked him to let Sinatra record some solo songs. Under pressure from his ambitious vocalist, Dorsey finally agreed, but only on the understanding that Sinatra's solo songs would be released on the cut-price Bluebird label.

On 19 January, 1942, with the guidance and help of Axel Stordahl as arranger and conductor, Sinatra held his first solo recording session and cut four sides—'Night And Day', 'The Night We Called It A Day', 'The Song Is You' and 'Lamplighter's Serenade'. Tommy Dorsey was credited with the orchestral accompaniment on the last two sides but both singles carried Frank Sinatra's name on top. He was the man up front for the first time in his life, a different experience indeed from being just one of the instrumentalists at a band recording date. Harry Meyerson was Victor's A&R man supervising the session: 'Frank

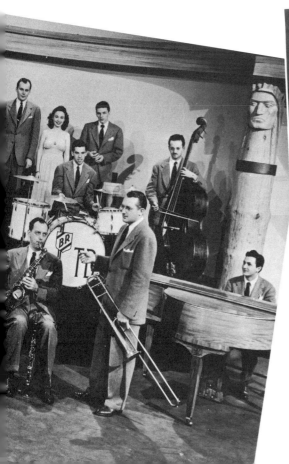

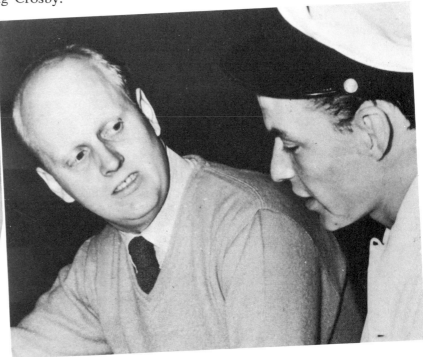

Left: Sinatra makes his Hollywood debut with the Tommy Dorsey Band in 'Las Vegas Nights'. Above: Sinatra with Axel Stordahl.

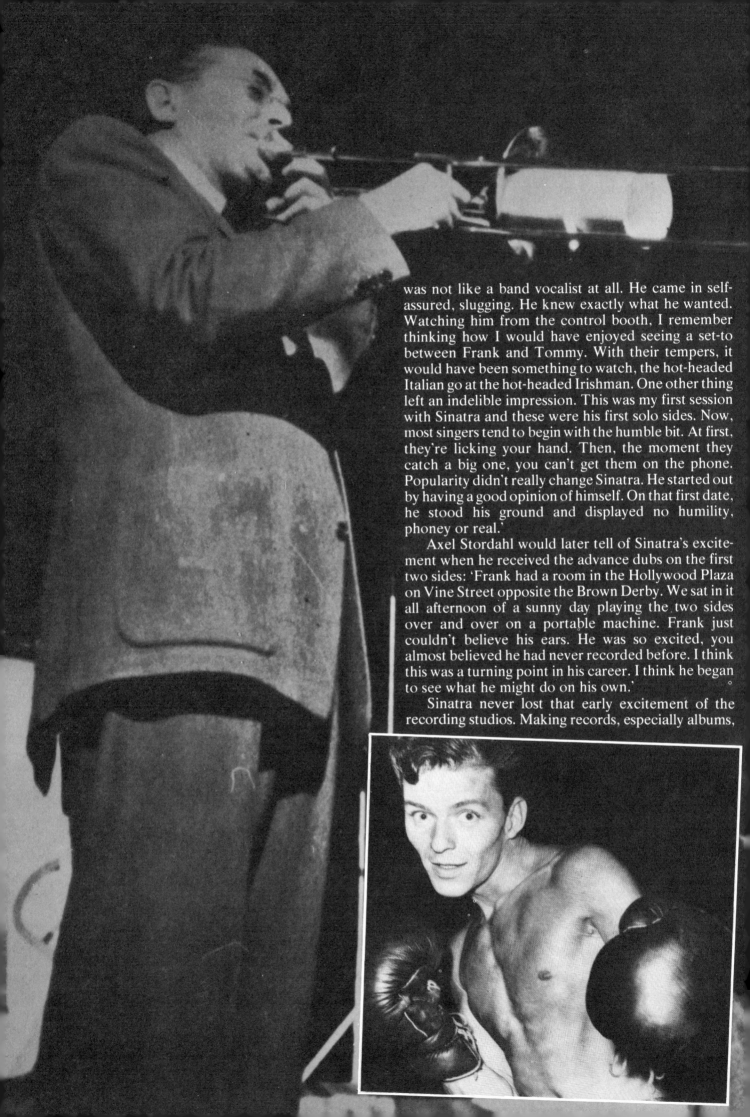

was not like a band vocalist at all. He came in self-assured, slugging. He knew exactly what he wanted. Watching him from the control booth, I remember thinking how I would have enjoyed seeing a set-to between Frank and Tommy. With their tempers, it would have been something to watch, the hot-headed Italian go at the hot-headed Irishman. One other thing left an indelible impression. This was my first session with Sinatra and these were his first solo sides. Now, most singers tend to begin with the humble bit. At first, they're licking your hand. Then, the moment they catch a big one, you can't get them on the phone. Popularity didn't really change Sinatra. He started out by having a good opinion of himself. On that first date, he stood his ground and displayed no humility, phoney or real.'

Axel Stordahl would later tell of Sinatra's excitement when he received the advance dubs on the first two sides: 'Frank had a room in the Hollywood Plaza on Vine Street opposite the Brown Derby. We sat in it all afternoon of a sunny day playing the two sides over and over on a portable machine. Frank just couldn't believe his ears. He was so excited, you almost believed he had never recorded before. I think this was a turning point in his career. I think he began to see what he might do on his own.'

Sinatra never lost that early excitement of the recording studios. Making records, especially albums,

Frank Sinatra with the great trombonist Tommy Dorsey on stage. Even from his early days as a boxer in Hoboken (inset) Sinatra was a fighter and a loner and it was inevitable that as the vocalist gained popularity in his own right he would want to break with the band.

Above: Frank and first wife Nancy. She hoped that leaving the Dorsey Band would give Frank more time with her and Nancy Jr. Right: Sinatra in the chorus line of 'Ship Ahoy!', one of his last appearances with Dorsey's Band.

would become the priority of his professional life. Not that his first two solo discs created quite the sensation he must have hoped for. *Down Beat* picked out 'Night And Day' as a 'potential juke winner', but the rest of the notices were luke-warm. It was another Dorsey band single, 'There Are Such Things', that took Sinatra back to the top of the hit parade in December 1942; ironically the session at which it was recorded turned out to be one of the last that Sinatra shared with the band (July 1942). By the time the record was on sale Sinatra was out on his own.

Even Dorsey himself was beginning to anticipate the inevitable. He had altered the programming of his shows through 1942, giving more prominence to his young male vocalist. Sometimes he would even use Sinatra to close the show with a song—uncustomary in a well-known band since it made the vocalist the focus of applause and encores. When Dorsey broke the house record at the Stanley Theatre, Pittsburgh, in July 1942, *Variety* highlighted the vocalist's achievement. 'It is unusual for a band vocalist to get the closing spot in a show. But that's the lot of Frank Sinatra. He fills it—and how! Crowd simply wouldn't let him get off and ran the opening performance overtime by at least five minutes.'

Live dance music and the culture of the Big Bands had dominated the pop scene so entirely that the only vocalist who had in modern terms succeeded as an independent solo pop star was Bing Crosby. And yet after another decade of radio the potential market and public were there. Jack Leonard had tried without success in 1940. Now Bob Eberly announced his intention of leaving the other (Jimmy) Dorsey band to go solo. The idea that someone might move out

into that world ahead of him spurred Sinatra to his own break with Tommy Dorsey. It was, as he later admitted, a gamble: 'I guess I must have had someone watching over me from the day I was born, because I seem to have made the right move every time. You see, I figured that no one had seriously challenged Bing Crosby since 1931. There were two other guys coming up (Bob Eberly and Dick Haymes) and if they had got the edge on me by even a few months, I might never have made it. When I left Tommy, I had Sanicola with me. Then I hired Axel Stordahl from Tommy to do my arranging. Tommy had paid him $150 dollars a week—I paid him $650, and Tommy got even madder with me. . . . !'

The decision to go would have been difficult for anyone to make. For Sinatra it must initially have seemed like a step back into the never-never world he had known in the 1930s. Singing with the Dorsey band was top spot in a regular well-paid profession where other people were hired to do the selling, the planning and the worrying. Cut off from the aura of a top band the singer was submitting his talent, his charisma, his

good luck, all of himself, to a final and potentially ruinous test. The step out into the cold was, if nothing else, an enormous act of faith.

It is not clear which of the Sinatra intimates at the time were for or against the move. Axel Stordahl who moved out with Sinatra, was probably the one who gave Frank the professional confidence to go it alone. As for the show-biz 'come-ons', Manie Sachs at Columbia had indicated interest in signing him up for recording and one of the larger agencies, GAC, offered to represent him.

The hopes, fears or despairs of the two Mrs Sinatras are not recorded. Mother Sinatra was still far from convinced and perhaps, as with another (future) Mrs Sinatra, Nancy Snr was secretly hoping for some ebb in her husband's fortunes. The cocksure, money-in-the-pocket Sinatra was not an easy man around whom to build a family. The coming of Nancy Sandra had made it more difficult for Nancy Sr to travel round with her husband while he, as star vocalist of a top band, had had more than his share of temptations. Relations between them were sometimes strained and

Frank's periods at home were punctuated with ill-temper on his part and sulking on hers. Perhaps she was hoping now that harder times or a new pattern of work would bring her man home more often. The Dorsey years had not been very happy ones for her. The breaking of the Dorsey contract gave birth to the first of the Sinatra gangster legends. The twenty-seven-year-old singer was known for his friendships in the rough and ready worlds of boxing and gambling, and had already acquired something of a reputation for surrounding himself with 'unsavoury characters'. The story was told that Dorsey had refused to release his vocalist from contract until the day a gangster and alleged friend of Sinatra— Willie Moretti, the *padrino* of New Jersey— took the matter into his own hands and pushed a revolver barrel down the trombonist's throat. Improbable? Untrue? Like most of the Sinatra anecdotes the story cannot be totally discounted. Like all of the legends, no one will ever be absolutely sure of the truth.

Whether he was frightened into it or not, Tommy Dorsey certainly held out for a lion's share of Sinatra's future. On the terms of the severance deal Dorsey was to take one third of Sinatra's future earnings and the Dorsey manager, Leonard Vannerson, ten per cent. A year or so later with the help of prospective new agents at MCA and with an advance from Columbia, Sinatra bought himself out of that severance deal for a reported $60,000.

But for all the bitterness of these deals and counter deals, Sinatra never denied his affection for his former band leader, nor his debt to the two-and-a-half years he spent with the Dorsey band. 'Tommy taught me everything I knew about singing. He was my real education. . . . It was a wonderful life, they were great days. I can remember every detail of them even now.' No surprise then that Sinatra had asked Dorsey to be godfather to Nancy Sandra. The other members of the band reciprocated the affection and the impression they gave of Sinatra is one of a generous, high-living companion, an immaculate dresser, fastidiously clean and tidy even in the uncomfortable routines of bus touring. 'Lady Macbeth' they called him, for the number of times he used to wash his hands. On the debit side was his quick temper. More than once he embarrassed the band by plunging out onto the floor to seek out the origins of someone's barracking or insults and even a music critic found himself flat on his back, nursing his jaw, after an anti-semitic remark at a cocktail party. Sinatra was quick to take offence, easy to anger and not one to forgive or forget very easily. 'Brittle', Dorsey had once called him. The insecurities were deep and more than one of the Dorsey musicians believed that the skinny, hollow-cheeked singer could not survive professionally or personally outside the corporate, mutually supportive framework of a big band.

3 OUT ON THE RAINBOW 1942-1947

Sinatra walked off the Dorsey stand for the last time on 19 September, 1942 and the early weeks alone did nothing to reassure him that he had made the right move. A musicians' strike had closed recording studios right across the continent and his hopeful new agents could turn up nothing more lucrative than a three-minute spot singing 'Night And Day' in the Columbia picture, *Reveille With Beverly*. His contract for the picture did not even stipulate a major credit and the expenses of the trip used up most of his fee. He returned from Hollywood further disheartened after an unsuccessful audition for the job of staff singer at NBC. A couple of months later and they would have been queueing up for him.

It was Manie Sachs at Columbia who found Sinatra his first solo break, a twice weekly radio slot on CBS that went out under the title *Songs by Sinatra*. The programme gave him enough kudos to land a booking in the Mosque Theatre, across the Hudson in Newark. It was home territory for Sinatra and he worked hard to build enthusiasm in what was a predominantly young audience. Luckily for him, his agent, Harry Romm at GAC, took New York Paramount manager, Bob Weitman, to see the show. As Weitman recalls, the performances were dead and the theatre half-empty. 'But then this skinny kid walks out on the stage. He was not much older than the kids in the seats. He looked like he still had milk on his chin. As soon as they saw him, the kids went crazy. And when he started to sing, they stood up and yelled and moaned and carried on until I thought, you should excuse the expression, his pants had fallen down.'

Weitman figured that much of the enthusiasm was due to Sinatra's local home-town support, but he was impressed enough to book Sinatra into the Paramount Theatre as an 'Extra Added Attraction' for Benny Goodman's post-Christmas show with Peggy Lee and pianist Jess Stacy. After all, that local audience was still only a bus-ride away from Broadway. Benny Goodman had never even heard of Sinatra, despite the singer's two-and-a-half years with Tommy Dorsey. But he agreed to take on the extra vocalist for a couple of songs during the show.

On the day before New Year's Eve, 1942, Frank Sinatra walked out onto the stage of the New York Paramount and turned the history of popular music upside down and inside out.

'That day at the Paramount,' he told Robin Douglas-Home, 'I'll never forget it. It was the day things got really started. It was my first real engagement after leaving Tommy, and the Paramount was at that time the Mecca of the entertainment world. Benny Good-

man was playing there with his band and there was a Crosby picture showing, so the kids were really being pulled in. Benny had the top band in the world then and it was the first time I'd sung with him. He'd never heard about me, and when he introduced me he just said kind of matter of fact: "And now—Frank Sinatra."

'Now Benny lived in a complete world of his own. All he was conscious of was his clarinet and his orchestra—nothing else. A true musician through and through. He never knew anything about new up-and-coming singers or anything like that. Anyway, when he introduced me I stuck my head and one foot out through the organdie curtains—and *froze!* The kids let out the loudest scream you ever heard. I couldn't move a muscle—I was as nervous as a son-of-a-bitch. Benny had never heard the kids holler before and he froze too—with his arms raised on the up-beat. He looked round over one shoulder and said, to no one in particular: "What the fuck was that?" That somehow broke the tension and I couldn't stop laughing for the first three numbers. . . .'

Well might Benny Goodman spin round in alarm. The noise he had heard heralded the end of the Big Bands. It was, as *Life* magazine announced, 'the

proclamation of a new era'. In the three months that followed Sinatra would conquer the widest age-group audience of any singer past or future. The days of the crooner and swooner made their first headlines on that December night in New York and within four years pop music had become exclusively singer and song, the bands and Kings of Swing scattered to the winds.

The Paramount stayed packed out from morning to night for the four week duration of Benny Goodman's show. The theatre hired extra guards to handle the crowds of bobby-soxers; the newspapers were full of articles trying to explain the secrets of the lean and hungry singer with the curl on his forehead; editorials spoke of mass hypnosis; and intellectual analysis likened the bobby-sox reaction to the Children's Crusade. Once the press stories started the hysteria achieved a momentum of its own. 'Not since the days of Rudoph Valentino,' said *Time* magazine, 'has American womanhood made such unabashed public love to an entertainer.'

When Benny Goodman moved on at the end of that January the Paramount signed up Sinatra for another four weeks with a couple of lesser-known bands. Sinatra's eight week run at the Paramount had only ever been exceeded by Bing Crosby, and only

Left: Benny Goodman.
Below: Sinatra in 1942—the lean and hungry singer with a curl on his forehead.
Right: From December 1942 Sinatra became the hero of a million bobbysoxers.

once equalled by Rudy Vallee at the height of his popularity. No one had ever seen the kind of audience reaction inspired by the kid from Hoboken. It was difficult for some people to accept it as a natural phenomenom and the question was asked then as it has been ever since, how much had that initial bobby-sox reaction been encouraged or even laid on by the Sinatra entourage? Certainly the two critical nights— that of Weitman's visit to Newark and the opening

night at the Paramount—had been helped on their way by local press stories and perhaps even with the distribution of some complimentary tickets. The schools were on holiday and there was no shortage of potential teenage enthusiasm. But Sinatra's organization was still very underdeveloped and under-financed and it would be a mistake to attribute too much to the manipulation of a publicity machine. George Evans, who was to join Sinatra as his press agent during this first solo year, would admit many years after to some orchestrating of fans and their reactions. But that was later when the phenomenon was well established.

In fact Connie Haines had witnessed some juvenile enthusiasm three years previously when Sinatra was still with the Harry James band, and, as she pointed out, no one in that outfit had money to spare on publicity stunts. 'It was something about him being so frail and skinny. Something about the way he'd hang onto that microphone. Something in his singing that reached out to the audience—like he was saying, I'm giving this to you with everything I got; what have you got to give me? I guess they came backstage afterwards to tell him.'

However the hysteria was explained at the time— the war, girls with soldier boyfriends far from home, emancipation, degeneracy—everyone seemed to agree that this Sinatra was someone exclusively for the kids and everyone expected the young star to follow the Paramount with a nationwide tour. But Sinatra had no intention of going back on the road. There were more important audiences to conquer, radio, cinema and the night clubs, and he wanted them all.

After the sensation of his appearance at the Paramount, offers from radio and cinema followed as a matter of course. Within a month he was signed to replace Barry Wood on the most influential of the networked pop shows, *Your Hit Parade*, a weekly Saturday evening concert of the current top tunes. And in Hollywood his three-minute uncredited appearance in *Reveille with Beverly* was suddenly promoted to star billing. That same month, January 1943, he negotiated a picture contract with RKO. Still kids' stuff, the columnists were saying and for all the potential publicity, none of the big night clubs seemed interested in him.

It was boom time for the 'Niters', with war contracts swelling the civilian pay packets and the New York streets full of wandering uniforms looking for the good time. But so far as the clubs were concerned, Sinatra was not sophisticated enough for the up-market atmosphere. The only club which could be persuaded to try him on was the one club then in financial embarrassment, the Riobamba. As at the Paramount, Sinatra was initially billed as a cautious

Sinatra fans queueing outside New York's Paramount Theatre to see their idol. The mass hysteria he engendered surprised the world.

'Extra Added Attraction', the stars of the show being Walter O'Keefe, comic and MC, and the commedienne/singer Sheila Barret.

Again we may assume that friends and members of the entourage worked hard to ensure a sympathetic first-night audience. But the sceptics were there nonetheless, the columnists and reviewers on whom the succeeding audiences depended. And Sinatra won them all over. They liked him as a personality—the self-effacing, modest, vulnerable image; and they liked the songs. Sinatra remembers the significance of that evening: 'I had to open the show walking round the tables and singing. There was no stage or anything and the dance-floor was only as big as a postage-stamp. I was nervous as hell again, but I sang a few songs and went off. Walter O'Keefe was the star of the show and he was to do his act last. That night he just walked on and said: "Ladies and Gentlemen, I *was* your star of the evening, but tonight, in this club, we have all just seen a star born." And he walked out without saying another word. I hadn't really been conscious of any great reception or anything during my act—maybe because I was so nervous—but next day there was a big explosion in all the papers and all round.' His act eclipsed the then top night club attraction, Jimmy Durante at the Copacabana; his fee was raised from $750 to $1,000 and finally to $1,500. He was signed for two extra three-week periods and throughout the ten weeks the Riobamba Club was regularly packed out each night. From the vulgar sensation stories of teenage orgasms ('urine' in those days) at the Paramount, Sinatra had climbed within two months into the society columns. He was obligatory material for the repartee of every night club comedian. Jackie Miles at the Martinique: 'He's so skinny that both of us are trying to get together to do a single . . . Everyone applauds every song he sings and I know why. They think each song is going to be his last.' Or Joe E. Lewis at the Copacabana: 'Frank Sinatra looks like the advance man for a famine. If he ever gets an Academy Award, it'll be for his sunken chest.' Sinatra rated a George Frazier feature in *Life* magazine, open-mouthed at his success: 'Every Saturday noon the sidewalk outside the CBS Playhouse at Broadway and 53rd, where he rehearses for the *Hit Parade*, is jammed with girls who want to bask in the radiance of his smile. . . . His voice does something extraordinary to women of all ages. At the Riobamba, the New York night club where Sinatra is now appearing, a man remarked the other night that what Sinatra's singing does to girls is immoral. "But," he added, surveying the sea of ecstatic expressions throughout the room, "it also seems to be pleasant!".'

After a spell at the Meadowbrook in Cedar Grove, New Jersey, Frank Sinatra was booked again by the Paramount, this time for $2,500 a week and New York's most exclusive club, the Wedgewood Room at the Waldorf, signed him for the autumn in the face of

competition from the Copacabana. He was to conquer at the Waldorf as he had done at the Riobamba, winning this time an even more 'determined-to-be-unimpressed' audience of Park Avenue sophisticates. He had become, as *Variety* pointed out in April 1943, 'the hottest thing in show-biz' and he had achieved it in only three short months.

That same summer Sinatra and his press agent George Evans arranged a series of concerts with four of the country's leading symphony orchestras: the Philharmonic, the National of Washington, the Cleveland and the Hollywood Bowl. Ostensibly the concerts were organized as an attempt to relieve the financial problems of the large orchestras, but whatever their origins they were good publicity, and aimed at an altogether different audience from those conquered so far in the theatres and night clubs. Although Sinatra's reference during one of the concerts to the players in the Philharmonic as 'the boys in the band' was heavily ridiculed in the press and the serious music critics were predictably outraged by the whole affair, the Sinatra entourage considered the concerts to have been a success.

His fame was now no longer restricted to Manhattan or the East Coast. *Your Hit Parade* had doubled its national audience since his debut in February. By the time he came west to Los Angeles in August for the first of his RKO pictures and his concert at the Hollywood Bowl, the bobby-sox fan club was operating nationwide. In an attempt to escape his admirers,

Sinatra captured a wider audience both with his intimate nightclub appearances (left) and his live broadcasts on 'Your Hit Parade' (below).

Sinatra left the Sante Fe Chief at Pasadena instead of Los Angeles but was still mobbed at the railway station by a vast crowd, a scene so well covered by newsmen that one suspects someone in the Sinatra entourage leaked word of the singer's intended train-jumping. The official reception committee from RKO had to take refuge in a garage for two hours until the riot subsided.

It would have been an instinctive reaction for the Hollywood show-biz world to reject this new East Coast sensation, but a series of well-handled interviews earned him the support of the daily press and the all important columnists. The *Los Angeles Times* made Sinatra's arrival a front page story, their lady reporter making no secret of her loyalties: 'He is a romanticist and a dreamer and a careful dresser and he loves beautiful words, and music is his hobby. He makes no pretensions at all.' Even the redoubtable Louella Parsons was won over: 'He was warm, ingenuous, so anxious to please.'

Hollywood decided to be pleased. Sinatra sang his Bowl concert to a capacity audience. He was a guest on Bing Crosby's Radio Show, he spent and entertained well, and in the weeks of work that followed on his first major picture, *Higher And Higher*, Sinatra built

himself the foundations of friendship and support that were to make him so quickly one of the most powerful figures in the Hollywood establishment. Like theatre and radio, the cinema had succumbed to the talent and charms of the young crooner.

It was taking far longer to establish Sinatra as a solo artist in the recording world. Columbia's A&R man, Manie Sachs, had been instrumental in Sinatra's early breaks as a solo man the previous autumn, but the musicians' union recording ban had effectively blocked the signing of new talent by the major companies. Even after Sinatra's dramatic success at the Paramount, Sachs' bosses at Columbia were content to 'wait and see', and the management at Victor were at that time still hopeful of signing the new solo crooner. Tommy Dorsey had as much as anyone else to do with Sinatra's final recording decision, for he had insisted that Victor keep the young singer on the subsidiary Bluebird label, and Victor were not convinced enough by Sinatra's long term prospects to risk offending Dorsey. Sinatra had no intention of recording for Bluebird and while

Below: Sinatra relaxes in his dressing-room at the Paramount Theatre, New York.

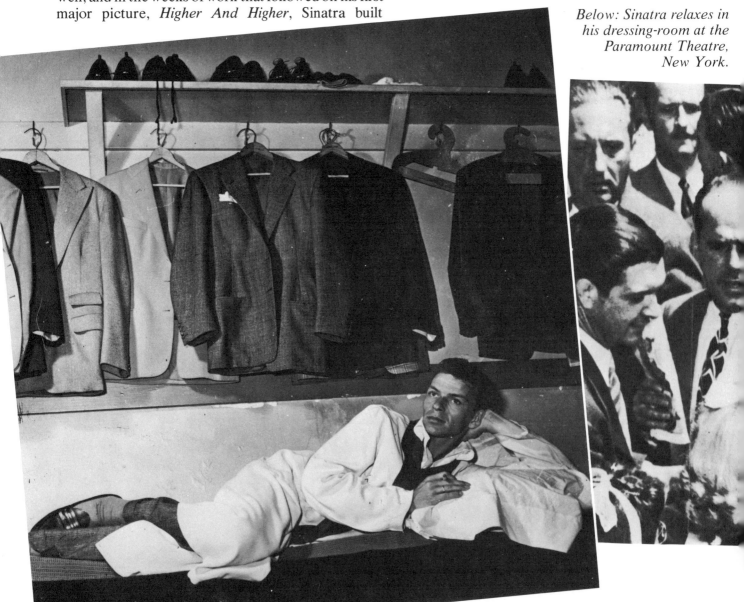

Victor were dithering, Manie Sachs had discovered the old Harry James single 'All Or Nothing At All' in the Columbia vaults. Columbia re-released it in May 1943, and Sinatra plugged it on his radio shows. In little more than a month the old 1940 recording had climbed to number one in the hit parade. Columbia had already been given a further spur towards signing Sinatra at the beginning of June when the then parvenu company, Decca, slipped Dick Haymes into the studios to record *a capella,* with a vocal instead of an instrumental background. Columbia decided to evade the musicians ban with the same tactic and Manie Sachs was at last given the go-ahead to offer Sinatra a contract. By 7 June, Sinatra was in a Columbia studio cutting the Warren/Gordon song, 'You'll Never Know', to a vocal background.

That first contract with Columbia was a sixteen song agreement over two years and gave Sinatra a mere $1,600 advance. Though Columbia would stand the full production costs of each record (artists were sometimes expected to pay for their own musical backing) it was in no way a generous deal and reflected the jittery state of the recording business, battered as it was not only by the musicians' ban but also by limitations set by the War Production Board. A second contract was drawn up well before the two year expiry date, and a third contract in 1948 would eventually give Sinatra a $6,000 a month advance, an amount more commensurate with the profits he was then earning for Columbia.

'All Or Nothing At All' and 'You'll Never Know' both made the top of the hit parade in the summer of 1943 and by the end of the year Sinatra pushed another two of the *a capella* songs into first place, 'People Will Say We're In Love' (from *Oklahoma*), and 'Sunday, Monday Or Always'. He dominated the hit parade for the whole of that second half of 1943.

On the third side of the pop music triangle of record, radio and sheet music, Sinatra had already established his own publishing set-up. Hank Sanicola and Sinatra joined music publisher Ben Barton in the summer of 1943, the first Sinatra venture into the business and financial side of show-biz. Among the properties Barton Music acquired during those early months were the Sinatra radio signature tune, 'Put Your Dreams Away', 'Close To You' (later to become the title of one of the Sinatra albums), and 'Saturday Night Is The Loneliest Night In The Week'. In 1944 they published the famous Van Heusen melody 'Nancy With The Laughing Face', (dedicated to young Nancy Sandra Sinatra, with lyrics by the comedian Phil Silvers).

As entertainer and businessman Sinatra was already on the way to his first million dollars, and all this still from an audience and public confined to the United States.

So far as a world-wide audience was concerned, his arrival on the screen and on the air could not have been better timed. 1943 was the year the Allied armies began their major territorial reconquest against the Germans and Japanese. The GIs with their allies invaded Sicily in August, the mainland of Italy in September, and they carried with them in their kitbags and on their radio shows, Sinatra V-discs, Sinatra pictures, 'Sinatrauma' in general. By the end of the war in 1945, before Sinatra had ever set foot outside the States, his name was already a household word wherever American forces had been stationed and wherever they were in occupation.

The war also caused Sinatra his first major publicity upset. Already in a New York club he had fought with a couple of Marines who had called at him across the tables—'Hey, wop. Why aren't you in uniform?' The same question, phrased in a dozen different ways, was easy copy for the scornful press. By the time Sinatra's name came up for draft classification he was hyper-sensitive about the whole issue. After his preliminary medical he was passed 1-A and professed himself 'restless and ready to go'. But in December 1943 he was called back for a second examination, accompanied, to the army's embarrassment, by a streetful of tremulous fans. This second time round the army doctors

Left: At the height of his fame, Sinatra was mobbed by fans wherever he went.

found a hole in Sinatra's left eardrum and rejected him for service as 4-F. While Sinatra claimed disappointment, the streetful of faithful fans cheered and cried their relief. Sinatra himself was probably none too sure how he felt about it all. One half of him, the fighter, the boxer, might have welcomed the challenge—a Maggio, a Prewitt or a Noah Ackerman. The other half had a lot to lose, in particular the momentum of a career that for all its success would still be vulnerable to a long absence from radio or from recording.

His 4-F lasted him until February 1945 when, with the war in Japan still apparently a long way from decision and the Germans prolonging the European agony, Sinatra was suddenly ordered to report for induction at a local board in Jersey City. Transferred to an induction in Newark, he had to be rescued from a mob of hysterical fans by the military police. He was moved on again for another medical on the suspect eardrum, this time to Governor's Island where he was finally classified 2A-F, implying that his normal employment was 'essential to the national health, safety and interest'. A month later the draft board, in response perhaps to cynical press comment, reclassified him as a medically unfit 4-F. And there the draft issue finally rested.

Not so the press comment on Sinatra's war. That same year, in midsummer and after VE day, Sinatra set out on a USO tour round the US forces based in Europe and North Africa. The columnist Lee Mortimer wrote: 'The 4-F from Hasbrouck Heights waited until hostilities were over in the Mediterranean to take his seven-week joy ride, while fragile dolls like Carole Landis and aging, ailing men like Joe E. Brown and Al Jolson subjected themselves to enemy action, jungle disease and the dangers of travel through hostile skies from the beginning of the war.'

His tour as such seems to have passed without trouble. With a clever blend of self-mocking repartee and whole-hearted singing he won over his military audiences, sceptics and all. But when he arrived back home he was outspoken about the conditions on tour, about the low standard of most of the USO shows and about the amateur arrogance of the 'shoemakers in uniform' who organized the tours.

Columnist Ed Sullivan and the music paper *Metronome* backed Sinatra in his condemnation of the shows, but the majority of press comment, including the service newspaper *Stars and Stripes,* was anti-Sinatra and the USO incident was one of his few setbacks in the early years of success.

The pattern of success had been established by that first incredible year. For the next six years Sinatra

would divide a hard-working schedule between theatre dates, night clubs, his weekly radio programme *Hit Parade*, films and, after the lifting of the musicians' ban in November 1944, recording.

Following the initial series of vocal-backed *a capella* recordings, the singers had decided to respect the Union picket lines and for a whole year there were no new recordings except from the one label, Decca, which had conceded the Union demands on royalties. The lack of new records put a far greater emphasis on Sinatra's live performances, whether in theatre, club or on the air. It also created rarity value. Sinatra's performances, where and when they occurred, were followed slavishly by his fans, his new songs carefully catalogued and the favourite numbers requested in the fan mail that inundated George Evans's P.R. office.

The climax to this period of ultra-fanaticism had come just one month before the end of the recording ban when Sinatra returned to the Paramount Theatre, New York, in October 1944. Bobby-soxers ignored the curfew imposed on juveniles by Mayor La Guardia and a thousand girls queued through most of the night for opening day seats. After press stories describing the first day scenes, the second day crowds were much larger and more unruly. The so-called 'Columbus Day Riot' started in the early morning with upwards of 10,000 kids taking advantage of a school holiday and extending the theatre queue a whole block round 43rd, Eighth Avenue and 44th. Police estimated another 20,000 fans were running wild in Times Square and they diverted reserves that had been called out for the

Fifth Avenue Columbus Day parade to deal with the juvenile crisis. When the theatre doors opened the box office was destroyed in the crush and adjacent shop windows broken. By mid-morning there were over 400 police reserves, 200 detectives and sundry mounted police, policemen, traffic cops and patrolmen trying to control 25,000 hysterical teenage girls.

Not surprising then if the Sinatra entourage began to worry about his personal safety. A suit of his impeccable clothes would often fail to survive a single evening. Already in one clothes-snatching session two girls on either end of his bow-tie had half-strangled him, bruising his larynx badly enough to cause future haemorrhage and voice failures at times of physical or emotional stress. Fans collected his butt-ends, stole the clothes pegs that hung his vests, the sheets from his hotel bedrooms. They even gathered his footprints from the snow to store in their ice-boxes.

Below left and centre: Frank Sinatra and vocal backing group enjoy themselves recording 'You'll Never Know' in 1943. Below: In the early forties Sinatra is always good copy.

It was E. J. Kahn in one of a series of articles in *The New Yorker* who pointed out that this hysteria was not wholly without precedent. 'When Franz Liszt played the piano, every now and then some woman listening to him would keel over. Women kissed the seams of Johann Strauss's coat and wept with emotion at the sight of Paderewski's red hair. In 1843, when the Norwegian violinist, Ole Bull, who had long, golden hair and a striking build, gave some recitals over here, his feminine followers unhorsed his carriage and pulled it around town themselves. Then there was Rudolph Valentino's funeral. . . .'

Sinatra offered his own, perhaps over-modest explanation: 'It was the war years. There was great loneliness and I was the boy in every corner drugstore, the boy who'd gone off, drafted to the war. That's all. It's directly in the troubadour tradition of the old days.'

Sinatra's frail physical image had a lot to do with it—the vulnerable, boyish appeal that was to last until his decline and the ravages of the Ava Gardner affair, began to change his face. When 'Sinatrauma' first hit London five years later *The Times* defined this un-American, anti-hero side to Sinatra's appeal. 'Here is an artist who, hailing from the most rowdy and self-confident community the world has even known, has elected to express the timidity that can never wholly be driven out of the boastfullest heart. To a people whose idea of manhood is husky, full-blooded and self-reliant, he has dared to suggest that under the . . . crashing self-assertion, man is still a child, frightened and whimpering in the dark.'

Robin Douglas-Home would later write: 'The voice I heard was that of an insecure man, alone, calling for understanding from the depths of a cold, private wilderness . . . of a vulnerable child, crying itself to sleep in the secrecy of his room.' If vulnerability was the secret of the image, reality, whether sad or happy, was the essential ingredient of his singing. After the casual, flippant, uninvolved, tongue-in-cheek self-mockery of the 1920s and 1930s, Sinatra had put passion, and even sex, back into popular white music for the first time since the Italian *bel canto* that grew out of nineteenth century opera. He had seen and heard Billie Holliday perform in the 52nd Street clubs when he was still an apprentice in the singing world and he had learnt from her the emotions that can grow from music and lyrics. In the sense that Billie Holliday and Sinatra were both 'living their songs' their approach could be paralleled with what was to be later called 'the method' in acting (a style or technique of acting Sinatra would profess to despise). The 'sex' came as much from this emotional commitment as from technique—the projection of that vulnerable, rather frail, intensely sincere young man who could give your heart and stomach a bounce with a *glissando,* a delayed beat, a quarter-tone. In *The Voice* E. J. Kahn quoted a description

and condemnation of the style by an unnamed contemporary critic: 'Soft, insinuating scoops and slides between the notes and a dropping away of the voice after every line. . . . [a] style very dangerous to our morale, for it is passive, luxurious and ends up not with a bang but a whimper. . . .'

Oh that danger and degeneracy could be measured in whimpers!

The Times of London would take a rather less serious look at the crooner when Sinatra played his first concert there in 1950: 'There is nothing mysterious, of course, about Mr Frank Sinatra's success. He is a trim, well-spoken, gay young man who laughs when the more excitable of his admirers punctuate his songs with fervent little "o-ohs" and "a-ahs", and who can kiss his hands to an audience without appearing foolish. He has as well exactly the manner for those rather trumpery little songs of to-day, which serious people deplore yet find themselves humming. The best of them deal in scraps of popular philosophy about falling in or out of love, and Mr Sinatra knows just when to seem moved himself and when to revert to his air of nonchalant amusement. When he tries his hand at songs we associate with very different singers, pieces such as "Old Man River" and the hero's rather shaming soliloquy in Carousel on learning he is about to be a father, it is fair to remember that Mr Sinatra's accomplished performance is given before a microphone. It must be easier far to "interpret" when there is no doubt that one's voice will carry.'

Sinatra's vulnerable boyish appeal delighted the readers of Movie Fan Magazine.

Many years later another English critic redefined both technique and image, and his re-assessment, after one of Sinatra's last appearances in London, is still valid for 'the Voice' of those earlier years. Tony Palmer, writing in *The Observer,* compared Sinatra's singing with the sound of the Tommy Dorsey trombone, 'endlessly flowing . . . six to eight bar phrases at a go, whilst most singers can't get to four. He used to swim underwater whilst reciting lyrics to learn breath control. He prefers a black microphone so that it will melt into his dinner jacket and moves it back and forth from his mouth so that you never hear the intake of breath, thus giving the voice that continuous purring quality. Each word is stretched and rephrased —"mine" becomes two syllables and not one, so his diction acquires a healthy succulence.'

Douglas-Home described the Voice even more extravagantly: '. . . a mouthful of Château Mouton Rothschild '49 chased by a teaspoon of celery salt and a sprinkling of cayenne pepper, or a spoonful of Hymettus honey washed down with the dryest of dry vodka martinis.'

Douglas-Home's personal reaction to the singing was more relevant. 'The pathos and dejection in that voice struck a range of hidden chords in my memory, bringing back vivid and searing fresh those moments, deep-buried and long-forgotten, when a cold hand gripped at the ardent heart of young love—when her telephone call did not come on the promised hour, when the longed-for letter never came, when you saw her dancing happily or leaving the party with someone else. . . . In the larynx of this man these banal phrases become poignant, pointful and even beautiful.'

Perhaps George Frazier, writing for *Life* in 1943, had come close to the inner secret: '[Sinatra] has the ability to believe implicitly the rhythmic goo he sings. He is utterly convinced that a kiss is still a kiss, a sigh still a sigh.'

We are left with the enigma of a man who gave sex back to pop music yet at the same time expressed himself with all the frilly, decorative pastiche of romantic love. Perhaps his one wholly convincing, wholly sincere, lasting and inborn theme was the cry of the lonely man, the despair of 'I'll Never Smile Again', the late night, empty solitude of 'Goodbye' and 'One More For My Baby'.

Sinatra's song-writers had their own considerable part to play in the development of his style and image as a singer. In those early solo years the combination of the Sammy Cahn/Julie Styne writing partnership and Axel Stordahl's arrangements gave the quality to Sinatra's concert repertoire and most of the best singles to Sinatra's studio work. Once serious recording had resumed in 1944 this team dominated statistically while songs from Richard Rodgers, Van Heusen, Cole Porter and Irving Berlin made up the best part of the other numbers issued under Sinatra's name.

The two major record companies, Columbia and

Late 1944 saw Sinatra's return to the Columbia studio, recording seventeen songs within a month.

RCA Victor, had finally settled their differences with the musicians' union in November 1944, and after a year's absence from the studios Sinatra started recording again in the middle of that month. Before the end of the year he had recorded no less than seventeen songs, including two hit parade successes, 'Saturday Night Is The Loneliest Night In The Week', and 'I Dream Of You'. The ultimately successful 'Nancy With The Laughing Face', recorded in a December session, was shelved by Sinatra until another and better version was recorded in August 1945.

Apart from his regular pop recordings, 1945 was also a year of experiment. He cut gospel songs with a Negro group called The Charioteers ('I've Got A Home In The Rock', 'Jesus Is A Rock In The Weary Land'); Latin songs with Xavier Cugat ('Stars In Your Eyes', 'My Shawl'); then even persuaded Columbia to let him conduct an orchestra in a recording of an Alec Wilder composition ('Frank Sinatra Conducts Alec Wilder'). Not surprisingly, Sinatra could not manage the reading of a full orchestral score and Alec Wilder prepared a special melody chart to help him follow the entries and phrasing. Columbia kept a professional conductor waiting in the building in case Sinatra could not cope, but, as Manie Sachs recalled, the young singer surprised them all: 'Here were all these symphony cats sitting around with their Stradivarius fiddles and goatees when Frank walks in, mounts the

platform just like Stokowski, and raps for attention with the little stick. The musicians didn't know what to make of it. But Frank was smart. "I need your help," he said right off, "and I want to help this music." By the time he was through, they were applauding him and hugging him and patting him on the back.'

In contrast to his singing the image, style or magic of Sinatra's early films are more difficult to define or analyze. His two appearances with Tommy Dorsey (*Las Vegas Nights* and *Ship Ahoy*) were confined to playing his real life role as the band vocalist and in *Reveille With Beverley* his performance had consisted of the one Cole Porter song, 'Night And Day'. But it was this last film that demonstrated Sinatra's potential as a box office draw. John T. McManus wrote in *PM*, 'Each time he so much as turns his dead-pan head or flickers an eye-lid, the adolescent set goes absolutely nuts! They squeal with delight; they rock and moan and make little animal cries. When he is finished, they are emotionally spent.'

Sinatra's first starring roles, the two RKO pictures, *Higher And Higher* and *Step Lively*, were not particularly memorable either as films or as Sinatra vehicles,

but they did rate him respectable notices. Critics found the shy personality put across in both films endearing and well enough portrayed. Howard Barnes in the *New York Herald Tribune* even admitted that Sinatra had 'far more performing range and assurance than many may have suspected'. *Higher And Higher* produced Sinatra's first indirect Oscar nomination with the Jimmy McHugh/Harold Adamson song 'I Couldn't Sleep A Wink Last Night'. *Step Lively* instead produced Sinatra's first 'walk-off' when he refused to film one day unless his co-star, Gloria De Haven, changed her high hat. Like Errol Flynn and Alan Ladd, Sinatra was somewhat sensitive about his height when playing opposite tall ladies. It was also noticeable in this second film that the novelty of film-set stardom was wearing off and that Sinatra was beginning to experience that frustration and boredom with the slow pace of film-making that was to handicap his whole acting career.

It was boredom or frustration that led to the meaningless 'pictures stink' controversy in 1945, when an off-hand remark of Sinatra's was seized on by both trade and daily press and blown up out of all proportion. 'Pictures stink,' Sinatra was quoted as saying. 'Most of the people in them do, too. I don't want any more

movie acting. Hollywood won't believe I'm through, but they'll find out I mean it.' Lack of gratitude seemed to be the accusation against Sinatra; someone had dared suggest something amiss with Hollywood's golden smile. Sinatra was working at the time with MGM and it is significant that the press department there felt it necessary to draft a statement for the rebellious young star: 'It's easy for a guy to get hot under the collar, literally and figuratively, when he's dressed in a hot suit of navy blue and the temperature is 104° and he's getting over a cold to boot. I think I might have spoken too broadly about quitting pictures and about my feelings towards Hollywood. . . '

In 1945 Sinatra swopped studios to do *Anchors Aweigh* with producer Joe Pasternak and director George Sidney. Teamed with Gene Kelly (Kelly doubling as actor and choreographer) Sinatra came up with his best performance to date, demonstrating a slick, fast exuberance, and, as occasionally in his previous two films, the timing of a natural comic. Controversy was forgotten when the film was released.

'Sock artists, sock tunes and sock dances,' was Louella Parsons' judgement of the film in the *Los Angeles Examiner,* and Sinatra's performance, she declared, moved him 'right up into the major star class'. In *Screen Guide's* anniversary poll *Anchors Aweigh* was voted best film of the year.

1945 was also the year that Frank Sinatra stepped out of line to make a ten-minute propaganda short against racial and religious intolerance, *The House I Live In.* Mervyn LeRoy of *Little Caesar* fame directed and Albert Maltz wrote the script that had Sinatra lecturing and singing to a gang of city kids. The film won a special Oscar and was given prominence by the liberal press. But it was one of a series of public political commitments that eventually turned the Republican press anti-Sinatra. Nor did the Hollywood establishment much approve. Politically committed stars remained unacceptable until the Brando/New-

man/Shirley MacLaine anti-racialist, anti-war radicalism of the 1960s.

A year after *The House I Live In* Sinatra's political image took something of a knock when he stood on a white pedestal in an immaculate white tuxedo to sing 'Ol' Man River'. It was, suggested *Life*, the year's worst moment on screen. Sinatra's part was a guest appearance in the Jerome Kern celebration, *Till The Clouds Roll By,* his next major role being the Danny Miller part in *It Happened In Brooklyn*. As in *Anchors Aweigh*, Sinatra won himself good, slightly surprised reviews. John McManus in *PM*: 'The big revelation of *It Happened In Brooklyn*. . .is the way Frank Sinatra seems to have loosened up and got into the swing of things as a film player and even as a comedian.' Sara Hamilton wrote in the *Los Angeles Examiner*, '. . .all of a sudden it's spring and Frankie is an actor'.

But Sinatra's films were still nothing much more than a reflection of his stardom as a singer. When his popularity began to fall off in the world of records and radio his box office magic diminished.

Left: Sinatra and Gloria de Haven rehearse for 'Step Lively'. Centre: Sinatra with co-star Gene Kelly in 'Anchors Aweigh!' Below: Hollywood acknowledges 'The Voice'.

39

The success of Sinatra's early years had been building to a climax in the two years following the end of the War. He had become the country's top night club entertainer; the country's strongest box-office draw in theatres; a 'major star' in the cinema. These were also Sinatra's heaviest recording years—51 numbers including his best-selling 'Coffee Song' in 1946; 72 songs in 1947. At the end of 1946 he won *Down Beat's* award as the country's favourite male singer for the third successive year. He signed a five year film contract with MGM for a guaranteed minimum of $1½ million, plus the music publishing rights in alternate films and the right to one outside picture each year. His weekly radio show was renewed at $12,000 a programme and on the theatre scene he was to break a city box-office record in Chicago—$93,000 for a one week run doing 45 shows in six days and singing upwards of 80 numbers each day.

Yet, for all such comprehensive success, 1946 and 1947 were in a sense the turning years, the beginning of a long, cold slide. Perhaps the pace was beginning to tell; perhaps there was nowhere else for him to go now but downhill. There were certainly enemies waiting for that process of decline to set in.

Late in 1946 a columnist in the Los Angeles *Daily News* ran a story that was in effect the prelude to battle; 'Where there is temperament I guess there's always a beef. First it was wife trouble. Then an argument with MGM over the singing of a song on the radio before its release in a movie. Before leaving for New York Frank was mad at the Los Angeles press. And now it's a battle with a recording company.' George Evans had stayed on the West Coast and when Sinatra read the article his telegraphed response from New York was drafted without his press agent's soothing advice: 'Just continue to print lies about me, and my temper not my temperament will see that you get a belt in your stupid and vicious mouth.'

Sinatra's relations with the press had been deteriorating for some time and the main area of contention was centred, not surprisingly, on his personal life. Early Sinatra fans adopted the whole family, wife and children, as part of their ritual of worship, sending presents and letters to them as well as to Frank himself. Their loyalties had made marital tensions between the two Sinatras even more significant and newsworthy than they might otherwise have been.

At the beginning of his rise to fame in 1943 Sinatra had moved his family into a $25,000 suburban detached in Hasbrouck Heights, New Jersey—a natural home for any well-to-do middle class Italian family on the

Despite press criticism, Sinatra was an active campaigner for Franklin D. Roosevelt in 1944. He is pictured here at one of the many meetings which relied on his 'magic' to draw the crowds.

west bank of the Hudson. The Sinatras had their ups and downs even in these early years, but the home was sacrosanct and Nancy far enough away from her husband's playground on Manhattan to be able to turn the blind eye on his wanderings. Had she been by nature jealous and possessive the marriage could not have lasted beyond the first year for there was, it seemed, no acceptance of sexual fidelity on his side by Frank. But even Nancy's careful detachment would not survive the hot-house gossip and scandal-mongering of Hollywood.

The Sinatras' second child, Franklin Wayne, was only six months old when Frank Snr moved wife and children to the West Coast, separating Nancy Snr from her own family background in New Jersey for the first time and throwing her into the glittering, competitive society of Beverly Hills. Their first Californian home, Mary Astor's ex-residence in the Toluca Lake area, was not a house Nancy particularly liked and instead of the comparative seclusion of Hasbrouck Heights and New Jersey, she now had to cope with gossip and the Hollywood columnists, always so intent on keeping Frankie's list of conquests up-to-date.

The two relationships that showed any permanence through Sinatra's early years of success were his affairs with Lana Turner and Marilyn Maxwell. It was Sinatra's press agent and friend, George Evans, who worked hardest of all to minimize the effects of these interludes, not only with the ubiquitous columnists, but with Frank and Nancy themselves. George Evans had learnt the effect of emotional tension on his volatile client. 'It absolutely destroyed him. You could always tell when he was troubled. He came down with a bad throat. Germs were never the cause unless there are guilt germs.' It was Evans who managed to persuade Sinatra that Lana Turner was using him as a lever in her courtship of Howard Hughes, and Evans again who rallied the Sinatra entourage to apply the pressure when Sinatra took Marilyn Maxwell off to New York for the 1946 Joe Louis/Billy Conn heavyweight fight. Frank planned to sit with Toots Shor at the fight but Shor objected to Frank's partner and following the further intervention of Manie Sachs, Sinatra arrived at the fight without Marilyn Maxwell, in the company instead of Marlene Dietrich and Joe DiMaggio.

Lana Turner's name re-emerged in October the same year when radio and press stories reported Frank Sinatra's first separation from Nancy. Nancy apparently told columnist Hedda Hopper that Frank wanted 'freedom without divorce'. Whatever the actual quarrel Sinatra packed his bags and moved out of the Toluca Lake house and into an apartment. Lana Turner was interviewed about the rift by Louella Parsons and denied being the home-wrecker, while George Evans, making allowances for the career pressures on 'Young Frankie' confidently predicted a reunion and was no doubt instrumental in the public

and sentimental reunion when Frank and Nancy met 'accidentally' on Phil Silvers' opening night at Slapsie Maxie's. Frank sang as an invitation artist and chose the song 'Going Home'. When he finished singing, Phil Silvers led him to Nancy's table and the couple embraced. In a subsequent radio interview Sinatra announced his intention of spending more time back east and of building a country home for the family in Connecticut, thus meeting at least one of Nancy's complaints—though somehow that country home never did get built.

Public scrutiny of Sinatra's private life had already left him with a strong dislike and suspicion of columnists and press photographers, and his anger was not always confined to verbal abuse. In December 1946 the Hollywood Women's Press Club named him 'the least co-operative star of the year', and early the following year Sinatra quarrelled with his one-time columnist ally, Louella Parsons. A telegram was Sinatra's characteristic response to allegations she had made about him in one of her monthly columns: 'I'll begin by saying that if you care to make a bet, I'll be glad to take your money that MGM and Frank Sinatra do not part company, permanently or otherwise. Secondly, Frankie has only been heard from when it concerns the improvement of the picture, which you will find happens in most pictures where you use human beings. Your article claims my pout was caused by something about a song [rumours that Sinatra had been refused the publishing rights to *It Happened In Brooklyn*]. Regardless of where you got this information, from some gossipmonger or otherwise, you can rest assured that if I pouted at all, it would have been for a much bigger reason than a broken-down song. As an added thought, I have always been one of the stalwart defenders of the phrase "nobody is

indispensable", so apparently your line about my being irreplaceable was all wet. Last but not least, in the future I'll appreciate your not wasting your breath in any lectures because when I feel I need one I'll seek such advice from someone who either writes or tells the truth.'

These skirmishings with the columnists can seem in retrospect the first and temperamental signs of decline, but it would be nearer the truth to attribute much of Sinatra's difficulty in 1947 to a deliberate press campaign, undeniably political in its origins.

Not all Sinatra's enemies were victims of his quick-tempered brawling or his bully-boy bodyguards. His social and political attitudes were abhorred by a large and powerful section of the press, in particular the Hearst and the Scripps-Howard empires. Their newspapers and their columnists have always been the vanguard of any anti-Sinatra campaign right up until his change of political allegiance in the late 1960s. Not altogether surprising then if their first campaign was to climax in that McCarthy year of 1947.

Frank Sinatra had been raised in a politically conscious background, his mother playing a not unimportant role in the fortunes of the Hoboken and Jersey City Democrat Party. She served her apprenticeship under the Hoboken Democrat chief Mayor Bernard McFeelers and it was in those early years that the young Sinatra learnt and recognized the ramifications of power and patronage. Those early years had also left him with an undying hatred of religious and racial bigotry. They were years when even the Italian immigrants of New Jersey had been visited by the Ku Klux Klan, childhood years of gang wars that were nearly always racial in character. It had

been an anti-semitic joke at a cocktail party that caused his first publically recorded brawl in the Tommy Dorsey years. The christening of Franklin Wayne in 1944 had provoked a similar reaction when a Roman Catholic priest objected to the nomination of a Jewish godfather—Manie Sachs. There had been an argument in church with Sinatra refusing categorically to nominate anyone else.

Apart from singing at local ward gatherings, Sinatra had taken no active part in Democrat politics during his adolescence and early professional years. But in 1944 he was a surprise tea party guest of Franklin D. Roosevelt at a White House reception, invited along with restaurateur Toots Shor and the comedian Rags Ragland through the Democrat National Committee chairman, Robert Hannegan, an old friend of Shor. 'The greatest guy alive,' Sinatra said of Franklin D. Roosevelt and not surprisingly he joined the election campaign later that same year. He was a member of the 'Independent Voters Committee of the Arts and Sciences for Roosevelt', and volunteered his services as a speaker both at rally meetings and on radio. When he contributed $5,000 to the election fund the news made headlines, and in so doing he made enemies with the nation's republican columnists. Westbrook Pegler condemned his meddling in politics and dubbed him the 'New Dealing Crooner'. Lee Mortimer, always an enemy of the hysterics of 'Sinatrauma', seemed to see two evils linked—hundreds of thousands of Sinatra bobby-soxers marching obediently in Democrat Party

Left: Sinatra at a baseball game with Marilyn Maxwell, Virginia Mayo and Ava. Below: With Lana Turner. Right: Lana Turner with her bandleader husband Artie Shaw.

parades. (For two weeks that autumn his fears seemed justified—the election campaign ran second best to the Paramount Theatre 'Columbus Day Riots' and Sinatra once used his public magic to draw Republican crowds away from a Thomas Dewey reception committee at the doors of the Waldorf.)

Sinatra himself wrote later: 'My first real criticism from the press came when I campaigned for President Roosevelt in 1944. A few columnists took me to task insisting that entertainers should stick to entertaining. Most stars agree with this. They also realize it is bad public relations to indulge in politics because you may lose fans who don't agree with you. However, I feel it is the duty of every American citizen to help elect the candidates of his choice. Ginger Rogers, George Murphy and other stars supported Tom Dewey during this campaign, and I noted that none of my critics lambasted them.'

On 31 October, 1944, Sinatra appeared at a Madison Square Garden rally along with Harry Truman and Fiorello La Guardia. It was his first public appearance at a mass rally and when he stepped forward to speak he found the emotion had dried up his voice. He recovered enough to present a brief and rather simplistic statement of belief in FDR: 'He is good for me and my kids and my country.'

Most of his electioneering that year went unrecorded but he was considered, along with Orson Welles, as the most effective radio performer in the Democrat cause. Election night saw Sinatra, Welles and Republican columnist Westbrook Pegler all in separate suites at the Waldorf, where it was later claimed Sinatra had baited the disappointed columnist as the election results indicated a Democrat victory. It was one of those 'incidents' where second-hand reporting recreated all possible permutations of the truth. One version, denied vigorously by Pegler, casually by Sinatra, had the Voice busting up the jounalist's room in an exuberant victory celebration. A second version saw Sinatra busting up his own room in frustration after finding Pegler's door locked. According to Orson Welles, he and Sinatra spent the evening in 'appropriate celebration' at Toots Shor's restaurant.

Whatever did or did not happen that evening at the Waldorf, Sinatra now had powerful and embittered enemies watching and waiting for his bandwagon to lose momentum. His social campaigning the following year did nothing to alleviate their hostility. The Republican press had already highlighted a Sinatra fisticuffs with a barman who had refused to serve a Negro musician. They were less enthusiastic about publicizing his trips to lecture school kids on racial prejudice after the Harlem riots of 1945. In the same year, and after a high school boycott protesting against the admission of Negro children, Sinatra visited an Indiana school, opening his meeting there against a chorus of jeering and booing. He ended up with the 5,000 students listening to him in silence.

It was after this flurry of activity that film director Mervyn LeRoy first approached Sinatra with the idea of making the propaganda short. RKO were persuaded to donate studio facilities and stock, and Axel Stordahl dug out an old revue song (written by Lewis Allen and Earl Robinson) to give the film both its title and main selling angle. *The House I Live In* (1945) collected a special Oscar for Sinatra and LeRoy and served to further irritate those hale, hearty and healthy Americans who believed that the entertainment world should remain forever politically colourless, odourless and inoffensive.

As a golden child of the Catholic community Sinatra did himself even more harm in 1946 when he blasted off against the Franco regime in Spain. The Catholic press now joined in the chase, telling their skinny singer to confine his social work to spastics and paralytics. At least one newspaper, the *Standard and Times* of Philadelphia, labelled him a pawn of 'fellow travellers'. The notorious House Un-American Activities Committee, feeding on smear and innuendo, was thus served up with Sinatra's name, but did not quite dare the ridicule that might have followed his subpoena. Consequently Sinatra had no opportunity to answer the 'pinko' charges that continued to appear spasmodically in the Hearst papers. In 1949 Senator Jack Tenney would bracket Sinatra in with Katherine Hepburn, Gregory Peck, Danny Kaye and Thomas Mann as a fellow traveller with communist leanings. Sadly, the USA took such wild mud-slinging with great seriousness at the time and headlines such as 'Red Scare Sinatra' and 'Sinatra Faces Probe on Red Ties'

contributed to his initial loss of public support in that
critical year of 1947.

1947 was also the first year that the singer's name
was openly cited by the press in connection with
alleged friends or acquaintances in the society of
organized crime—the year of the infamous Lucky
Luciano incident.

Sinatra's fascination with the underworld dated
back to his childhood in Hoboken and his early singing
days in the roadhouses and clubs of New Jersey, venues
more often than not under the protection or control of
some local Mafia. He became friendly with the *capo*,
Quarico 'Willie Moore' Moretti, the man who, it was

*Right: Lana Turner. Below: In spite of
increasing harrassment at the hands
of the Republican press, Sinatra
was still welcomed by Hoboken
as their most famous 'son'.
At a parade held in his honour
Sinatra greets the crowd from
a fire truck driven by his
proud father, Captain Martin
Sinatra, commander of
Engine No. 5 in Hoboken, N.J.*

said, pushed the revolver barrel down Tommy Dorsey's throat when the band leader was refusing to release Sinatra. As late as 1950 Moretti was sending telegrams to Sinatra reminding him in a paternalistic Sicilian way that he had a 'decent wife and children'—this presumably in reference to press stories about Sinatra's traumatic and very non-Catholic romance with Ava Gardner. (Moretti was eventually to die the traditional gangster's death—a bullet in a back street, victim of gang warfare or some obscure vendetta.)

The 'gun in the mouth' Tommy Dorsey episode was alluded to in *The Godfather* and led to a general assumption that the Johnny Fontane character was a fictional development of Frank Sinatra. In fact then, and later, there was no factual evidence with which to gauge the depth of Sinatra's involvement with the 'Organization'. Contrary to popular belief Sinatra had no hereditary link with the Mafia. His father's family came from the relatively prosperous east coast of Sicily, originally from the orange grove country around Paterno and later, in his father's time, from the city of Catania. The Mafia had failed to infiltrate in this part of Sicily beyond some control of wholesale commerce and urban crime. There was no endemic secret society, as in the towns and villages of the interior and west of the island, although his Sicilian blood certainly gave him a natural bond with the Morettis, Lucheses, Patriarcas and Fischettis of New Jersey, New York and Chicago. Friendship would have been offered and accepted with less than usual reticence and a two-way traffic of favours might have resulted from such associations. Sinatra's night club, boxing and gambling interests would have increased a traffic of favours, but the implications of these relationships remain a mystery.

Accidental or not, a visit by Sinatra to Cuba in February 1947 coincided with a syndicate 'summit conference'. He arrived in Havana on the same flight as Rocco and Joe Fischetti, members of a Chicago underworld family and cousins of Al Capone. Sinatra's visit was shadowed and reported on by a journalist, Robert Ruark, an employee of the Scripps-Howard chain of papers—a Republican group where Sinatra was already, if not a marked man, certainly *persona non grata*.

The 'summit conference' in Havana had been called by Lucky Luciano, then considered to be chief of chiefs in the Mafia clans. He had been responsible for the unification of Italian Mafia factions following the end of prohibition in the 1930s and had then combined with the most powerful elements in Irish and Jewish crime to create the basis of what later came to be called the Syndicate or the Organization. Imprisoned on a prohibition charge in 1936 he managed to manoeuvre himself a parole after the war, following the help he was supposed to have given to American forces during the invasion of Sicily in 1943. The conditions of parole included deportation, but apparently there was a tacit understanding that Luciano

would be allowed to return to the States after a few years. His visit to Havana in 1947 was a preparation for this return. He held court there and the Syndicate bosses flew over from their territories in the States to confer with him.

'Charlie' Lucky's gathering was being watched by agents of the Federal Narcotics Bureau, and it was these agents who first reported officially on the alleged meetings between Sinatra and Luciano. The Narcotics Bureau chief, Henry Anslinger, was already a declared opponent of Sinatra's liberal 'pinko' attitudes, and, coincidentally or not Bureau information was leaked to journalist Robert Ruark, who wrote up the story with an emphasis by now familiar in the Scripps-Howard chain of newspapers: 'Sinatra was here (in Havana) for four days last week and during that time his companions in public and in private was Luciano, Luciano's bodyguards and a rich collection of gamblers and highbinders. The friendship was beautiful . . . Mr Sinatra, self-confessed saviour of the country's small-fry, seems to be setting a most peculiar example for his hordes of pimply, shrieking slaves.'

Sinatra would later claim coincidence for the meetings with the Fischettis and Luciano: 'I had some time off and decided to vacation in Havana and Mexico City. On the way, I stopped off at Miami to play a benefit for the Damon Runyon Cancer Fund. I ran into Joe Fischetti there and when he found I was headed for Havana, he told me he and his brothers were going there too. He changed his reservation to be on my plane. . . .

46

Left: Sinatra and Judy Garland in 1946. Above:
Sinatra with Moss Hart and Ethel Merman,
harmonizing for F.D.R.

'That night I was having a drink at the bar with Connie Immerman, a New York restaurateur, and met a large group of men and women. As so often happens in big groups, the introductions were perfunctory. I was invited to have dinner with them and while dining, I realized that one of the men in the party was Lucky Luciano. It suddenly struck me that I was laying myself open to criticism by remaining at the table, but I could think of no way to leave in the middle of dinner without creating a scene.

'After dinner I went to the *jai alai* games and then, with an acquaintance, toured the night spots. We finally wound up at the Havana Casino where we passed a table at which were Luciano and several other men. They insisted that we sit down for a drink. Again, rather than cause a disturbance, I had a quick drink and excused myself. These were the only times I've ever seen Luciano in my life.'

According to Tony Scaduto in his biography, *Sinatra,* Narcotics Bureau information stated that the singer had spent four days with the Syndicate chief, 'gambling and partying until the early hours', but that he had never been included in any of the business conferences that took place during those four days.

Ruark himself later moderated his views on Sinatra's Mafia associations, but not before the same Havana incident had been revived around election time in 1951, this time by Lee Mortimer. Again the information he used had apparently been leaked by the Narcotics Bureau, the charge against Sinatra being that he had smuggled $2 million of Mafia funds in his overnight valise—investment 'dues' for Luciano. The story killed itself in exaggerated detail. The $2 million were said to have been smuggled in dollar bills. 'Picture me,' answered Sinatra, 'skinny Frankie, lifting $2 million in small bills. For the record, $1,000 in dollar bills weighs three pounds, which makes the load I am supposed to have carried 6,000 pounds. Even assuming that the bills were $20—the bag would still have required a couple of stevedores to carry it. This is probably the most ridiculous charge that has ever been levelled at me. . . .' By then even the credulous American public had raised an eyebrow and the insinuation was never followed up with any more definite evidence. If the Narcotics Bureau had gathered something of a case against him the leaking of information to a newspaper columnist was no way to bring such a case to a satisfactory conclusion. The motivation behind Mortimer's charge, whether per-

sonally or politically inspired, was undoubtedly his intense dislike of Sinatra.

Lee Mortimer had been the centre of Sinatra's most notorious public brawl to date—another bad incident from that worst of all years, 1947. Sinatra had already felt the sting of Ruark's Lucky Luciano story from Havana and suffered the ill-effects of his quarrel with Louella Parsons. The 'fellow traveller' smear had hung over from his 1946 outburst against Franco. He was, to put it mildly, paranoiac about his press relations. In mid-March *It Happened In Brooklyn* had premiered to a largely favourable reception for Sinatra's performance. The one exception in content and tone was Lee Mortimer. He praised the film, but condemned the actor: '. . . this excellent and well-produced picture . . . bogs down under the miscast Frank (Lucky) Sinatra, smirking and trying to play a leading man.'

Less than one month later, on 8 April, Sinatra and Mortimer were both dining at Ciro's on Sunset Strip. On his way out Lee Mortimer had an exchange of words with Sinatra and later admitted to passing a couple of cracks about Sinatra's relationship with Lucky Luciano. The insults escalated and Mortimer ended up on the floor at the end of a Sinatra punch and, depending on which version of events you read, being pummelled or not being pummelled by two, three, or four, Sinatra associates.

The whole Hearst organization moved into action behind Mortimer—editors, attorneys and columnists. Sinatra was arrested by police during a date at a radio station and bailed out for $500 after his request for a jury trial. The incident rated Hearst headlines for five whole days and divided the rest of the country's press fairly equally between the two camps. Ed Sullivan, for example, argued in the *Daily News* that Sinatra had had more than enough provocation from Mortimer, and Earl Wilson in the *Post* reminded his readers of Mortimer's insulting attitude towards Sinatra's young fans. But what might have turned into an interesting legal discussion of provocation and justification was cut short by the intervention of Louis B. Mayer, head of MGM Studios. He pointed out to Sinatra that should the case go against him the charge of battery carried a possible six months jail sentence. Sinatra was persuaded to settle the affair. Nearly two months

after the incident, on 4 June, 1947, the two protagonists faced each other in the District Court at Beverly Hills. Sinatra read out a statement without once acknowledging the presence of his antagonist. The statement expressed the usual regrets at what had happened, and also acknowledged that there had been no provocation from Mortimer. Mortimer, in turn, expressed himself satisfied and the court ordered the charge to be withdrawn. The out of court settlement made to Mortimer was thought to have been $9,000 but the whole affair with legal expenses cost Sinatra over $20,000.

Westbrook Pegler was the next man into the ring from the Hearst corner in September, dragging up a stillborn seduction charge against Sinatra that dated back to 1938 and the young singer's days at the Rustic Cabin. Again Ed Sullivan helped the Sinatra camp set the record straight: 'The attempted smear of Sinatra on 1938 charges is rather stupid. The woman was thirty years old, mother of an eight-year-old child, not unmarried as alleged. The Grand Jury twice threw out her charges of "seduction". . . '

The first ominous signs that the press campaign was beginning to affect Sinatra's popularity came that autumn of 1947 when he played a three week season at the Capitol Theatre in New York (this being the occasion of Sammy Davis Jr's first appearance on stage with him). At the opening of the show the Hearst empire substituted critic Harold Conrad's favourable review in the New York *Mirror* with an unfavourable one written jointly by Lee Mortimer and editor Jack Lait, but left under Conrad's name. The audience, whether or not dissuaded by the efforts of the Hearst press, stayed away from the show, and takings were less than half the expected figure. Lee Mortimer positively gloated: 'Broadway whispers this will be Sinatra's last appearance here and that didn't kill my appetite for the family turkey dinner.'

Even Hollywood's show-biz columnists began their ladylike climb off what they felt was a sinking ship. 'What's wrong with Frankie?' was Hedda Hopper's query; 'he isn't a well boy', was Louella Parsons' summary of the situation. 'The old screamers are now in their sedate "twenties",' wrote Sheila Graham, 'and without the hullabaloo, Frank's voice doesn't seem quite so potent.'

A bad year. And there was worse to come.

The culmination of a bad year for Sinatra: arraigned in a Beverly Hills Justice Court on a battery charge, he chats to a reporter while ignoring Lee Mortimer (standing behind him). Mortimer, a reporter with one of the Hearst newspapers, brought the charge against Sinatra after a night club brawl in April 1947.

5 LOVE AND DISASTER 1948-1952

1946 had been Sinatra's last year as indisputable king of pop. 'The Coffee Song' and 'Five Minutes More' were his big sellers of the year, together with 'The Things We Did Last Summer' and the Rachmaninoff inspired 'Full Moon And Empty Arms' with its theme from the Second Piano Concerto. But by the end of the year even Sinatra seemed to be anticipating the need for a change in musical fashion when he discarded the Cahn-Styne-Stordahl sound in his final recording session of the year and cut 'Sweet Lorraine' with Sy Oliver and a group of leading jazz musicians.

During the following two years Sinatra found himself picking the right songs, but seeing them 'hit' with other vocalists: 'Once In Love With Amy' that became Ray Bolger's triumph and 'Nature Boy' that made the top with Nat 'King' Cole. But even the songs were beginning to change. The world of pop was moving towards a harder sound, the full, muscular voice of a Frankie Laine, the country traditions of Nashville's Hank Williams. Tony Bennett ('Cold, Cold Heart') and Perry Como began to steal Sinatra's crooning, *bel canto* audience and Nat 'King' Cole his clubland status.

The situation was made no easier for Sinatra in that he still occupied the centre showcase in Tin Pan Alley, the Saturday evening Hit Parade he shared with Doris Day on radio. The songs were more often than not out of his style and he could scarcely disguise the fact that there were none of his own singles in the top end of the record selling charts. Already in 1947 *Metronome* had condemned the Hit Parade shows as 'alternately dull, pompous and raucous'. Even if the format of the show was not Sinatra's responsibility *Metronome* found his singing equally unconvincing: 'Frank sings without relaxation and often at tempos that don't suit him or the songs. Axel (Stordahl) plays murderous, rag-timey junk that

For the next few years Sinatra's life entwined itself with that of the incomparable Ava Gardner (left and centre). Inset: Frank and Ava on their wedding day at the home of the record company executive, Lester Sachs.

he, with his impeccable taste, must abhor . . . Frank sounds worse in these Saturday nightmares than he ever has since he first became famous.'

Sinatra persisted with the show through 1948 and the first four months of 1949. But in May that year he finally gave up, condemning both the songs he had to sing, and the style in which he had to sing them. To add to his discomfort the *Down Beat* poll at the end of 1949 pushed him out of the top spots for the first time since 1943. Billy Eckstine headed the poll; Frankie Laine was placed second; Bing Crosby tied with Mel Tormé in third place; and Sinatra could only manage fifth spot. The singers who figured that year in a 'Best Discs of the Year' compilation were Eckstine and Doris Day with two each, Frankie Laine, Perry Como, Vic Damone, Nat 'King' Cole, Sarah Vaughan, Ella Fitzgerald and even Metropolitan Opera star, Dorothy Kirsten. But not Sinatra.

In 1950 the eclipse of swooning 'Sinatrauma' was completed with the arrival of Johnnie Ray out of a Detroit cabaret. Following the Sinatra pattern of 1943 Ray not only conquered the teenage market of theatre, radio and record sales, but won over the swells and sophisticates of the Copacabana. He was to reign more or less intact until the arrival of Presley six years later.

Fortunately Frank Sinatra had the good sense to let all this happen without attempting any radical change of style in his own singing. There were new faces in his recording entourage: Sy Oliver, Xavier Cugat, Mitchell Ayres, Phil Moore. But the development from Sinatra croon to Sinatra swing was a gradual evolution and each stage of the evolution was unmistakably a Sinatra style. There was no attempt on his part to ape the full-voice, foot-stamping opulence of the Frankie Laine sound or the histrionics of Johnnie Ray.

In January, 1950, Sinatra's most steadfast ally in the recording world, Manie Sachs, resigned from the board of Columbia records. The new recording boss at Columbia, Mitch Miller, preferred the modern noise — the 'belters', Frankie Laine, Eddie Fisher and Georgia Gibbs. He tried to push Sinatra towards the new sound (such as on the 1950 album 'Sing And Dance With Frank Sinatra'), but he was more interested in his own 'discoveries' — Rosemary Clooney, Guy Mitchell, Tony Bennett and Johnnie Ray. Unlike his predecessor, Manie Sachs, he had little time or inclination to boost the flagging Sinatra. Sinatra was later to allege that Miller had presented him with inferior songs in which he had financial or publishing interests. Miller pointed out that his job was to record songs that were profitable to Columbia: 'I would not select unpromising material deliberately. I would be defeating my own purpose.' Sinatra's accusations were submitted in 1956 as evidence to a House Judiciary and Senate Committees investigating the TV industry and its associated business interests and even years later,

at a chance meeting with Miller in a Las Vegas hotel, Sinatra ignored the request to let bygones be bygones, with a 'Fuck you, keep walking' to Miller's outstretched hand.

Sinatra had a lot to forgive and forget from these years of decline, even if Miller himself had had little to do with the ensuing collapse of his recording career. Sinatra recorded some good songs in his last year at Columbia ('The Birth of the Blues', 'I'm A Fool To Want You' and 'Why Try To Change Me Now') but when his contract expired in December 1952 he owed the company over $100,000 in unearned advances and neither Columbia nor any of the other

*Despite fading popularity at the end of the forties,
Sinatra appeared in several films. Above: 'On the
Town', and right, 'Take Me Out to the Ball Game'.*

record companies made a move to sign him up. That
same year he had played to a half empty Paramount
theatre in New York and worse still to a night club
audience at the Chez Paree in Chicago that scarcely
filled one tenth of the tables.

Even his cinema following was falling away. In 1948
he returned to RKO and attempted his first out of

53

type acting role as the priest in *The Miracle Of The Bells*. He restricted himself to a single song ('Ever Homeward') and played a quiet-spoken third string to Fred MacMurray and Alida Valli. As a restrained piece of acting he makes out all right as Father Paul, but the film was not well received and a non-singing Sinatra did not tempt fans to the cinemas in anything like their old numbers. MGM pushed him back into musicals with a terrible costume picture, *The Kissing Bandit* (1948), then finally returned him to song and dance routines with Gene Kelly. As the first of a 1949 pair, *Take Me Out To The Ball Game* was not so successful. Gene Kelly and Stanley Donen had conceived a thin story outline which never quite managed to fill out and the film ends up as a series of laboriously connected songs and dances. The Kelly/Donen partnership proved more successful as a directing team later in the same year. *On The Town* (1949) had started life as a musical play and was dramatically a tighter and more consequential piece — three sailors on a 24 hour furlough in New York, '. . . a film so exuberant', wrote the *Time* critic, 'that it threatens at moments to bounce right off the screen.'

Significantly it was promoted more as an old-style Hollywood bonanza musical than as a Sinatra movie. The decline in his fortunes was now in full free-fall and the undoubted success of his acting as Kelly's shipmate and the number two sailor did little to help him. By this time he was up for grabs, moving back to

RKO for the 1951 production *Double Dynamite* and on to Universal for *Meet Danny Wilson* later the same year. In *Double Dynamite* he was eclipsed by co-stars Groucho Marx and Jane Russell and ended up looking something like an uninvited guest. Already in this film the face is changing. The boyish look, around which his part is built, has gone. The facial lines and the taut nervousness did not fit in with the ingenuous Johnny Dalton. Sinatra must have seemed then to studio executives a has-been on his fast way out.

In practical terms *Danny Wilson* treated him no better. The film and his performance passed by with no great effect on the public or at the box-office. In fact the part is his most underestimated piece of acting and perhaps we see for the first time in this role the commitment and toughness that were to help him from obscurity to an outright Oscar three years later. The biographical parallels between Danny Wilson

Right: Sinatra with Jane Russell and the indomitable Groucho Marx in 'Double Dynamite'. Below: An impromptu concert with (l. to r.) Ed Wynn, Ethel Merman, Bob Hope and Tallulah Bankhead.

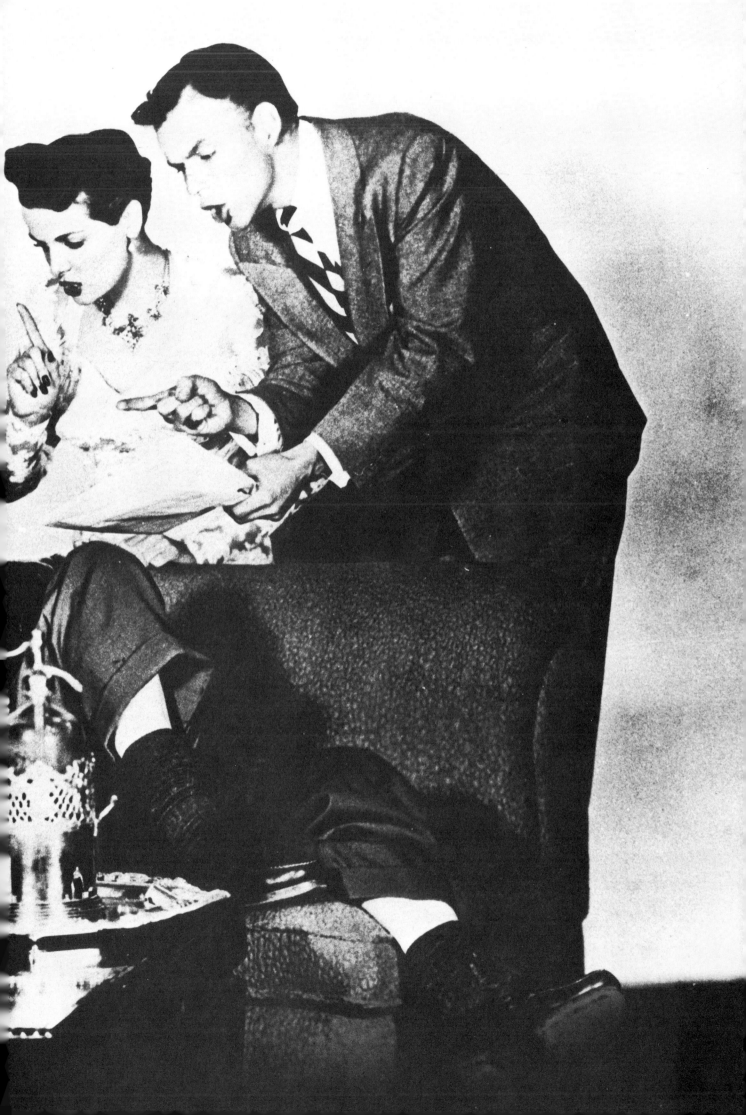

and Frank Sinatra are not hidden and Sinatra plays him at times with an almost masochistic anger—'a convincing portrayal, *Newsweek* was to say, 'of a nasty little success boy'. The story was set in a racketeering night club background and Kay Proctor in the *Los Angeles Examiner* commented that 'for the first time on the screen he seems completely at ease, and sure of himself and what he is doing. . . . I suspect it is because the role of Danny Wilson quite openly parallels Sinatra's own career. . . .'

Such recognition appeared to have come too late. However good the acting, this was the last of the 'first decade' Sinatra films. By the end of 1951 there was not a Hollywood studio that wanted to hear his name and when CBS cancelled Sinatra's TV contract that same autumn his last show-biz stage had disappeared.

The growth of the television audience in the late 'forties must have diminished the size and potential of Sinatra's live audiences in much the same proportion as it cut into cinema box-office receipts. In May 1950 Sinatra had bowed to the inevitable and accepted an invitation from Bob Hope to appear on a show. He impressed enough people with his first TV appearance to land himself a five-year contract with CBS that guaranteed a minimum quarter million dollars income a year. The amount of money involved probably reflected more the open-pocket hustle of the early TV entrepreneurs than the drawing power of the failing Sinatra. Perhaps would-be sponsors figured that the crooner's swooners, now married couples in

their twenties, were an important element in the captive sitting-room audience.

But Sinatra's debut in October that year was disappointing. As an M.C. and anchor-man in a musical show he demonstrated an unease that was poison on the close-up screen. CBS had lavished a budget to pull in Frankie Laine, Perry Como and the Andrews Sisters but Sinatra, over-casual and under-scripted, couldn't disguise the effort involved in introducing talents that had been usurping his public. Perry Como stole the Sinatra show and the ratings on the rival Milton Berle show (Tony Bennett, the Mills Brothers and Rosemary Clooney) never dropped far enough to impress the sponsors. Eventually they pulled out altogether, giving CBS the wherewithal to cancel their contract.

His failures in these early TV shows reflected Sinatra's apparently inescapable decline. But they were not necessarily representative. Television, live or recorded, remained and still remains the one medium he has never wholly conquered, his one public face that seems perpetually and irredeemably ill-at-ease, a reflection almost of his tempestuous and unhappy personal life.

the third Sinatra child, Christina, arrived in June 1948. That same year the family moved into a luxurious new home in the Holmby Hills area of Beverly Hills and George Evans, together with most of Sinatra's friends, now predicted the long-term survival of the marriage. They had reckoned without Sinatra's 'Hurricane' Ava.

Sinatra had first met Ava Gardner at a Palm Springs night club during his separation from Nancy in 1946, when he and Howard Hughes had swopped respective partners, Lana Turner and Ava Gardner, for a couple of dances. According to a friend of hers, Ruth Schechter, Ava found him 'conceited, arrogant and overpowering', and for nearly three years she maintained her public dislike and disapproval of the brash young Italian singer. Perhaps it was significant that the two of them never really hit it off together until Sinatra had become something of a lost cause and a lost soul, still a public personality, but privately vulnerable and lost—half male hero, half stray dog. Dethroned king.

Ava Gardner had arrived at Hollywood in 1941, a nervous unsophisticated eighteen-year-old country girl from North Carolina, talent-spotted in a photograph by a young errand clerk working in MGM's New York office. She had been through the full MGM training and grooming as an apprentice starlet; had married Mickey Rooney in 1942; divorced in 1943; had been dated over three years by Howard Hughes; married Artie Shaw in 1945; divorced in 1946. Beyond her countless walk-on parts and studio mis-castings—her 'clothes-horse years', she called them—she had made two films that had done some justice to her talent and image—*Whistle Stop* (1945) with director Léonide Moguy, and *The Killers* (1946) under Robert Siodmak.

The Frank/Ava love affair burst into life it seems on the evening of 8 December, 1949, when the two of them met at the premier of a New York show, *Gentlemen Prefer Blondes*. Their mutual enjoyment of each other's company was obvious enough on that occasion to become a talking point around New York next day, though the affair did not, as it were, lift off the ground until they met again two weeks later at a Palm Springs party. By Christmas they were frequently being seen together and when Sinatra was booked into a two week date at the Shamrock Hotel in Houston, Texas, after New Year, he decided against everyone's better judgement, to take Ava along with him.

Before travelling south to Texas, Sinatra flew into New York to see his press agent, George Evans. The two of them had been on uneasy terms for some time, their differences of opinion not unconnected with the crisis in Sinatra's private life. The meeting in New York seemed to restore something of their original

Sinatra's years of decline coincided with the final break-up of his first marriage, and the wild, destructive trauma of his love affair with Ava Gardner. Earl Wilson, the columnist and biographer perhaps closest of all to Sinatra, called this grand passion 'one of the wildest weirdest love stories ever told about a show business couple . . . a two year soap opera with screaming fights heard around the world'. The London *Daily Sketch* called it 'the most exhausting game of transatlantic ping-pong ever played'. And yet, similarly to the more recent Richard Burton/Elizabeth Taylor epic, biographers can still only relate the externals of the affairs—journeys, public fights, public laughter, public scandal, separation, reunion, re-separation. It is the one period of his life when Frank Sinatra seems wholly insecure, wholly vulnerable and wholly out of control of a situation. But it is impossible to know, perhaps even for him, how far this was due to his infatuation, and how far to the collapse of his career and public life.

The ups and downs of the Sinatra marriage had continued after that first brief separation in 1946. Hedda Hopper, on a visit to his home, found Frank 'restless and bored'. It was Hollywood's surprise when

friendship and respect, but three days later George Evans died suddenly from a heart attack. That same fateful week in January 1950 the other 'prop' in Sinatra's clan, Manie Sachs, had resigned from the Columbia board and in the middle of his own personal crisis Sinatra was left without the only two colleagues capable of influencing his public and private behaviour. Sinatra returned to New York for Evans' funeral—the end of a close, seven year friendship—then rejoined Ava Gardner in Houston to complete his engagement at the Shamrock, the two of them by now spot-lit in the public eye. A disagreement with a Houston photographer was misrepresented and made headlines across the nation, and once this 'aggro' had been established the romance became hot news for every editor or cub-reporter in the western world.

At times even, press and public opinion seemed to dictate the very geography and chronology of the affair. After a second Sinatra separation on St Valentine's day—this time on Nancy's initiative—columnists turned on Ava Gardner, dubbing her the home-wrecker and calling her a variety of the synonyms that passed in those days for the five letter word 'whore'. MGM had cast her in Albert Lewin's *Pandora And The Flying Dutchman* due to be shot in Spain that spring and early summer, and she decided to anticipate her departure. But not before she had travelled to New York with Frank in March for his first Copacabana date since his years of peak success. It was the only important engagement Sinatra had had for many months and he was terrified of failure. On his opening night he seemed to be on the verge of collapse and had to have treatment from a doctor. Through his first ten evenings Ava sat up front in the audience willing him to succeed. Who knows but that the audience had not come predominantly to goggle at the pair of them. The public was given its moment of lynch-mob passion on the opening night when Sinatra was foolish or unthinking enough to sing 'Nancy With The Laughing Face'—and the Park Avenue sophisticates turned and laughed openly at Ava.

The tensions between the two of them were

58

Left: Sinatra with Ava Gardner at a Hollywood premiere. Above: Sinatra in London in 1950.

To no avail. On 26 April, 1950, Nancy filed for separate maintenance and the same day at the Copacabana, New York, Sinatra lost his voice for the first time in his life. He had been having trouble with his throat for some days but there were those in his entourage who remembered George Evans' assertion during a similar period of voice trouble that Sinatra's voice crises were caused by nervous stress — the 'guilt germs'. Ordered to take two weeks' rest, Sinatra left for Spain on day eight of his enforced vacation. He spent a few uncertain and uncomfortable days at Tossa del Mar in and out of Ava Gardner's company, while the papers wrote stories of how Mario Cabre had shut himself up in his room writing poems to Ava while he waited for the American singer to return home.

As in New York the two of them parted unhappy and uneasy, Ava back to the external frills of the romance with Mario Cabre, Frank back home to his disintegrating career. He arrived in Los Angeles in time to read the *Los Angeles Times* report on his Spanish departure (the sequence described was part of the film Ava was working on, not the spontaneous love scene it is made out to be): 'Tossa del Mar. Ten minutes after Frank Sinatra left for Paris Ava Gardner ran into the street blowing kisses to Mario Cabre. Frank Sinatra left thirty seconds before Cabre rode down main street in a horse-drawn carriage to an ovation by flower-throwing villagers and peasants, all staged for *Pandora and the Flying Dutchman* in which Ava Gardner co-stars with James Mason.

'Miss Gardner ran to the village from her villa a few minutes after bidding good-bye to Frank Sinatra. She elbowed her way to the front ranks. When the carriage passed, Ava shouted: "Mario mio, Mario mio", and blew kisses, but stayed out of camera range. Cabre beamed. After the scene, Cabre walked over and gave Miss Gardner a bouquet. The crowd in the square applauded as he kissed her on each cheek and hugged her saying: "Hello, baby. Okay, Baby".

'Cabre bared his chest, showing where bull's horns penetrated yesterday. Cabre (in Spanish): "I was thinking of Ava even when the bull had me up against the rail. I think of her all the time. She is sublime."

'Ava dined with Frank Sinatra last night, breakfasted with Frank Sinatra this morning. Tonight, Miss Gardner dines with Cabre.'

Sinatra's response to the report was uncharacteristically cool, considering his state of mind. . . . 'I hadn't counted on that bullfighter. He was an added starter they ran in at the last minute. I never did meet him. I assume that what he said was just a publicity stunt.'

In July *Pandora* moved to the MGM studios in London and Sinatra, with an impending date at the London Palladium, flew to join Ava again. For once the interlude was happy. London treated them well: their privacy was respected (they lived in separate

screwed up tighter during this unhappy New York stay. One night Ava Gardner went out night-clubbing with the writer Richard Condon and a girlfriend. They visited Bop City where Ava's ex-husband Artie Shaw was singing, and when Sinatra heard where she had gone he threatened suicide over the telephone to her, firing shots from a revolver into a mattress as he was talking. According to which version of the story one believes Ava either coolly hung up on him, or hurried round to his Hampshire House suite in a state of hysteria. A few days later, nervous and unhappy, she left New York for London en route for her work in Spain.

If she had hoped to escape the attentions of journalists and photographers she was to be disappointed. Spain was unused in those days to film units and Hollywood stars, and the Spanish press were glad enough of a story that would not be subject to political censorship. They discovered Ava's love for Spain, and seemed also to discover romance between Ava and her co-star, bullfighter Mario Cabre, news which delighted Sinatra's columnist enemies back in the States. They gave the rumours great prominence and speculated that the official Frank-Nancy separation need not after all take place.

flats in Berkeley Square); and the London audience, seeing the live Sinatra for the first time, received him with an ecstatic fervour reminiscent of his early solo days at the New York Paramount. His voice had recovered and his confidence, briefly, returned. London society feted him, accepted Ava and let them live perhaps their happiest two months together.

'They were drawn to each other,' wrote Charles Higham in his biography *Ava*, 'not only because of sexual attraction but because they were so much alike. Both were night people, barely capable of sleeping at all, liking to sit up into the small hours. Both loved Italian food, hard liquor, boxing matches, both were generous, warm, fiercely honest, violent-tempered, afraid of being used, deeply insecure and sceptical of their own talents, neurotic, tension-ridden. Their energies fused, and their relationship was from the outset passionate and yet deeply frustrating, tormenting because, similar as they were, they had a terrifying ability to seek out each other's weaknesses.'

Back in the States that autumn the tensions returned. Neither of them was yet secure in the relationship, Sinatra intensely jealous whenever they were apart, Ava Gardner impatient at the delays in Sinatra's attempts to secure a divorce.

Nancy Sinatra won her suit for separate maintenance on 28 September with an award of one third of her husband's annual salary on the first $150,000, ten per cent on the second $150,000, and a decreasing scale thereafter. Nancy also kept the Holmby Hills house, some shares in the Sinatra Music Corporation, and not unnaturally, custody of the three children. She was reported to have been in tears throughout the court proceedings, and steadfastly refused to contemplate the possibility of divorce. Frank had left home several times before; it was not yet for her the end of the marriage, and indeed throughout the winter Sinatra continued to make regular visits home to the family.

Sinatra's work was concentrated on his TV shows during the autumn and winter—'a drab mixture of radio, routine vaudeville and pallid pantomime', Jack Gould called it in the *New York Times*—while Ava Gardner instead was working on her most important and successful role to date, the part of Julie in the film *Show Boat*. The contrast in their work did not improve relations between them and by the following spring Ava was threatening not to see Sinatra again until he had obtained his divorce. It was at the end of that March (1951) when Sinatra recorded his intensely moving and despairing version of 'I'm A Fool To Want You'—a song for which he shared the writing credit. The agony in that song prolonged itself through spring and summer. In May Nancy finally agreed to allow divorce proceedings to start. 'I refused him a

divorce for a long time,' she told Louella Parsons, 'because I though he would come back to his home... I am now convinced that a divorce is the only way for my happiness as well as Frank's.' Hedda Hopper suggested later that Nancy had changed her mind because she felt public opinion was beginning to turn against her. In many people's eyes the ill-starred lovers were no longer villains, but hero and heroine.

Legal complications were still postponing freedom or decision. At the end of July the two of them gave the press another field day when they 'slipped away' for a quiet holiday in Mexico. Their departure from Los Angeles was delayed when Sinatra demanded that the tarmac and ramp be cleared of photographers. At the plane's stop-over in El Paso photographers and newsmen were waiting again. In Mexico an estimated 70 newsmen and photographers had been assigned exclusively to the job of following the couple around and cataloguing their movements. They stayed in Acapulco, had a fight with a cameraman in a night club, denied rumours of a Sinatra divorce and quick marriage and on their return to Los Angeles side-swiped a newsman in the airport car-park when a barrage of photographers penned them in.

In early September newspapers carried stories about Sinatra's attempted suicide following another quarrel with Ava. Sinatra was vehement in his denial. 'This would be a hell of a time to do away with myself. I've been trying to lick this thing for two years and I've practically got it licked now.' According to

60

Sinatra the incident had been caused by a combination of sleeping pills and alcohol. 'Tuesday night, Miss Gardner, my manager Hank Sanicola and Mrs Sanicola dined at the Christmas Tree Inn on Lake Tahoe. Ava was returning to Hollywood that night. We came back to the Lake and I didn't feel so good. So I took two sleeping pills. Miss Gardner left by auto for Reno and the plane trip back to Hollywood. By now it was early Wednesday morning. I guess I wasn't thinking because I am very allergic to sleeping pills. Also, I had drunk two or three brandies. I broke out in a rash. The pills felt kind of stuck in my chest. I got worried and called a friend who runs the steak house here. He sent a doctor who gave me a glass of warm water with salt in it. It made me throw up and I was all right. That's all there was to it—honest'.

At the end of that same month it was Ava who fell ill with a severe virus infection. She spent most of the next four weeks in hospital while the press speculated in their usual way on the nature of her illness.

Finally, on 30 October, an interlocutory decree of divorce was granted to Nancy in Santa Monica, the terms of alimony being the same as the suit of maintenance the previous year.

Below: On another visit to London, Ava and Frank had ringside seats for a Randolph Turpin fight at the White City Stadium. Right: Nancy Sinatra in court at Santa Monica for her divorce.

On 1 November Sinatra picked up a Nevada divorce and 24 hours later Frank Sinatra and Ava Gardner applied for a marriage licence in Philadelphia, where State law required a three day waiting period before the licence could be issued. During the wait, back in New York, the pair quarrelled yet again and Ava Gardner, in a fit of jealousy, flung her engagement ring out of the window and locked the door against her husband-to-be. The two of them sat in their separate suites brooding and it took the intervention of friends to patch up the quarrel.

The wedding finally took place on 7 November, 1951, at the Philadelphia home of Lester Sachs, cousin of Manie. Last minute switches of venue did not fool the press and Sinatra had one more outburst at them as he drove up to the house with his bride-to-be. The party was small, a few relatives with some of Sinatra's closer friends—Axel Stordahl, who was best man, his wife, the Sachs, Ben Barton, Sinatra's music publishing partner, Dick Jones, ex-Dorsey arranger. Ava Gardner survived a slip downstairs during the playing of 'Here Comes The Bride', the ceremony was completed and the couple took off for a short honeymoon in Miami andCuba.The departure was so hurried to avoid the press, that Ava left behind her trousseau case. They waited in Miami for a day, while

Unlike Nancy, Ava Gardner took an active part in her new husband's life. Centre: Caught unawares, the honeymoon couple stroll on the beach at Miami. Insets, below: Ava and Frank at the Empress Club in London for a Charity Midnight Matinee; far right: At the Washington Hotel, before leaving for a performance at the London Coliseum.

Ava's clothes caught up with them and it was there on the beach near the Green Heron Hotel that a photographer stole a picture of the couple strolling hand-in-hand, their backs to the camera, a picture that for all its implied happiness seems overcast and ominous.

Frank Sinatra was now approaching the lowest ebb in his professional life, while Ava instead had grown from a little-known starlet to the status of an international star, following her part in *Show Boat*. She had paid for wedding and honeymoon and now set about trying to rebuild some of the old Sinatra image.

On a trip to London for a charity concert one month after the wedding, newspapermen began to detect a change in Sinatra's tone. He agreed to interviews and conducted one of them at his own expense on a transatlantic call with Fern Marja of the *New York Post*. But this time there were tiffs with the English press and the visit was further soured by a jewel robbery and a disagreement with the band during a rehearsal of the charity show. After his London success in 1950 Sinatra was bitterly disappointed at what was now only a luke-warm reception for his singing.

In the spring of 1952 he used the influence of his old friends to get him another show at the New York Paramount. Again the press saw a new, humble, almost humiliated Sinatra ride into town. 'I'll always be made up and ready,' he told photographers, 'in case you ever want to shoot any pictures of me.' Not many of them did and Sinatra's 'woo-the-press' campaign, the result of pressure from both Ava and his new press agent Mack Miller, was virtually stillborn.

That summer he tried to write his own *apologia*, signing two articles for the Hearst *American Weekly* in which he apologised for his previous disagreements with newsmen and tried to refute the accusations about his 'pinko' political attitudes and his links with the Mafia. Lee Mortimer had revived the old 1947 (Lucky Luciano) charges in an article sub-titled 'Gangsters in the Night Clubs', an attack condemned by the *Hollywood Reporter* as 'the filthiest piece of gutter journalism ever composed'. One may assume that the timing of this had not a little to do with the then current build-up to the presidential elections in which the Sinatras were already committed as Adlai Stevenson supporters.

It was at a Hollywood Democrat rally that husband and wife publicly made up after one of their stormy quarrels had inadvertently leaked into the gossip columns. In fact columnists had already dubbed them 'the battling Sinatras' and it was obvious to friends and family that the two of them were living in a constant state of mutual siege, both of them hard-headed, proud and totally unable to concede even the smallest point during an argument or quarrel. 'Hurricane' Ava, casual and undomesticated, was determined not to be owned or bossed or taken for granted. Frank instead was still the spoilt Italian Mamma's boy, demanding his family-orientated wife and his well-ordered home, needing, especially now in his moments of doubt and self-pity, a great deal of reassurance and encouragement. Both of them were intensely jealous: Sinatra was particularly paranoiac about Ava's previous husband, Artie Shaw; Ava Gardner about Frank's former flame, Marilyn Maxwell. Their quarrels became increasingly violent and thus increasingly public. Police were called to one scene at the Palm Springs cottage when Frank Sinatra had apparently found Ava Gardner and Lana Turner comparing his sexual performance with that of their mutual former husband Artie Shaw. It was this quarrel that the pair healed in public at the Adlai Stevenson rally in the Hollywood Palladium.

The low point of Sinatra's decline coincided with the Republican victory that fall, as though the tearing up of contracts and agreements was all part of the victory celebration. Dropped by CBS from television and recording contracts; 'box-office poison' in Hollywood; and now even Sinatra's agents, MCA, were claiming that he owed them $40,000 in back commission. Trade papers rumoured that MCA might ditch their 'has-been' client. Sinatra laughed publicly at such stories—an agency drop a client who had earned over half a million dollars the previous year? But drop him they did, to press comments like 'Kiss-off of a Former Idol', 'The Last Goodbye', 'Final Indignity'. Sinatra would ask in disbelief, 'Can you imagine being fired by an agency that never had to sell you?'

When he flew off to accompany Ava Gardner on location work for *Mogambo* in Kenya he was talking to friends in despair about the 'nothingness' ahead of him and about the futility of going on with it all. He was in trouble with tax debts and by all accounts his money was running out. He seemed at the time to be heading for a complete breakdown and total obscurity. But he had left one card on the table back in Hollywood—the offer made to Harry Cohn that he would play the part of Maggio in *From Here To Eternity* for a mere $1,000 a week. His previous asking price had been $150,000. 'We'll have to wait and see,' Cohn had told him. 'We're doing screen tests for the part.'

Ava's career began to overshadow Frank's in the early fifties. Far left: Ava on location in Kenya during the shooting of 'Mogambo'.

In the early fifties Sinatra (above) continued to perform in spite of continued disfavour. By 1954, however, he had re-established himself in the most complete storybook comeback that Hollywood had ever known as Angelo Maggio in From Here To Eternity *(right).*

6 FROM HERE TO ETERNITY 1953-1954

'I knew Maggio. I went to high school with him in Hoboken. I was beaten up with him. I might have been Maggio.'

Maggio—the quick talking Italian boy from the mean streets of 1930s America, an enlisted man fighting the army system like he was going to break all of them for the way they made life so difficult. Maggio was only a supporting role, a fifth billing on the credits, a character part in a war novel set in the Hawaii of Pearl Harbour days. But Sinatra wanted him desperately, as though some instinct beyond his mere familiarity with the character told him just what he could achieve, and where he could arrive with this role. When he first read the James Jones novel upon

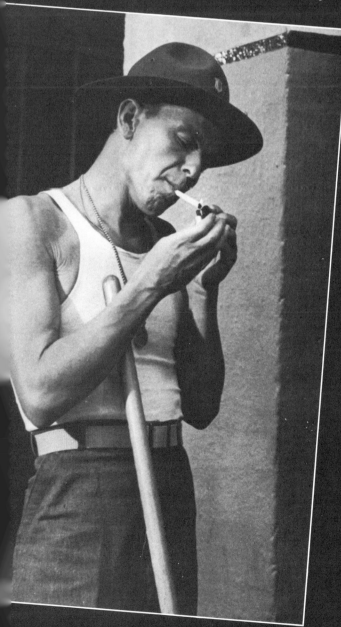

which the film is based, Sinatra was a has-been professional struggling to pick up even the odd club dates, dropped by his record company, sacked from a TV contract, an unwanted piece of 'box-office poison' in the studioland of Hollywood, a performer without even an agent hustling to find him work. Eighteen months later he had re-established himself in the most complete storybook comeback that Hollywood has ever known.

Sinatra's efforts to land that part have been the subject of documentary and fictional speculation for the last 25 years, with especial reference once again to the character of Johnny Fontane in Mario Puzo's *The Godfather*. One thing is clear, that Frank Sinatra moved heaven and earth and every friend he had in the universe to persuade Columbia and 'King' Harry Cohn to cast him as Maggio.

His first line of attack was through Ava Gardner and her link with Harry Cohn's wife Joan. When this approach produced no positive result it is alleged that Sinatra asked his Copacabana drinking companion Frank Costello to pull his weight in the Syndicate world. Whether or not Sinatra appealed to Costello personally, the New York mobster later announced that he had interceded on Sinatra's behalf using Syndicate influence in the West Coast film unions. Apparently to no avail. The doors at Columbia stayed firmly closed.

Sinatra was in a dilemma, due to leave for Africa with Ava Gardner, and still his name not even chalked up on the studio wall. Shortly before his departure he went in person to see Harry Cohn, swallowing the humiliations of rebuff and delay in the ante-cameras.

'Shit Frank,' was Cohn's reported comment when Sinatra made the big man's desk. 'Maggio is an actor's part. You're a singer, not an actor. We want an actor.'

Sinatra talked his way through the time allowed him for the interview without apparent success. By way of farewell, and appealing to Cohn's tightfisted reputation, Sinatra offered to play the part for a mere percentage of his usual fee. Cohn, still unconvinced, wanted the exact figure out of Sinatra. 'I'll play Maggio for a thousand a week,' was the answer he got, and by all accounts this was the one argument that finally persuaded Cohn to let Sinatra take a screen test on the part.

Columbia's original choice to produce the picture (Sylvan Simon) had died and when Buddy Adler took over Frank renewed the appeal he had made to Cohn. Adler was, after all, an old friend—not that friends had meant very much in the way of help or support in these bad years. Adler promised to try and have Sinatra called for a screen test but warned him that the studio had the last word even on tests, and that already the short list for the part had been narrowed down to Eli Wallach. Maggio was in fact one of the last parts to be cast and this probably reflected a true dilemma in the minds of producer, director and studio. Whether the dilemma was artistic or financial is more difficult to decide.

Frank flew out to Nairobi as a camp follower on *Mogambo*. Humiliation was digging deep now: his wife playing a lead in one of the year's big budget pictures, while he couldn't even land a screen test for a supporting role. He sat on the sidelines, buddying with Clark Gable, Grace Kelly and director John Ford, consuming every line of every West Coast gossip column that came their way. The *From Here To Eternity* cast list grew day by day: Burt Lancaster, Donna Reed, Deborah Kerr, Montgomery Clift. Clift was already bad news. 'We'd look like brothers or something,' Sinatra said. 'It's put me out of the race.'

But in the end a telegram came, the invitation to take a screen test, without any offer or even mention of expenses. Sinatra, or Ava Gardner, had to pay the air ticket for the 27,000 mile round-trip. He surprised everyone at Columbia by arriving less than two days after the telegram had been sent, slipping in unnoticed at Los Angeles airport where no one much cared any more about his comings and goings.

Sinatra did two scenes for his test, at the saloon bar where he plays poker with the olives and in the hotel garden where he is found drunk and AWOL. 'I was scared to death,' he admitted later. 'The next day I flew back to Africa, probably the longest route an actor ever travelled for a fifteen minute screen test.'

Buddy Adler still believed Sinatra was out of the running for the casting of Maggio and had preferred not to go down on stage to watch his friend's performance. He was summoned by director Fred Zinneman: 'You'd better come down here. you'll see something unbelievable.'

The 'unbelievable' was Sinatra's acting in the drunk scene which impressed both men as far and away the best they had seen on any of the five screen tests shot to date. And Sinatra knew his Maggio so well by then that he played both pieces without one reference to a script.

Whether this screen test was the final decider in Sinatra's favour is not known. Last word on casting still lay with Harry Cohn and though he later claimed to have been persuaded by the test, he was more likely swayed in the end by the financial argument he was having with Eli Wallach's agents. The part of Maggio had been budgeted for $16,000, Wallach was demanding $20,000, Sinatra would do it for $8,000. Perhaps Eli Wallach himself resolved the dilemma when he signed for the Tennessee Williams play, *Camino Real* on Broadway.

Back in Kenya, Ava Gardner was suffering a crisis of her own. She was pregnant and the difficult conditions of living and working—rain, humidity and now extreme heat—had made her unwell. She flew to London for a four-day stay in a nursing home. In 1956 she told Joe Hyams that she had had a miscarriage: 'I was hospitalized secretly . . . with what was called in the newspapers "a severe case of anaemia." All my life I had wanted a baby and the news that I lost him (I'm sure that it was a boy) was the cruellest blow I had ever received. Even though my marriage to Frank was getting shakier every day I didn't care. I wanted a baby by him.'

The reunion with Sinatra back in Kenya was happy, and the *Mogambo* film unit celebrated Christmas as boisterously as might be expected on the set of a John Ford movie. Sinatra had brought presents for everyone; he led carol singing with the unit and their native helpers; and he was, indirectly as Robert Surtees recalled, the star of a party thrown for the local British officials. 'John Ford thought it would be funny to have the Governor and his lady meet Ava. He tried to put her on by saying, "Ava, why don't you tell the Governor what you see in this 120 pound runt you're married to". And she said, "Well, there's only 10 pounds of Frank but there's 110 pounds of cock!" Ford went green and said, "I'll never talk to that girl again", but the governor loved it. He and his wife fell over laughing.'

Despair started creeping back into Sinatra as the *Mogambo* unit returned to filming after the festivities.

Right: Ava arranges a camp-site Christmas for stars and crew of 'Mogambo'. Below: Sinatra in 'From Here to Eternity' with Montgomery Clift.

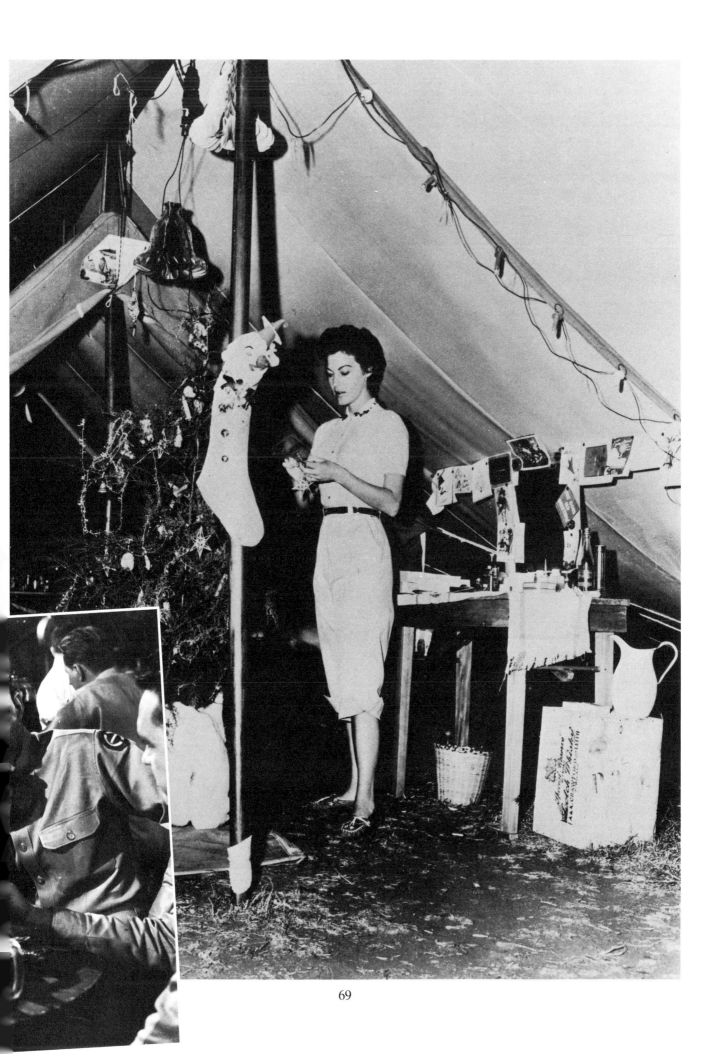

He now could not bear even watching them at work, but spent all day back at the camp brooding. He wondered if his screen test had really been that good. Apart from the technicians on stage, no one had bothered to compliment him or even suggest that he had done well.

Then one day, while he was alone in the camp, the long-awaited telegram arrived. The part of Maggio was his if he agreed to the $8,000 fee. He cabled acceptance and when the film unit came back that evening they found him aggressively exultant: 'Now I'll show those wise guys!' he shouted. 'I'll show all those mothers!'

And show them he did, in his portrayal of the little laughing 'wop' with the talc bottle and cherished photo of his kid sister; the enlisted man living his army routine from one week's furlough to another; the winning sly grin holding a pass to the best brothel in town; the only friend of ex-bugler and ex-boxer Prewitt (Monty Clift); the loser working, with Prewitt, more fatigues than any other man in the unit; and the 'tough monkey' who gets busted by Sgt. 'Fatso' beaten finally to a whimpering death in the arms of his buddy on the very day he jumps the stockade in the back of a garbage truck.

When Prewitt walks out into the middle of the barracks square to play 'taps' on the evening after Maggio's death, the moment is one of the classic screen throat-catchers: the bugle, the soldiers coming out in the darkness on their stairs and verandahs to listen; and the little dead Italian who has left himself so strong an image in a film full of outstanding performances.

It was as though Angelo Maggio somehow encapsulated the various Frank Sinatras—the battling 'guinea', the saloon-bar, wise-cracking wise guy, the loyal, defiant and romantic friend, the doomed 'take on all comers and bust' fighter. Producer Buddy Adler would say 'He dreamed, slept and ate his part'. Even the film unit began to call him 'Maggio' or 'Angelo'. Zinneman described Sinatra's playing as entirely natural: 'He played Maggio so spontaneously we almost never had to reshoot a scene.'

But acting is acting whatever the motivations and preparations. The characters and words are fictitious, the inhibitions of display and identification always have to be overcome. The 'natural performance' of Sinatra required as much control and concentration as the 'studied performance' of Montgomery Clift required precision and intensity. It was the timing in Sinatra's performance that impressed Zinneman, the ability, learned from his singing, to shade a line to its natural length, or to drop in an extra word or phrase

Frank Sinatra as Maggio is restrained by Montgomery Clift during a brawl in 'From Here to Eternity'.

to lift the mood of a portrayal that one critic would describe as 'doomed gaiety'. The powerhouse of both the Clift and Sinatra performances was emotion. As actors they complemented each other perfectly, creating the reality of that particular kind of buddy-buddy barrack-room friendship which had the audience rooting for both of them against the whole of the outside world. (Monty Clift would later partner one of Sinatra's closest friends in a similar and successful war-time relationship when he played Noah Ackerman to Dean Martin's Michael Whiteacre in *Young Lions*.)

As a piece of story-telling and film-making, *From Here To Eternity* was a complex enough operation and the schedule, with its location work in Hawaii, taxing for all the players. But for once Sinatra was not worried by the delays and frustrations associated with filming. His commitment was absolute and apart from one recording session early in April 1953 he had little to distract him. And as he worked on Angelo Maggio, so his own confidence came seeping back to him. A member of the production staff later described the

metamorphosis: 'It was like watching a man grow day to day. When he first walked on that set he was like a school-kid playing hookey with the adults. Then he kind of filled out and his head went back and he started looking you straight in the eye again. And when he walked off at the end of the picture, he walked out like he was King once more.'

Not quite King, for the coronation was yet to come. But he was on his way back not just as an actor, but as singer, recording star and all-round entertainer.

The William Morris office were the first to anticipate a possible revival of Sinatra's fortunes—and to their credit they signed up as his new representatives before Sinatra had even heard the result of his screen test. They were not apparently involved in the dramas of the Angelo Maggio casting but devoted all their early efforts to search for a new recording contract. Columbia had dropped him after a ten year run, and there was little enthusiasm from anyone else: no offer of advances, expenses or front money of any kind. Even Manie Sachs, now an executive at RCA Victor,

Sergeant 'Fatso' Judson (Ernest Borgnine) pulls a knife on Sergeant Milton Warden (Burt Lancaster) while Maggio (Sinatra) and the rest look on, in another gripping scene from Fred Zinneman's 'From Here to Eternity'.

could not persuade his colleagues that Sinatra was still a hot property. In the end the dice, however meagre, fell right for Sinatra; Capitol Records signed him up for just one year, without advances or expenses; Sinatra would have to foot the bill for musicians, arranger and all associated costs; but at Capitol he would eventually team up with the producer and arranger/conductor who consolidated his next and perhaps most successful stage of musical development.

One of Sinatra's former musical partners, Axel Stordahl, had helped to promote the move to Capitol and it was with Stordahl that Sinatra cut his first two sides in that late April session of 1953—'I'm Walking Behind You' and 'Lean Baby'. The record sold well enough but producer Voyle Gilmore felt the lush romantic approach unsuitable for a market used to the harsher sound and syncopated rhythms of the new generation of singers. His instinct proved correct for it was Eddie Fisher who had the hit version of 'I'm Walking Behind You'.

Stordahl himself resolved a possibly embarrassing situation by taking a TV job in New York and leaving Sinatra and Gilmore free to choose another arranger. Billy May and Nelson Riddle were the two favoured names, though for reasons of availability it was Riddle who worked all the arrangements for Sinatra's second Capitol session at the end of April—'I Love You', 'South Of The Border', 'Don't Worry About Me', 'I've

Got The Whole World On A String'. A few days later they recorded their classic version of 'My One And Only Love' and the new brass and string backed swinging Sinatra was on his way to being born. It was a style and a sound, said Robin Douglas-Home, 'epitomizing the Age of Romantic Cynicism as exactly as Chopin epitomized the Age of Romantic Idealism'.

'He's stimulating to work with,' Riddle later said of Sinatra. 'You have to be right on mettle all the time. The man himself somehow draws everything out of you. He has the same effect on the boys in the band—they know he means business so they pull everything out. Frank and I both have, I think, the same musical aim. We know what we're each *doing* with a song, what we want the song to say . . . In working out arrangements for Frank, I suppose I stuck to two main rules. First—find the peak of the song and build the whole arrangement to that peak, pacing it as he paces himself vocally. Second—when he's moving, get the hell out of the way; when he's doing nothing, move in fast and establish something. After all what arranger in his right mind would try to fight *against* Sinatra's voice?'

For all the good omens, 1953 was not an easy year. Sinatra had played *From Here To Eternity* for $8,000 and recorded for Capitol with no advance payment at all. He was short of money and waiting in some anxiety for the success, or failure, of Angelo Maggio. Columbia had already led off with strong pre-release publicity for the film in which Sinatra figured as a potential Academy Award winner and Sinatra feared they were courting disaster with such high-flying claims.

A few days after recording 'My One And Only Love' Sinatra left for a concert tour in Europe with Ava by his side, but it was an uneasy and fretful time. He quarrelled with airport officials in London when a BEA flight failed to wait for them; an audience in Stockholm booed him when a tight schedule denied them an encore; there were skirmishes in Rome with the insistent *paparazzi* photographers; and in Naples Frank alienated his audience by walking off stage when they interrupted his songs with cries of 'Ava, Ava!'. Ava Gardner, already alarmed by the attentions of the Neapolitan crowds, had fled north to Milan, though it was becoming obvious by then that these public incidents, above all Sinatra's short temper with audiences and musicians, were being provoked by his own domestic unhappiness. The whole trip was, it seems, punctuated with quarrels, their only time for relaxation coming briefly at the end of the tour when the two of them settled down for two months in London while Ava Gardner was filming *Knights Of*

The Round Table. Sinatra had a successful English concert tour, and recorded two good broadcast shows for the BBC. But even this interlude ended in a quarrel so violent that neighbours complained and the landlord threatened eviction. The motive for their quarrel was their next move: Sinatra had a night club date at the 500 Club in Atlantic City and wanted Ava to come along with him. Ava, exhausted both by her film and her husband's moods, insisted on going to Madrid for a holiday.

Sinatra returned to the States on 12 August, completed his Atlantic City engagement, earned $6,000 for a guest appearence on Milton Berle's new TV show, then settled for a month in New York for a short season at the Riviera. Ava returned from Europe at the beginning of September without telling Sinatra of her arrival, but was nevertheless offended not to find Sinatra on the tarmac waiting for her. With Frank installed at the Waldorf, Ava moved into Hampshire

Below: Frank and Ava continued to travel together, though their relationship was stormy. Right: Sinatra in rehearsal.

House, the two of them too petulant and proud to ring the other and make up the quarrel. It was Frank's mother Dolly Sinatra who brought about a brief reconciliation when she invited them both to supper in Weehawken. Sinatra moved into Hampshire House to join his wife, but alienated her again only a couple of days later by staying out all night with his entourage of cronies.

On 2 October, they both attended the premiere of *Mogambo*—something of a personal triumph for Ava—and next day flew to Hollywood. But while Sinatra had a date at the Sands in Las Vegas, Ava went off to Palm Springs by herself. Three weeks later, on 27 October, on Ava Gardner's behalf, MGM announced their separation and impending divorce, a move that apparently took Sinatra quite by surprise, and seems in retrospect to have been an attempt by Ava Gardner to test her husband's feelings. The combination of two proud and insecure people, both unwilling to retreat or make the first step towards reconciliation, made it

unlikely that they could ever have held together for very long. Ava herself said: 'When he was down and out he was sweet. But now he's got successful again he's become his old arrogant self. We were happy when he was on the skids.' She had dominated the early months of the relationship. She could not now tolerate the brash, but still uneasy self-assertion of the King coming out of the shadows. The courtiers were gathering round again, the famous and the infamous, whose occasional drinks she had been buying for the last eighteen months. In New York that September, instead of the occasional, often patronising, drink with 'poor old Frankie', they had settled down in clubs or in restaurants for whole evenings and nights. She resented them for what they were—and for the intrusion they caused into an already not very private life.

On his side Sinatra suffered the heartache without having the first idea how to rebuild the relationship. 'Don't cut the corners too close on me, baby,' he had told Ava the first time she objected to an all night stag party. Then when she walked out on him he would sit and brood and suffer. Already that autumn his recordings were beginning to reflect the melancholy, sometimes even the despair, of that breaking dream— 'A Foggy Day In London Town', 'Little Girl Blue', 'I Get A Kick Out Of You'.

Ava had had hopes that autumn of making *Saint Louis Woman* with Frank, but when plans for the film failed to materialise she once again asked MGM for a film role that would take her back to Europe and away from a situation she could no longer cope with. In the end it was United Artists who offered her just such a role in *The Barefoot Contessa*, a part written specifically for her by Joe Mankiewicz. Weeks of haggling followed while MGM and United Artists negotiated the terms for her loan-out, and Sinatra, conscious of her intended move, busied himself taping advance shows of his new twice-weekly radio programme on NBC to leave himself free to accompany her. He knocked himself out trying to do too much and was taken to the Mount Sinai Hospital in New York suffering from 'complete physical exhaustion, severe loss of weight and a tremendous amount of emotional strain'.

Apparently worried about his condition, Ava Gardner saw him briefly on his return to Hollywood, but left for Europe a few days later with the talk of divorce still in the air.

Sinatra flew out at Christmas to join an apparently reluctant Ava in Madrid and Rome. Ava was suffering from an attack of German measles, and Sinatra from a cold, and the whole reunion was something of a let-down. In Madrid Ava Gardner had already met the man who would, however temporarily, supplant Sinatra as the emotional centre of her life. Perhaps her thoughts were more occupied with the bullfighter Luis Miguel Dominguin, than with the confused needs and insecurities of her husband.

Insofar as Sinatra's career was concerned that period of vulnerable insecurity was all but over and his comeback almost established: a new radio show, an impending TV contract, the offer of two leading film roles—in *Pink Tights* with Marilyn Monroe at 20th Century Fox and the lead in *Pal Joey* back with Columbia. Even more important for his day to day bread and butter he had re-established himself in the Niter world with a spectacular success at the Riviera in New York. The chemistry to make it all come finally together was timed for 1954 and, though he did not yet know it, the two catalysts were already in the can and on tape. He had been given his expected Oscar nomination for Angelo Maggio, and in a December session, he had recorded the single 'Young At Heart', a romantic ballad with a bit of swing that Pat Boone might have made his own a couple of years later. A few quarter-tone slides and quarter-beat hesitations supply the Sinatra magic and they were all the song needed.

At the beginning of March 1954 'Young At Heart' climbed spectacularly and unexpectedly to the top of the singles hit parade; on 25 March he took his eldest daughter and his son along with him to the Academy Awards ceremony in the Pantages Theatre, Hollywood. The will-he won't-he speculation had already turned this into one of the more dramatic and emotional Academy years and most of Hollywood, friend or foe, seemed to be rooting for Sinatra. They had, along with the critics, unanimously applauded his portrayal of Private Maggio and there was a strong feeling that this was one of the more deserving 'natural' Oscars of recent years. But they were also watching him with the sidelong looks of people saying: 'There, but for the grace of God, go I.' They wanted to be reassured that there was a way back from disaster. As columnist Sid Sikolsky said: 'He proved you could flop and make a comeback.'

Perhaps Sinatra's chief rival in the Best Male Supporting Actor category was the child actor Brandon De Wilde for his performance as Joey Starret in *Shane*. The other contenders were all strong pros: Jack Palance as the sinister gunfighter, again from *Shane;* Eddie Albert in the Irving Radovich part from *Roman Holiday;* and Robert Strauss, Stosh in *Stalag 17*.

Already the previous evening, Sinatra's family—the original family of Nancy Sr plus children—had presented him with their own miniature Oscar at a family supper party. Nancy had kept an open house for Frank ever since their divorce, offering him maximum access to the children and, as it turned out, a refuge for himself in times of emotional stress. This supper was the first formal reunion of the full family aside from birthdays, and their gold medal Oscar had been inscribed 'Dad, we'll love you—from here to eternity'. Privately, if he had inherited Sicilian superstitions, he might have felt threatened by such an emotional anticipation of success. He might, as presenter Mercedes McCambridge opened the magic envelope on the following evening, have been composing himself in what David Niven later described as the 'generous-hearted loser face'.

When his name was read out the theatre roared its longest and loudest applause of the evening. The moment compared with the melodrama and sentiment roused by Liz Taylor's *Butterfield 8* award in 1960, or Humphrey Bogart's for *African Queen* in 1951.

It is not difficult to imagine Sinatra's feelings at that moment, though his traditional speech of thanks to director, producer and film unit followed strict protocol. He had been at the top of show-biz for long enough in the 1940s to know what this Oscar would mean for him and he must have felt in that moment like throwing out a few inverted V-for-Victory signs at the agents and front office parasites who had so humiliatingly dismissed him over the previous three or four years. And he must also have said to himself, then or later, never again will I be at the mercy of their whims and statistics.

On the disc jockey's poll in *Billboard* at the end of 1954 he scooped best song ('Young At Heart'), best LP ('Swing Easy'), and top male vocalist. *Metronome* named him Singer of the Year and for the first time since 1947 he was polled top of *Down Beat's* Most Popular Male Vocalists. Sinatra had re-established himself against all the usual show-biz odds. Over the next eight years he would build himself a Siegfried Line of private companies to own his various activities. For better or for worse he was going to be his own man, in his own way, at his own tempo.

Below: Frank Sinatra accepts his golden Oscar from Mercedes McCambridge for Best Supporting Actor in 'From Here to Eternity'. Now he could afford to relax (right).

–7 THE SECOND TIME AROUND 1954-1958–

'People often remark that I'm pretty lucky,' Sinatra would later tell Joe Hyams. 'Luck is only important in so far as getting the chance to sell yourself at the right moment. After that, you've got to have talent and know how to use it.'

And use it he did. During the next six years Sinatra was to star in seventeen films and record maybe his best, certainly his most famous albums. His asking price at the top night clubs approached $50,000 a week, with perks, and his gross income within one year of his Oscar triumph had put him near the millionaire bracket. All this after his $1,000 a week gamble as a supporting actor in a war movie.

Considering the circumstances of his comeback it was hardly surprising that the working pattern of his life became dominated for the next few years by his acting. From 1954 onwards recording sessions and Niter dates were fitted in as and when a heavy filming schedule permitted. Even so, more than a year passed after the filming of *From Here To Eternity* before Sinatra walked onto another film stage. Originally he had been signed up by 20th Century Fox to star opposite Marilyn Monroe in *Pink Tights*. The film was postponed after Monroe's objections to the script (she refused point-blank to play the part and was suspended

by 20th Century Fox as a result) but the company paid Sinatra to keep an option on his services while they tried to find an alternative subject. Both Warner Bros and MGM were offering Sinatra roles (*Young At Heart* and *St Louis Woman*) though it was United Artists who gathered him at the expiry of 20th Century Fox's option, signing him up for the part of a psychopath assassin in *Suddenly* (1954).

'He holds the screen,' wrote a reviewer in *Cue*, 'and commands it with ease, authority and skill that is, obviously, the result of care, study, work and an intelligent mind.' And indeed producer Robert Bassler later confirmed that Sinatra had suggested script changes ultimately incorporated into the film. 'There is nothing more disturbing than the cerebration of an actor, but Frank wasn't making demands to exploit himself at the expense of the picture. The suggestions he offered made sense . . .'

Perhaps because of the film's thriller genre and B-feature values, Sinatra's performance as the presidential assassin has always been undervalued, though at the time of its release he was given a good reception. *Newsweek* thought the film refuted any suggestion that Sinatra's Oscar winning performance was one-shot stuff: 'In *Suddenly* the happy-go-lucky soldier of

Sinatra in 'The Man With the Golden Arm'. His portrayal of Frankie Machine ensured his position as one of the most promising of all cinema actors.

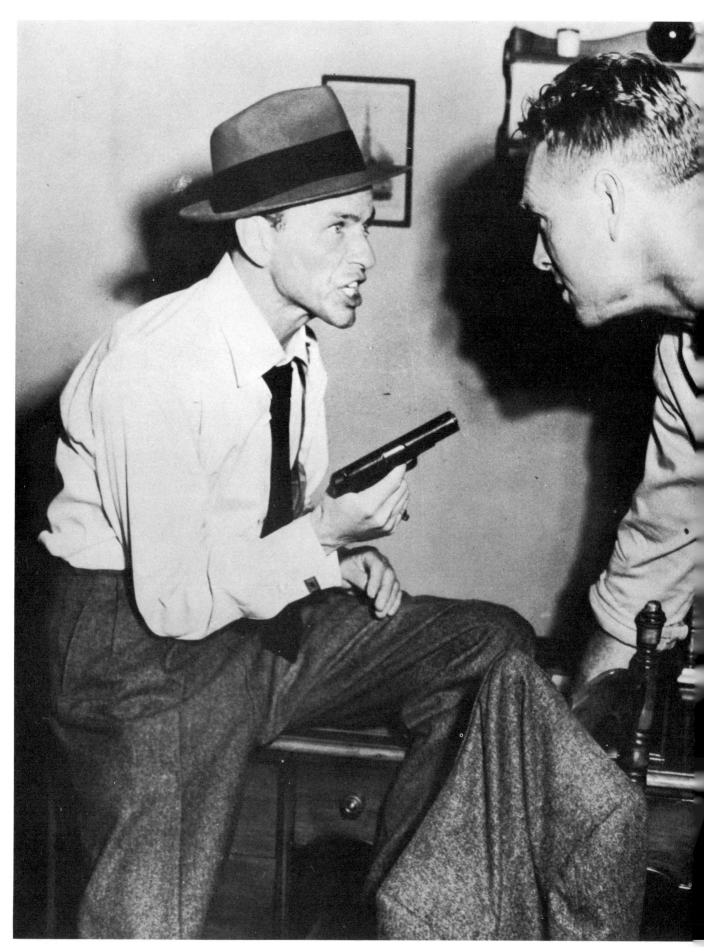

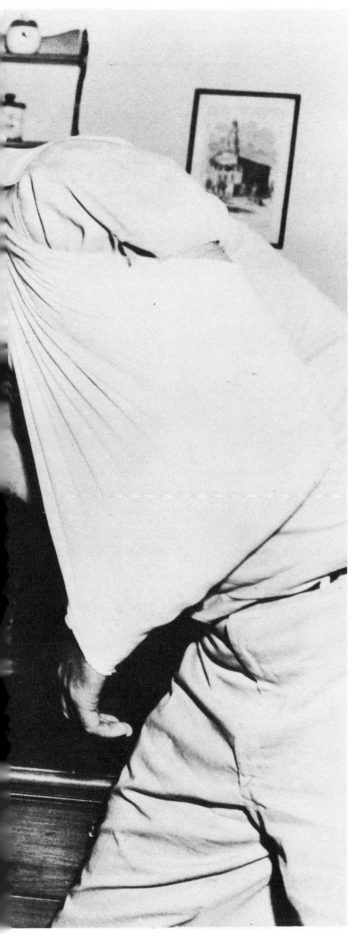

Eternity becomes one of the most repellent killers in American screen history. Sneeringly arrogant in the beginning, brokenly whimpering at the finish, Sinatra will astonish viewers who flatly resent bobby-soxers' idols.' Strange that after ten years' work as a professional actor, Sinatra could not lose that bobby-sox connotation. *Citizen News* still referred to him as the 'one-time crooner', *Cue* as the 'song and dance man'. At least the critic in *Cue* also mentioned the strength of Sinatra's dramatic playing in *Meet Danny Wilson,* and it is worth emphasizing the continuity of Sinatra's development as an actor. It would be a mistake to divide his acting career into pre and post *From Here To Eternity* periods. A talent had been evolving, through the comedy timing of the quick-tempo Gene Kelly films and the harder, angry commitment of *Meet Danny Wilson.* Angelo Maggio, even if in retrospect the best of his acting achievements, was part of a continual development that did not stop until the films of the late 1950s. *The Joker Is Wild* (1957), *Pal Joey* (1957) and *Some Came Running* (1958) are perhaps the last Sinatra vehicles that stretched his talent, the last performances to suggest an even deeper talent fighting to get out.

In October 1954 Sinatra was working again at United Artists' studios in a Stanley Kramer picture *Not As A Stranger* featuring Robert Mitchum in an unlikely hospital soap opera. Sinatra as Mitchum's jokey and cynical doctor buddy was again much praised, not only in the eventual reviews, but more significantly by his colleagues on the film. He had not been the easiest of actors to work with — Kramer, in his dual capacity as producer-director, vowed never to use Sinatra again — yet an associate on the production staff, quoted by Arnold Shaw, claimed Sinatra had salvaged a disaster: 'When the film was lying on the floor dead, along came Sinatra as Dr Boone and revived it by the force of his personality. It was a beautiful thing to watch.' Robert Mitchum would also claim that Sinatra had 'saved the film' — in spite of reviews that suggested Sinatra had 'stolen' the picture from him. Even Kramer's vow to boycott Sinatra did not survive more than eighteen months.

Mitchum made another observation about his co-star that throws some light on Sinatra's state of mind at the end of what had been an emotionally traumatic year: 'Frank is a tiger — afraid of nothing, ready for anything. He'll fight anybody, and about anything. He's really an amazing guy — frail, undersized, with a scarred-up face who's ready to take on the whole world.'

Sinatra was, beyond his various successes and six months of great activity, a lonely man. Ava Gardner

Sinatra as John Baron threatens Sterling Hayden as Tod Shaw in the 1954 film 'Suddenly'.

Some of Sinatra's finest film roles coincided with his years as Clan leader. Far right: Shirley MacLaine's first starring role was opposite Sinatra in 'Some Came Running'. Right: Robert Mitchum and Frank Sinatra get to grips with each other in 'Not As a Stranger'. Below: Sinatra with Raymond Burr (seated) and Alex Nicol during the shooting of 'Meet Danny Wilson', the first film to show Sinatra's potential as a straight actor. Below right: Clan members Sinatra and Sammy Davis Jr. Their long standing friendship was briefly threatened by allegations of an affair between Ava and Sammy.

had returned from Europe at the end of May 1955, apparently in love with the bullfighter Luis Dominguin, apparently intent on ending her marriage with Sinatra. She rented a cottage on Lake Tahoe and seemed set on establishing Nevada residence to qualify for a divorce. Sinatra, in Palm Springs, posed for photographs beside his swimming pool, holding hands with actress Mona Freeman. Was he feigning indifference?

Julie Styne who shared a bachelor maisonette with him through most of this year had a different impression of Sinatra's innermost feelings: 'I enter the living room and it's like a funeral parlour. The lights are dim and they just about light up several pictures of Ava. Frank sits in front of them with a bottle of brandy. After I get into bed, I can hear him pacing back and forth. It goes on for hours. At 4 am I hear him dialling someone on the phone. It's his first wife, Nancy. I hear him say, "You're the only one who understands me". After he hangs up, he starts pacing again. He seldom falls asleep until the sun's high in the sky. He can have almost any girl he wants by wagging a little finger. And he has lots of them. But he gets no satisfaction. And he suffers as much as the guy who never had one.'

One evening he tore up his favourite picture of Ava, then would not be calmed until he had found all the pieces and stuck them together again. A piece was missing from the reconstruction—Ava's nose—and it only appeared by the door when a delivery boy arrived with a crate of liquor. Sinatra was so relieved that he presented the astonished boy with his gold wrist-watch.

The agony of a disintegrating relationship prolonged itself, as though neither party was sure of their actions or intentions. Ava Gardner left Lake Tahoe without the divorce and set off on a tour of South America to publicize *The Barefoot Contessa*. Dorothy Kilgallen ran a story suggesting that the William Morris agency had had to assign one of their employees to guard against possible suicide attempts by Sinatra, and *Confidential Magazine* capped a year of gossip by publishing allegations about an affair between Ava Gardner and Sinatra's buddy, Sammy Davis Jr.

Sinatra's immediate reactions to such allegations are not recorded, but a few weeks later, when Sammy Davis smashed himself up in a car accident, Sinatra was his most regular visitor at the San Bernardino hospital: 'He was the first one to talk to me seriously after they removed my eye,' Davis said. All the others—Dad, Uncle Will Martin, Jeff Chandler, Tony Curtis, Janet Leigh, Jesse Rand, Charlie Head—they were being gay, as if it never happened. Not Frank. He knew I was sick with worry about how it would affect my career, and he was the first to try to help me face it.'

Sinatra offered Davis his Palm Springs home as a base for convalescence, and later, in person, broke an attempted colour bar when his friend was refused accomodation in Beverly Hills: a fight on the right side of the barricades. It was a pity that the year had to end with headlines about yet another night club brawl. After a house warming at Sammy Davis' home on 9 December, Sinatra adjourned with three others to the Crescendo on Sunset Strip where Mel Torme was singing. Judy Garland, Bob Neal and Cindy Hayes were the members of Sinatra's group and they were challenged as they were leaving by the club's press agent Jim Byron, who accused them of smuggling out drinks under their coats. During the exchange Byron apparently asked Bob Neal who his date was, and that question provoked Sinatra into an angry retort. 'What business is it of yours?' he is alleged to have asked. 'You're either a cop or a reporter. And I hate cops and newspapermen.' According to Byron, Sinatra went on 'ranting and raving' and finally hit him in the face.

Sinatra's version of the incident had Byron asking him who his date was. 'Two guys held my arms,' Sinatra told reporters, 'and Byron tried to knee me. He succeeded in denting my shinbone and clawing my hand. I couldn't do anything because I was held by the two men. I broke loose. It ended when I gave him a left hook and dumped him on his fanny.'

Some years later another reference to this fight by Sinatra showed just why he was so sensitive to the press agent's interference that night. 'If I hadn't hit him, he'd have had in the columns that I was dating Judy while Sid—her husband—was out of town. For cripe's sake! I wasn't with Judy. We were both in the same crowd, that's all.'

The papers had made great play of Sinatra's 'I hate cops' remark, and the incident kept him in the headlines until the end of the year. The columnists were also hinting at romance, first with Anita Ekberg, then with conductor Leopold Stokowski's estranged wife, Gloria Vanderbilt. Again, there were those who portrayed Sinatra as the marriage-breaking villain. It is not too surprising, then, that the following year, 1955, showed Sinatra at his most belligerent.

'Little Frankie Sinatra's all boiled up at the world again,' the *Morning Telegraph* told its readers, 'threatening people, sending them notes, yelling over telephones, taking paid ads to send bitter notes to people he hates.' Sinatra was in the process then of suing a London club, Les Ambassadeurs, who had cancelled his membership; an English columnist and newspaper chain for libel; and Sam Spiegel with his production company Horizon-American, who, Sinatra claimed, had promised him the part of Terry Malloy in *On The Waterfront* (the role that won Brando an Oscar in that year's Academy Awards). This last suit was not resolved until 1960 when Sinatra settled for the installation of a Hi-Fi system, rather less than the half-million dollars he had originally sued for.

Sinatra's personal battle that spring of 1955 was with his old friend and supporter Ed Sullivan, their quarrel being over Sinatra's planned appearance on Sullivan's show to promote *Guys And Dolls* (1955). Sinatra was demanding a fee for the appearance, while Sullivan claimed that as it was a plug for the film a fee was not called for. Sinatra had chosen to make this a test case on a point of principle, though he might have

thought twice about alienating someone so influential and hitherto friendly. Sinatra took the case to the Screen Actors Guild, asking them to tighten up the rules on free TV appearances. Sullivan replied with a full page advertisement in *Variety,* an open letter which concluded with a reference to Sinatra's earlier enthusiasms over Sullivan's friendly columns at a time when the rest of the national press was stacked against him—'Aside to Frankie Boy. Never mind that tremulous 1947 offer: Ed, you can have my last drop of blood.' Sinatra's reply, also in full page advertisements, was not conciliatory: 'Dear Ed, you are sick.—Frankie. PS—sick, sick, sick.'

'The little man with broken dreams,' was how the *Morning Telegraph* described Sinatra in that spring of 1955. 'But instead of nursing them in private like a man, he stands on a corner and scratches everything that passes by.'

The broken dreams were his private nightmare. Elsewhere 1955 was a period of intense activity and achievement. The beginning of the year had seen him top of the *Metronome, Down Beat* and *Billboard* polls as number one male vocalist; his single 'Young At Heart' had been the year's number one disc; and 'Swing Easy' the number one album. In February 1955 he cut the songs for the album that seemed so successfully to echo his own mood—the bittersweet 'In The Wee Small Hours' that became an instantaneous bestseller. A jazz critic, Barry Ulanov wrote: 'Sinatra

Left: Frank and Doris Day help Ethel Barrymore celebrate her 75th birthday on the set of 'Young at Heart'. Below: With Marlon Brando in 'Guys and Dolls'.

Left: Sinatra as Barney Sloan, the moody and frustrated genius from the gutter, serenading Laurie Tuttle, the quiet homely girl played by Doris Day, in a scene from 'Young at Heart', the musical remake of John Garfield's first movie, 'Four Daughters'.
Above: In 'The Tender Trap' it is Debbie Reynolds who, as Julie Gillis, traps the erstwhile good-time guy, Charlie Reader, played by Sinatra.

has always had a taste and an intuition for jazz nuances, for improvisational ornaments, for swinging beats, far beyond the call of popular singing duty.'

A session in March produced a Sinatra nod in the direction of rock and roll when he cut a rhythm-and-blues single 'Two Hearts, Two Kisses'. *Metronome* liked the heavy rock backing and commented, 'the master can do no wrong even out of his natural habitat'. But it was a one-off experiment for Sinatra, and most critics were glad to see him return to his own natural style. Another session in March and one in September produced two singles 'Learnin' The Blues', and 'Love And Marriage' that held second and third places in a hit parade already dominated by the Bill Haley sound. Once again Sinatra ended the year top of the polls in *Down Beat* and *Metronome*, and all of this while he starred in four major movies and a large scale TV production.

Sinatra had already overcome the suspicion that Maggio was something of a lucky swan song. In the film, *Young At Heart*, released in 1955, he was ready to prove it again, risking all kinds of odious comparison when he played the John Garfield role in a re-make of

Four Daughters. Brando had established the rebel and noble savage in half a dozen roles and James Dean was winning himself a new and predominantly teenage audience with his haunting performance as the outsider in *East Of Eden*. The critics were set to pounce on any attempt by the 'song and dance man' to climb aboard the rebels' bandwagon. But Sinatra just about charmed his way out of that trap, substituting the cheeky smile and song for Garfield's cynic-at-the-piano image. Lee Rogow wrote in *The Saturday Review:* 'Sinatra, although he smokes enough cigarettes for six cynics, doesn't burst from the screen with the old Garfield excitement, but he obliges with "Just One Of Those Things" and "Someone To Watch Over Me" to carry us along the way.'

The Tender Trap (1955) was less pretentious and infinitely more successful, the perfect vehicle for Sinatra's brand of quick-talk, quick-tempo comedy. The film never quite manages to move beyond its theatre play origins, but in the slightly claustrophobic surroundings of the shared bachelor flat Sinatra, as always with a competent fall-guy, hits sparks off his co-star David Wayne. The often critical Bosley Crowther wrote in *The New York Times:* '... his performance is well-nigh a perfect demonstration of the sort of

Left: Sinatra discusses technical details with producer Sam Goldwyn on the set of 'Guys and Dolls'. Above: Sinatra with four-legged friend in 'Johnny Concho'.

flippant, frantic thing he can do best. It catches the nervous restless Frankie at the top of his comedy form.'

The same mixture with a bit more grit was the recipe for *Guys And Dolls* shot immediately before *The Tender Trap* in the summer of 1955. Joe Mankiewicz directed Sinatra with half a dozen fall-guys to bounce him off whenever the Sinatra-Brando chemistry grew uneasy, and the result is a nice casual performance that never seems to betray the tensions between the two co-stars. Sinatra had not forgiven Brando for landing the Terry Malloy part in *On The Waterfront,* and the partnership in *Guys And Dolls* did nothing to improve relations between them. Sinatra had claimed the romantic singing role, Sky Masterson, only to find Brando already cast in the part and when the two of them started work together, Brando's acting temperament and preparations were a constant irritant on the 'one-take' Sinatra. 'Don't put me in the game, coach,' he would say to director Mankiewicz, 'until Mumbles is through rehearsing.' He was determined to act the method man off the screen and if he did not quite succeed in that, at least his 'oldest established' Nathan Detroit is more successful in detail of gesture and behaviour. For all its ethnic origin in the story, the 'worried man' portrayal of the crap game

proprietor is the nearest Sinatra comes in any of his roles to the facial attitudes and gestures of a Sicilian and it seems possible that he modelled the part on one of the Sinatra relatives.

He may also have had his models for Frankie Machine in *The Man With The Golden Arm* (1955), but the success of that performance stemmed as much from Sinatra's emotional commitment as from his observation of a drug addict's behaviour patterns. Frankie Machine, card-dealer, would-be drummer, was the hardest role in terms of sheer work that Sinatra ever undertook, but he approached it with almost fanatical dedication. As in *From Here To Eternity,* the frustrations and boredom of film making did not seem to affect him. Throughout shooting his life-style changed completely — few late nights, no clan revelries, only a couple of party dates with co-star Kim Novak. He would work at the studio twelve hours each day and then be too exhausted to do anything else but sleep. The dramatic high point of the film is the 'cold turkey' withdrawal agony, when Frankie shuts himself in a room for three days to break himself free of the hypodermic. The physical and mental violence of the scene was such that Preminger told Sinatra he could have as many rehearsals and takes as he needed, but to his surprise Sinatra played the whole climax in one single take. Preminger, by now convinced he had an Oscar performance in the can, hurried the editing to bring the film out in time for the Academy Award nominations. Sinatra was duly nominated, but in the end the award went to Ernest Borgnine for his performance in the title role of *Marty.* Even Sinatra had given up hopes of the Oscar by then, for the film itself was too controversial. Drug addiction was on a par with homosexuality and communism as an un-American activity and even Preminger's objective portrayal was considered by many as unfit for a general audience. The Production Code Seal of Approval was withheld, though the many critics who applauded the film made sure it did not suffer at the box office. All the critics, for or against, singled out Sinatra's perform-ance as something special. 'Truly virtuoso' was the way Arthur Knight described the Frankie Machine per-formance in *The Saturday Review:* 'The thin, unhand-some, one-time crooner has an incredible instinct for the look, the gesture, the shading of the voice that suggest tenderness, uncertainty, weakness, fatigue, despair. Indeed he brings to the character much that has not been written into the script, a shade of sweetness, a sense of edgy indestructibility that actually creates the appeal and intrinsic interest of the role.'

The combination of Frankie Machine and the part of Charlie Y. Reader in *The Tender Trap* persuaded Bosley Crowther of *The New York Times* that Sinatra was now one of the most promising of all cinema actors. United Artists seemed to share this view for they had agreed to finance Sinatra in independent productions. The first such production came before

Left: Sinatra performing at the Sands Hotel in 1956.
Among the enraptured audience are Jack Benny,
Kim Novak and, sporting a white carnation,
songwriter Cole Porter. Above: Sinatra sings with
daughter Nancy at Santa Monica High School.
Above right: A brief reunion with Ava.

played a delinquent cowboy who eventually reforms in the last reel and, while he convinces as the not so tough nasty, the sameness of story tempo and setting make of the character transformation an acting problem he did not manage to solve. As far as his film future was concerned his central weakness had now been revealed: a genius that never seemed to fail in its choice of material for the recording studio had let him down in the film front office where his prime responsibility was the choice of script, writer and director.

Apart from recording sessions in February, March and September, an almost continuous year of filming had only been interrupted twice—in August when Sinatra refused to go ahead with his scheduled part in *Carousel;* and in September when he worked for NBC on a major TV production of 'Our Town' with Eve Marie Saint and Paul Newman. There was a lot of contractual trouble between Sinatra and NBC before and during production of 'Our Town' but although he was said to have missed two of the final rehearsals the show turned out to be one of the best musicals ever staged on television. *The New York Times* described it as 'magnificent entertainment', and from Sinatra's point of view the show launched one of his big hit songs, 'Love And Marriage'.

Contractual misunderstanding was also at the root of his quarrel with 20th Century Fox over *Carousel.* Due to play the part of Billy Bigelow in the Rodgers and Hammerstein musical, Sinatra arrived on location in Maine in mid-August to find filming set up both for Cinemascope and Todd A·O. From Sinatra's point of view this meant the shooting of each scene twice and a

the cameras in December 1955, Sinatra's fifth film in thirteen months. It was called *Johnny Concho* with director Don McGuire, producer and lead actor, Frank Sinatra. Unfortunately the least said the better. Sinatra satisfied the childhood ambition of playing cowboys, and proved to himself and to the industry that he could control the administrative chores of film production. Beyond that, neither the film nor his performance are worthy of special note. Sinatra

considerable amount of time wasting while they changed camera and lighting set-ups. For two days he fought 20th Century Fox, the William Morris office and a bevy of lawyers, over long distance telephone. Then four days after his arrival, he went out for a presumed joy-ride with three henchmen in a car. They parked on the local airport perimeter, and, after pretending to admire the scenery, Sinatra suddenly sprinted across the field to a waiting private plane. The *Carousel* unit never saw him again, and five days later 20th Century Fox sued Sinatra for a million dollar breach of contract. Gordon MacRae was hired to take over Sinatra's role, but when filming resumed the dual set-up had disappeared. Sinatra had won another point of principle and *Carousel* was, in the end, only shot in 55mm. The breach of contract suit was dropped.

No wonder they were beginning to call him king of Hollywood. By next year, 1956, the king would have his own mountain-top castle, a custom-built home at the top of Coldwater Canyon from where he could watch over his kingdom. For most of the eight years he was to live there, the notice by the bell push on the gate read: 'If you haven't been invited, you better have a damn good reason for ringing this bell.'

'Nasty, rude, inconsiderate, uncooperative and ungrateful', said Kendis Rocklin in a Los Angeles *Mirror News* article on Sinatra. But, unlike cover-stories in *Time* and *Look* magazines, Rocklin also gave prominence in his article to the Sinatra that could be 'quietly generous and considerate without even expecting thanks'. Rocklin told his readers of the help and encouragement Sinatra gave to Bela Lugosi when he was committed to hospital as a narcotics addict. That same year Sinatra had held out helping hands not only to his friend Sammy Davis Jr, but to a man he hardly knew, actor Lee J.Cobb. Cobb had had a heart attack in the summer of 1955 and he recalled later, 'Frank in his typically unsentimental fashion, moved into my life. I was in a low mental state then, I was divorced and pretty much alone in the world. I was sure my career had come to an end. Frank flooded me with books, flowers, delicacies. He kept telling me what fine acting I still had ahead of me . . . He built an insulating wall around me that shielded me from worry, tension and strain.' Sinatra also gave Cobb his Palm Springs home for convalescence and paid the bills for a Hollywood apartment when Cobb moved back. 'After I recovered,' said Cobb, 'our relationship tapered off until I hardly saw him at all. He seemed to disappear as my need for him was over.'

Not only king it seemed, but protector in the best traditions of Sicilian paternalism—the *padrone* helping his chosen friends, though there were those who regarded his closest entourage with suspicion and even fear. As in his years of success in the 1940s Sinatra had again gathered around himself the professionals and

bodyguards who moved with him wherever he was working or playing: his manager Hank Sanicola; his accompanist, the pale-faced Bill Miller, otherwise known as Sun-Tan Charlie; the make-up man 'Beans' Pondedell; the writer Don McGuire; songwriter Jimmy Van Heusen; and the sundry heavies, the 'mob' that antagonized or terrified photographers and newsmen who crossed their path.

This 'court' was often confused in people's minds with the so-called Holmby Hills Rat Pack, Humphrey Bogart's irreverent if often misquoted gathering of like hearts and minds. Sinatra and Humphrey Bogart had been friendly ever since the Sinatras moved into the Holmby Hills area in the late 1940s, and Bogart was one of the few Hollywood acquaintances who did not write Sinatra off in the dark days of 1951 and 1952. The Holmby Hills mob was nothing more than the clique of anti-establishment friends that tended to congregate around Bogart, baptised at one supper party by Lauren Bacall as the Rat Pack. Joe Hyams of the New York *Herald Tribune* was the first journalist to acknowledge the existence of such a group: 'The Holmby Hills Rat Pack held its first annual meeting last night at Romanoff's Restaurant in Beverly Hills and elected officers for the coming year. Names to executive positions were Frank Sinatra, pack master; Judy Garland, first vice-president; Lauren Bacall, den mother; Sid Luft, cage master; Humphrey Bogart, Rat in charge of public relations; Irving Lazar, recording secretary and treasurer; Nathaniel Benchley, historian.

'The only members of the organization not voted into office are David Niven, Michael Romanoff and James Van Heusen. Mr Niven, an Englishman, Mr Romanoff, a Russian, and Mr Van Heusen protested that they were discriminated against because of their national origins. Mr Sinatra, who was acting chairman of the meeting, refused to enter their protests into the minutes.

'A coat of arms designed by Mr Benchley was unanimously approved as the official insignia of the Holmby Hills Rat Pack for use on letter-heads and membership pins. The escutcheon features a rat gnawing on a human hand with a legend, "Never Rat on a Rat".

'Mr Bogart, who was spokesman, said the organization has no specific function other than "the relief of boredom and the perpetuation of independence. We admire ourselves and don't care for anyone else". He said that membership is open to free-minded successful individuals who don't care what anyone thinks about them.'

Other individuals associated with the Pack included Sammy Cahn, Joey Bishop, the Kovacs,

Top right: With Grace Kelly and Bing Crosby in 'High Society'. Right: The 'Swell Party' number. Far right: With Cary Grant in 'The Pride and the Passion'.

92

Angie Dickinson and Paul Douglas. Activities included marathon weekends in Las Vegas, dinners at the Romanoffs or the Villa Capri, voyages with 'Captain Queeg' on the Bogart yacht *Santana*.

David Niven in his autobiography *The Moon's A Balloon* described a gathering in one of Bogart's last Fourth of July celebrations when the *Santana* dropped anchor in Cherry Grove and Sinatra, with Jimmy Van Heusen at a piano, sang to the assembled yachts and dinghys: 'Frank sang as only he can, with his monumental talent and exquisite phrasing undimmed by a bottle of Jack Daniels on top of the piano.

'He sang till the dew came down heavily and the boys in the listening fleet fetched blankets for their girls' shoulders.

'He sang till the moon and the stars paled in the predawn sky — only then did he stop and only then did the awed and grateful audience paddle silently away.'

Sinatra's personal life seemed to settle into an easier rhythm during 1955 and 1956. He had a well-publicized affair with Gloria Vanderbilt, which faded away after her unsuccessful attempt to play his co-star in *Johnny Concho* (she was replaced after a few hours shooting by Phyllis Kirk). More important to his peace of mind Sinatra was seeing a great deal of his children, taking Nancy Jr with him on a short twelve day tour of Australia, and singing with her at a PTA function for her school. Even the doomed relationship with Ava Gardner had achieved some sort of stability. There was no more talk between them of either divorce or reconciliation but whenever Ava visited Hollywood she would go out with 'my old man, Francis'. Her own world was now centred on the home she had bought herself a few miles out of Madrid, her way of life there a restless but apparently contented exploration of the city and country that so fascinated her. But even in the privacy of 'La Bruja', Sinatra would still accompany her late nights, for his were the songs she most enjoyed playing and she possessed a collection in triplicate of every record he had ever made.

In contrast to the hurried and infrequent sessions of the previous years, Sinatra's recording programme for 1956 included no less than 22 studio dates, and proved to be his first year of major impact in the LP market. Notwithstanding continued success in the singles hit parade ('Hey, Jealous Lover', and 'Wait For Me' in 1956), Sinatra's years with Capitol records were dominated by the albums. His comeback in 1953 and 1954 had coincided with the development of the ten inch, eight song LP which gave Sinatra not only the natural alternative to a hit parade battle with the young rock and roll stars, but also a show format that exploited the best of his talents as a compiler and performer. In 1956 *Metronome* named 'Swinging Lovers' as one of the best jazz albums of the year, and *Jazz Today* described 'This Is Sinatra' as 'alternately

swinging and swaying, sensitive and searing, with at least half a dozen pure jazz performances'. 1956 was also the year when a *Metronome* poll of jazz artists picked out Sinatra as the 'Musicians' musician'.

Sinatra took time out this same year to reconquer a few old battlegrounds. In August he played the New York Paramount for the first time since his disastrous reception there in 1952. He was in the same programme as his film, *Johnny Concho,* and after the critics' poor reception of the film it was obviously the stage show alone that drew the long queues to the box-office — ex-bobby-soxers and a younger generation curious to witness the live stage magic of the Crooner and the two Dorsey bands.

In December 1956 Sinatra returned to the Niter scene playing to capacity audiences at the Copacabana in New York and the Sands in Las Vegas, projecting to them the carefree jokesy image he had perfected earlier in the year on the set of *High Society*.

Sinatra's filming during this year had been a curious mixture of the enjoyable and the unbearable, the hilarity of *High Society* and *Around The World In 80 Days* spoiling him in a sense for the sheer hard work of a long location schedule on his summer film, *The Pride And The Passion* (released 1957).

High Society was fun to make and fun to be in, from beginning to end. Bing Crosby, Grace Kelly, Celeste Holm, John Lund, Louis Armstrong — the cast itself was good enough company for a five week vacation and Sinatra, playing the cheeky journalist around Grace Kelly's dress hem had a character and songs that made even the hard work enjoyable; his duet with Bing Crosby of 'What A Swell Party This Is' taking the sophisticated musical comedy routine to an all-time high. Both Crosby and Sinatra were on top of their form for this film, their respective nicknames on set, 'Nembutal' and 'Dexedrine', suggesting the effect they had on the rest of the unit.

A piano-man cameo in *Around The World In Eighty Days* was just as good fun and even less hard work, and both these spring experiences made the hot summer, sixteen week, $4 million slog of Kramer's *The Pride And The Passion* seem, by comparison, something of a nightmare. Sinatra's Spanish peasant guerilla is good, gritty realism — so far as the conventions of the day allowed — but the result was achieved at the cost of long hot days in remote Spanish country locations and, for the fastidious Sinatra, long early mornings and evenings driving, sometimes hundreds of miles, to and from his Madrid accommodation. The rest of the crew and cast (among them the not unsophisticated Cary Grant and Sophia Loren) made do with billets or even tents on location and eventually the atmosphere around Sinatra was stretched so tight that Stanley Kramer shifted his schedule to finish the Sinatra part four weeks early.

Not that Kramer complained about Sinatra's dedication once he arrived on set. 'Sinatra didn't appear to be happy, but he worked hard and he insisted on doing a lot of things you'd normally expect a star to leave to a double. He ran through explosions and fires. I had him trudging up and down mountains, wading in rivers, crawling in mud from one end of Spain to the other, and he never complained once.' The problem, as always, was with the rhythm of filming. 'Frank is a tremendously talented man, intuitive and fast, which is good for him but not always good for the other actors. During the filming of *The Pride And The Passion,* he didn't want to rehearse. He didn't want to wait around while crowd scenes were being set up.'

Sophia Loren obviously found it easier to get on with him than either Kramer or Cary Grant. 'Before he came to Spain, I hear all sorts of things. He is moody, he is difficult, he is a tiger, he fights. Here he is kindly, friendly. He has even helped me with my English, has teached me how people really speak in Hollywood. He is a regular gasser. I dig him.'

Part of Sinatra's tension was undoubtedly caused by his proximity to Ava Gardner—and to the feeling that their last chance of reconciliation had now vanished. Before he arrived in Madrid, in April 1956, Ava had been anticipating his visit to the extent of preparing a guest suite for him at 'La Bruja'. Whatever her hopes or intentions, Sinatra openly insulted her by arriving in Madrid with the starlet Peggy Connolly as his partner, and the few times Ava and Sinatra met—in restaurants

or clubs—they pointedly ignored each other.

Significantly, on 31 July, the very day that Sinatra flew back to the States, Ava announced in Rome that divorce papers had been signed, though she did not actually file for the divorce until one year later in Mexico City.

The whole experience in Spain seemed to have a doubly negative effect on Sinatra's career as a screen actor: it convinced him that films were better as fun interludes, preferably to be lived through in the company of friends; and it warned potential producers and directors who might have cast Sinatra in more

Below: Jeanne Crain and Sinatra in 'The Joker Is Wild'. Right: Sinatra plays the gilt-edged heel in 'Pal Joey'.

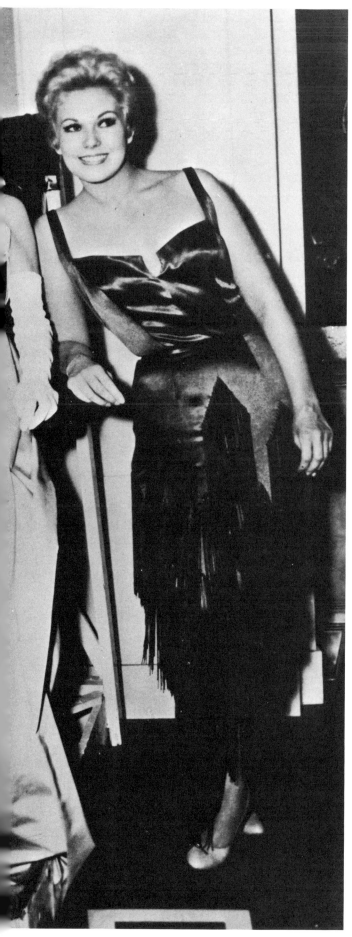

committed roles, that he could be a difficult and sometimes costly colleague on a film unit. It is a reputation that has crippled many brilliant but temperamental screen careers, for however good the performance, the hassle if bad, is seldom worth the trouble and money to employer and financier.

Sinatra's next two films, the Joe E. Lewis biography, *The Joker Is Wild* (filmed in the autumn of 1956), and the Rogers and Hart musical, *Pal Joey*, (early spring 1957) were both productions part-owned by one of his own companies. They were stories from a background familiar to him and roles with which he had no difficulty in identifying—comparable in some ways to the pre-*Eternity* picture *Meet Danny Wilson*. In retrospect, twenty years later and without the Joe E. Lewis originals to compare against, Sinatra's *Joker* works well both as film and portrait: a singer in a cafe falls foul of mobsters who cut his vocal chords; he turns to burlesque, succumbs to the bottle, loses girl and friends, then starts the long road back all on his own. It was Sinatra scenery—his own professional background, with something of his early days as a roadhouse singer. The film also gave him two of his best songs in 'Chicago' and 'All The Way' (an Academy Award nomination).

Pal Joey offered Sinatra an even more downbeat hero to play, a slick, fast-talking night club heel, King Rat among the mice. The film was toned down considerably from its stage musical original and though the Sinatra part still comes over with a strong, hard edge, the attempts to increase sympathy for the Joey Evans part and the tagged-on 'happy ending' seem to leave story and character unresolved. As played by Frank Sinatra, Joey comes out too classy as singer and swinger, whereas the original John O'Hara story made Joey Evans a second-rater. Sinatra could play the heel, but not the second-class singer, and with songs like 'The Lady Is A Tramp' and 'There's A Small Hotel' it would have been nonsense if he had. Joey Evans was one of the few good episodes in a predominantly bad year. Indeed there were moments when 1957 threatened to become as much of a negative turning point for Sinatra as 1947 had been.

The year had begun sadly with the death of Humphrey Bogart from throat cancer on 14 January, and however well prepared his friends were for the loss the distress was acute. Sinatra had intended to keep on as normal with his evening engagement at the Copacabana, but rang his agent at the William Morris office a few minutes before showtime and told him, 'I can't go on. I'm afraid I won't be coherent'. Two members of the audience, Sammy Davis and Jerry Lewis, stood in for him, while Sinatra tried to walk off the pain of his friend's death through the cold

Left: Sinatra with Rita Hayworth and Kim Novak in 'Pal Joey'. Far left: This 'symbolic' sequence illustrates the choice Joey has to make.

Manhattan streets.

Three weeks later a moody and irritable Sinatra broke a date at the Stadium in Sydney, Australia, when a series of airline bookings went wrong in Honolulu. Sinatra turned back for home where he was due to start work on *Pal Joey*, and had to make a settlement of $75,000 dollars with the Australian promoter.

Seven days later he was again in trouble, this time from the California State Senate Committee when he received a subpoena relating to a bizarre incident that had happened three years previously. The 'Case of the Wrong Door Raid', a comedy of Italian pride and errors, had arisen from Sinatra's friendship with 'Joltin' Joe DiMaggio of the New York Yankees. Back in 1954 Joe had been left by his wife, Marilyn Monroe, and big Joe was in much the same state over her as Frank was over 'Hurricane Ava'. A private detective reported to Joe that his wife was having a lesbian affair with some unnamed lady in an apartment block on Waring Avenue. The two outraged Italians joined up with private detectives Barney Ruditsky and Philip Irwin, and accompanied by Sanicola, Patsy D'Amore from the Villa Capri and a photographer, organized or helped organize a raid on the offending lady's apartment. Depending on which version of events one believes, Sinatra himself waited in a car round the corner while the raiding party attacked (Irwin claimed that Sinatra had been with the break-in party). Unfortunately Ruditsky or Irwin chose the wrong apartment and a strange woman was shocked from her sleep to find a splintered door and a group of strange men in her bedroom.

The differing details between Irwin and Sinatra's testimonies seemed to constitute possible grounds for a perjury charge, but the Grand Jury eventually accepted Sinatra's version of events, and at a second Grand Jury sitting in July 1957 Ruditsky himself took full responsibility for the raid, claiming that both Sinatra and DiMaggio had remained outside.

The woman concerned, a Mrs Florence Katz Ross, sued all the men concerned for $200,000 worth of damages—a suit ultimately settled out of court for an undisclosed sum.

A contentious year continued when, in May 1957 it was Sinatra's turn to file a complaint—a $2,300,000 libel suit against *Look* magazine and the writer of a three-part profile published in the magazine that month. The first episode of the profile, entitled 'Talent, Tantrums and Torment', had made Sinatra out to be, in its own words, 'a neurotic, depressed and tormented person with suicidal tendencies and a libertine'.

The suit never reached the courtrooms. In December that year Sinatra altered his grounds from libel to invasion of privacy, and after years of legal haggling he finally dropped the case altogether in 1963.

By the autumn of 1957 Sinatra's vulnerable public image was under pressure. If he had looked on his new TV series as an augury for the future he would have ended the year a distinctly worried man.

ABC had paid him $3 million for a series of thirteen half-hour musicals, thirteen half-hour drama shows, and two one-hour spectaculars. Filming had started in the summer of 1957 and the thirteen musical half-hours had been shot in something less than twenty days. Transmission started in October, and although the programmes were heralded by a successful hour-long special with Bing Crosby, Sinatra's own series seemed to betray its conveyor-belt methods of production. The *New Yorker* commented: 'Everything seemed under-organized and a little desperate'; and that for a show described as 'the most expensive half-hour programme in history'. John Crosby in the New York *Herald Tribune* found Sinatra 'one hell of a performer . . . his first TV show a triumph in almost all departments'. But he was apparently in a minority. Already in the second week ABC started a post-mortem into the falling ratings, and within a month the series had been written off by *Variety* as 'a flop, rating and otherwise'. In December Sinatra tried to introduce a live element into the shows, but even his Christmas show with Bing Crosby was condemned by *Variety* as 'static, studied, pretentious and awkward'. The same critic pinpointed the central weakness: 'Even discounting the often sloppy production . . . the absence of a central theme or point of view, the fact is that Sinatra never seemed at his best or at his easiest, and the attitude infects his guests.'

Sinatra celebrated pre-Christmas that year on the set of *Kings Go Forth* (1958), still king of Hollywood with his weekly party for cast and crew laid on at the studio by the Villa Capri. But he must have been wondering as that year closed whether those vultures were not gathering again. Only three years previously he had described his career as 'the rise and fall and rise again . . .'. Was there another free-fall written into the scenario?

Frank Sinatra and Tony Curtis in 'Kings Go Forth', a mediocre war movie set in the South of France in 1944. Sinatra got mixed reviews for his role as Sam Loggins, the tough yankee lieutenant who falls in love with the beautiful exiled American girl of mixed blood (Natalie Wood).

8 THE TOUGH MONKEY 1958-1961

1958 saw the TV show fade out on a whimper with *TV Guide* describing it in February as 'one of the biggest and most expensive disappointments of the current season'. There was a further disappointment when *Kings Go Forth* premiered in the summer to a very cool reaction, and in August location trouble on Sinatra's *Some Came Running* sparked off a new press campaign against him. Yet, when he played the Fontainebleau, Miami in March Sinatra broke all night club records grossing over $100,000 in one two week season, and his attendance at the Carmen Basilio-Sugar Ray Robinson fight that same spring attracted more attention from the crowds than the fighters themselves.

The truth was that while the actor, the TV personality and man might falter, the voice still reigned supreme, and the 1957-58 awards had confirmed his standing: top male singer in the *Down Beat* poll; top by such a margin in *Metronome* that the paper commented, 'Sinatra literally devoured this one: there was no chance for anyone else'; he was singer of the year with Billie Holiday in *Jazz 1957*; top male vocalist for the *Playboy*; and 'all round entertainer of the year' for *American Weekly*.

That previous year, 1957, he had cut three bestselling albums, 'Come Fly With Me', 'Where Are You?', and 'Sinatra's Christmas Album'. The song 'All The Way' from *The Joker Is Wild* would win the Academy Award, and Sinatra even scored in the difficult singles market with 'Witchcraft', under the ever-inspiring direction of arranger/conductor Nelson Riddle.

'Frank undoubtedly brought out my best work', Nelson Riddle told Robin Douglas-Home in a 1961 interview. ' . . . He'd pick out all the songs for an album and then call me over to go through them. He'd have very definite ideas about the general treatment, particularly about the pace of the record and which areas should be soft or loud, happy or sad. He'd sketch out something brief like "Start with a bass figure, build up second time through and then fade out at the end" . . . Sometimes he'd follow this up with a phone call at three in the morning with some other extra little idea. But after that he wouldn't hear my arrangement until the recording session . . . He'd

In spite of continuous press sniping, the Voice still reigned supreme. Left: Sinatra acknowledges his debt to the ever-faithful concertgoers and the fans who continued to put his records into the bestseller lists.

never record before 8pm and we'd knock off sometime after 11. We'd get about four numbers finished at a session with an average of three takes a number.'

Frank Sinatra reciprocated the praise when Douglas-Home asked him about his arranger/conductor. 'Nelson is the greatest arranger in the world . . . He's like a tranquillizer—calm, slightly aloof. Nothing ever ruffles him. There's a great *depth* somehow to the music he creates. And he's got a sort of stenographer's brain. If I say to him at a planning meeting, "Make the eighth bar sound like Brahms", he'll make a cryptic little note on the side of some scrappy music sheet and, sure enough, when we come to the session the eighth bar will be Brahms. If I say, "Make like Puccini", Nelson will make exactly the same little note and that eighth bar will be Puccini all right and the roof will lift off.'

Nelson Riddle has slightly more qualified memories about these planning meetings: 'Frank's instructions were painful at the beginning of a session, a meeting to decide an album. I would wonder how long my patience would hold out, taking all these notes down. But one thing I learnt about Frank—if there were twelve arrangements to be mapped out he would get tired around the sixth one and by the eighth he'd say, "do what you please!".'

Sinatra found the rhythm of work with Billy 'lets-go-then-cats' May entirely different. 'Recording with Billy May is like having a cold shower or a bucket of cold water thrown in your face. Nelson will come to the session with all the arrangements carefully and neatly worked out beforehand. But with Billy you sometimes don't get the copies of the next number until you've finished the one before—he'll have been scribbling away in some office in the studio right up till the start of the session . . . Billy is driving, Nelson has depth, with Gordon Jenkins (the third of his favourite arrangers in the post-Stordahl years) it's all so beautifully simple that to me it's like being back in the womb. That "No One Cares" album I did with Gordon is one hell of an album.'

Sinatra never made any secret of his delight in recording and his particular satisfaction in the successful production of an LP from the moment of its conception, through to the choice of songs and its planning and pacing. It was an old lesson he had learned from his Tommy Dorsey days. '. . . Dorsey did this with every band show we played. Paced it, planned every second from start to finish. He never told me this; it just suddenly came to me as I sat up on that stand night after night. But this is what I've tried to do with every album I've ever made.'

In May 1958 Dave Cavanaugh took over Gilmore's job supervising Sinatra's recording sessions, and during the next three years had occasion to watch, enjoy and sometimes suffer the excitement of Sinatra's studio dates: 'It was always challenging to work with him because his musical intuitions were always right. But he had his wrinkles, as all artists do. Once when he had a "frog" in his throat. I flipped the talkback switch and said gently over the mike: "Got a little fuzz there, huh?" He came back like a flash: "Hell, that's sexy." It got a big laugh from the studio audience. And that's really the crux of it. For Sinatra, a recording session is like a night club appearance. He has his crowd and he's putting on a show. He gets a kind of vibrancy into his records because he's not just singing. Man, he's acting. And you're not just an A&R producer. You're straight man for his jokes.'

'Only The Lonely' was the first album Cavanaugh collaborated on, in May and June 1958, and it stands out as perhaps the best conceived and planned of all the Sinatra/Nelson Riddle LPs. Mood and theme build through both sides, to the fade-out in 'Angel Eyes'—'Excuse me while I disappear'—and the late-night bar solitude of 'One For My Baby' with its predominantly piano backing losing the orchestra in a beautiful and unusual down-beat climax to the whole record.

'Come Fly With Me' (recorded with Billy May)

was the bestselling album that year, but 'Only The Lonely' was not far behind in second spot, and in its later 'Music For Pleasure' edition, 'One For My Baby', it became a top-selling Sinatra album.

By 1959 Sinatra's run with Capitol was beginning to taper off. Disagreements started with various executives on the Capitol board and, remembering the Mitch Miller situation at Columbia, Sinatra decided to cut loose and take the risk of forming his own record company. His contract with Capitol already gave one of his companies (Essex Productions) the copyright of master tapes and there is little doubt that Sinatra had been working quietly towards independence for some time. Not unnaturally Capitol were reluctant to let him go. The contract was not due for renewal until 1962, but after their refusal to terminate Sinatra stopped recording—14 May was his last studio session in 1959. The 1959 releases included the 'No One Cares' album he cut with Gordon Jenkins, and the Cahn-Van Heusen single 'High Hopes', theme song for the film *A Hole In The Head* and Academy Award winner that same year. The second album in 1959 'Come Dance With Me' (recorded with Billy May) was certified in 1961 as a Golden Album, though music critics were now beginning to suggest a certain monotony in Sinatra's singing. Sinatra himself admitted a falling off during these two years: 'I wasn't happy during that period with Capitol and I'm afraid some of those later albums show it—definitely they do. I had said I wanted to quit Capitol and even if it meant not recording at all for two years until the contract ran out. But they let me go on condition I cut four more albums for them to wind up the deal.'

Voluntary or otherwise, independence seemed to be the keynote also in his private life. The early months of 1958 saw the break-up of a relationship that had,

during the latter half of the previous year, become Hollywood's favourite affair. In the months following Bogart's death Sinatra had been Lauren Bacall's constant escort and the affection between them had seemed to be growing towards something more than just the solace and companionship of old friends. Unfortunately for their peace of mind, the show-biz columnists decided that this was an affair to be encouraged and constant speculation in the press about an impending marriage made it impossible for the relationship to develop normally. Bacall later said herself: 'I eventually did get involved with Sinatra on a boy-girl basis. It worked out marvellously for a while until the press went absolutely mad and drove both of us mad.'

Below: Billie Holliday — one of the greatest influences on Sinatra's musical development. Below left: Sinatra accepts an award for being one of the top two Box Office draws for 1961. Below left and far left: Recording sessions for Sinatra were like night club appearances.

Sinatra puts the same energy into recordings, rehearsals or performances, no matter where he is. Above: With Duke Ellington; left: Rehearsing in London; below: With Bing Crosby and Dean Martin (right).

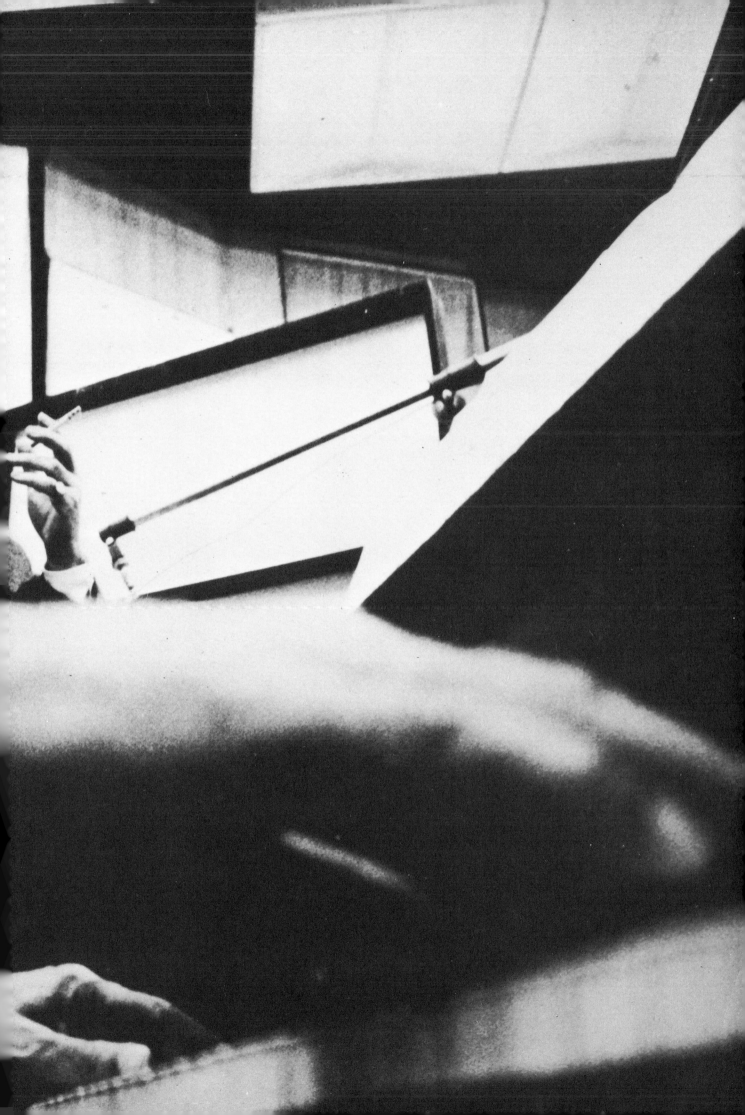

Louella Parsons applied the *coup de grace* to the romance in March 1958, when she published a headline in her column: 'Sinatra and Bacall to Marry.' Miss Parsons had received the news from the literary agent I.P. Lazar, Lauren Bacall's escort at a party given by Zsa Zsa Gabor, but the original source of information was never disclosed. Perhaps Lauren Bacall herself had wished to provoke Sinatra into stating his intentions. Whatever the motive—or mistake—Sinatra's reaction was entirely negative. He made no press statement, but as from that moment the affair from his side was over. There was more than a trace of bitterness in Bacall's retort to a journalist a few weeks later: 'Do me a favour: never mention me again in the same breath with Frank Sinatra.'

Another romance made headlines for Sinatra later the same year when he became the attentive escort of Lady Adele Beatty during a week's visit to London in September. American-born Adele Beatty, divorced earlier that year from Earl Beatty, was a society beauty in London and Sinatra's romance with her through a succession of upper-crust Mayfair parties excited columnists and newsmen on both sides of the Atlantic. Once again a wild newspaper report helped torpedo the affair when the London *Daily Mail* announced, after only two days of the courtship, that Sinatra and Lady Beatty planned to marry. Sinatra left London at the end of the week and within a few months the affair had been forgotten (Adele Beatty eventually married film director Stanley Donen).

As before with Lauren Bacall, the intrusions and machinations of the newsmen had angered Sinatra and another brush with a photographer on his return to New York seemed to set the battle-lines for a hard campaign. Needless to say, his press enemies had given little news-space to the fact that both his European trips that year had been for charitable functions—he sang at a UN Refugee Fund concert in Monte Carlo after the special premiere there of *Kings Go Forth* on 14 June; and acted as M.C. for the gala premier of Danny Kaye's *Me And The Colonel* in London on 19 September for the British Empire Cancer Fund.

Sinatra's relations with the press had taken a further beating that summer when the crew and cast of *Some Came Running* camped down for location work in the Ohio River town of Madison, Indiana. The outspoken, brash attitudes of the sophisticated Hollywood stars antagonized the townspeople from the outset and it would appear that Sinatra made little effort to understand the backwoods mentality of a small mid-west community. He and Dean Martin ignored an invitation to a local dance in favour of a gambling jaunt over the border in Kentucky, while

Above: Sinatra with Lady Beatty, attending a Mayfair party. Right: Sinatra became a family friend when Grace Kelly married Prince Rainier of Monaco. Below right: Sinatra and Lauren Bacall.

Shirley MacLaine, who attended the party, sat playing solitaire all evening. A local hotel clerk was abused and 'shoved around' after some misunderstanding over an order of hamburgers; autograph hunters were ignored; disparaging comments made about the town girls and the facilities. Director Vincente Minelli, while himself condemning Sinatra's restlessness on location, pointed out that members of the unit were shut up in the small town like animals in a zoo, with half the state of Indiana driving down in their cars to gawp at them all.

The atmosphere did not help ease Sinatra's usual location impatience, though there were reportedly long drinking sessions through the nights with the girls flown in for their pleasure from Hollywood and Las Vegas. 'Some mornings', a studio publicist said, 'Sinatra's eyes would look like two urine spots in the snow.'

Perhaps it was Sinatra's night-orientated metabolism that persuaded him to force changes in the daily shooting schedule when the *Some Came Running* unit moved back to the MGM studios. He broke Hollywood's sacrosanct nine-to-five working day, and insisted on adopting the French timetable he had experienced when on location for *Kings Go Forth*—namely a noon-to-eight working day with a break for a meal at four in the afternoon. That an actor with his independent production company could force such radical changes on a major studio was surely indicative of the new power structure beginning to emerge in the movie industry. The big studios were losing their omnipotence, big names

were what counted at the box-office and Sinatra was one of the first superstars to work that situation to his advantage.

Some Came Running opened in January 1959 to very mixed notices, though most reviewers picked out Sinatra's performance as the film's strong point. Bosley Crowther of the *New York Times*, once one of Sinatra's fiercest critics called him, 'downright fascinating . . . what the youngsters would call "cool" . . . beautifully casual with a bottle, bull's eye sharp with a gag and shockingly frank and impertinent in making passes at dames'.

Bosley Crowther was one of the few critics to be positively enthusiastic about Sinatra's second 1958 production, *A Hole In The Head*. 'Soap opera', was *Newsweek's* summary of the plot though critical interest in the film was heightened by the fact that it was director Frank Capra's comeback assignment after eight years in the Hollywood wilderness. 'Mr Frank Capra is back with us,' Bosley Crowther announced for the *New York Times*, 'and not only back, but also in such form as to make one toy vaguely with the notion that maybe it is good for a director to rest a bit once in a while. For *A Hole In The Head*, which is based on Arnold Schulman's Broadway play and has the carbolic Sinatra playing the character whose head is so endowed, is a thoroughly fresh, aggressive and sardonic comedy of the sort that sets one thinking about the comedies of the good old days.'

A Hole In The Head, shot only a month and a half after *Some Came Running*, had run into similar problems on location as the earlier film. The press had been waiting for the unit in Miami, determined, it seemed, to find production troubles, in particular any that centred on the controversial figure of Frank Sinatra. They filled their gossip columns with stories about his preference for parties rather than work; about his disagreements on set with co-star Edward G. Robinson; about his aggressive behaviour. The

107

reports were so consistent and so bad that Joe Hyams came down to visit the set. He could find no basis for the press stories, but found instead a man who, at the peak of success was afraid—'expecting to be cut down from the heights at any moment'.

Premonitions of possible disaster made 1959 and 1960 two uneasy years. The disagreement with Capitol led to Sinatra's decision not to record after May 1959 and neither of the two films he made that year, *Never So Few* and *Can-Can*, would prove to be a wild success.

Never So Few had a not uninteresting plot about the use made by the Chinese Nationalists of their American arms and supplies during the war—they were traded with the Japanese and 'war-lord' bandits and eventually turned against America's own soldiers. Unfortunately the structure of the story and development of the characters were rather flat and pedantic, and the political anger of the plot lost in the conventional melodramas of wartime action. Philip K. Scheuer of the *Los Angeles Times* called the film 'an old-fashioned movie about an old-fashioned war' —exactly what Sinatra's acting image could have

Below: Frank Capra directs Sinatra in 'Hole in the Head'. Below right: Sinatra with Edward G. Robinson—they share the same birthday. Right: Sinatra and Shirley MacLaine in 'Some Came Running'.

done without at this particular moment.

Can-Can—colour, Todd-AO, a saucy French story, and Cole Porter songs—seemed a better if familiar recipe, but somehow the magic did not quite come together. Shirley MacLaine, lauded by everyone after her debut in *Some Came Running*, overdid the Parisienne Cabaret owner, and Sinatra's performance seemed by contrast too off-hand and detached for the style of the story. 'The book becomes stale and foolish', wrote John McCarten in the *New Yorker*, 'and the Porter tunes are dispensed without any particular verve.'

All the more surprising then that ABC Television should choose this year to sign up Sinatra for a series of four expensive shows. Sinatra would again prove unable to dominate the small screen as he did the cinema or the live stage, but at least this time, with some outside help, he made an impact on those all-important ratings. The last two shows, recorded and broadcast in 1960, attracted the sort of audience figures Sinatra's sponsors must always have hoped for, the final show in March 1960 achieving a 41 percent rating against NBC's 21 percent and CBS's four percent. The third of the shows had been a St Valentine's Day tribute to the ladies with Eleanor Roosevelt reciting the lyrics of *High Hopes* to music by Nelson Riddle, and a young South African dancer, Juliet Prowse, providing the romantic interest as Sinatra's current girlfriend.

The fourth and last of the TV spectaculars, broadcast in March 1960, was a costly welcome-home-from-the-army party for Elvis Presley cannily

put together by Sinatra to attract the younger generation of viewers. Presley's fee for a ten minute appearance was said to have been around $100,000, nearly half the budget for the whole show. *Variety* would say that the show 'did not generate a quarter of a million dollars worth of excitement', but it was nevertheless a success of sorts for Sinatra. He had at last conquered the ratings and generated enough newsprint around the show to confirm himself the equal of the rock and roll star. When *Variety* commented that Presley's contribution to the show did not achieve the expected 'climactic wallop', it would seem that the king of show-biz had by way of a bonus upstaged the king of pop.

Certainly Sinatra's standing in the night club world during these two years had never been higher. He played to record breaking audiences in Las Vegas, Miami and Atlanta City—a measure of his popularity being the $50 tip paid to a waiter for one of his discarded cigarette ends. Women were hanging around dressing-rooms again, screaming at the sight and sound of him. And men were watching him with the grudging admiration usually reserved for a football or baseball star—after all here was the world's leading 'swinger', the man who had allegedly made love to every beautiful girl he had ever desired.

They were not claims Sinatra ever made on his own behalf. Indeed much of his unpopularity with newsmen originated in his well-observed rule never to talk in public about his women, whatever the circumstances.

The unpopularity reached an all-time high or low on Sinatra's short concert tour of Australia in April 1959. Ava Gardner was then in Melbourne filming *On The Beach*, and the Australian press were determined to rekindle the romance. Sinatra was pestered with questions wherever he went, a campaign that not unnaturally reached its climax when he arrived in Melbourne. Entering the stadium in a phalanx of bodyguards, Sinatra rounded on the newsmen, addressing them as slobs, and threatening them: 'If I see you again you'll never forget it. If you're around later,

they'll find you in the gutter.'

Ava Gardner had attended the performance and the two of them had their brief reunion in a hotel, where, in the words of the Australian paper *Truth*, 'the cranky crooner and his glamorous ex-wife drank wine together'. The reunion had in fact been a restatement of friendship after a quarrel they had had during another brief meeting in Rome the previous year—a quarrel sparked off by the fuss the press had then been making of Sinatra's affair with Lady Beatty. In Rome Ava had thrown her wedding ring back at Sinatra; now in Melbourne they were friends again, and Sinatra's visit a welcome break for Ava Gardner at a difficult time in her emotional and working life.

With the press lined up against him all across the world it was just as well that Sinatra's relationship with Marilyn Monroe remained a secret at the time of its consummation. Sinatra's previous friendship with Monroe's former husband, Joe DiMaggio, had cooled off after the 'Wrong Door Raid' affair, and when Marilyn Monroe took up with the Peter Lawfords a cooled friendship would turn into open hostility (DiMaggio banned Sinatra and the Lawfords from Marilyn Monroe's funeral in 1961). Peter Lawford, married to a Kennedy sister, was also a member of Sinatra's 'Clan' and it was almost inevitable that the King and Queen of Ring-a-ding-ding would eventually come together.

Norman Mailer describes the affair in his biography of Monroe: 'An intimate tells of driving her [Marilyn] to the Waldorf where Sinatra is staying. . . . Next day there is huge curiosity, but she indicates there was something wrong with the way the twin beds had been put together, some crack between the mattresses into which one or the other kept falling . . .

"Was Sinatra good?" asks the intimate.

"He was no DiMaggio. Of course she is wicked in most of her remarks about new lovers these days and will yet proceed to have a continuing affair with Sinatra.'

Continuing and discreet. Perhaps it was Marilyn Monroe herself who knew better how to organize such

Right: Bob Hope (left) and Sinatra entertain Mrs Mamie Krushchev at a luncheon given in the Krushchevs' honour at 20th Century Fox Studios. Below: Stars and officials toast Premier Krushchev (centre). Sinatra stands in the foreground, back to camera, with David Niven. Below, left: The Russian Premier was treated to a preview of 'Can-Can', starring Sinatra and Juliet Prowse, which Krushchev denounced as 'immoral'.

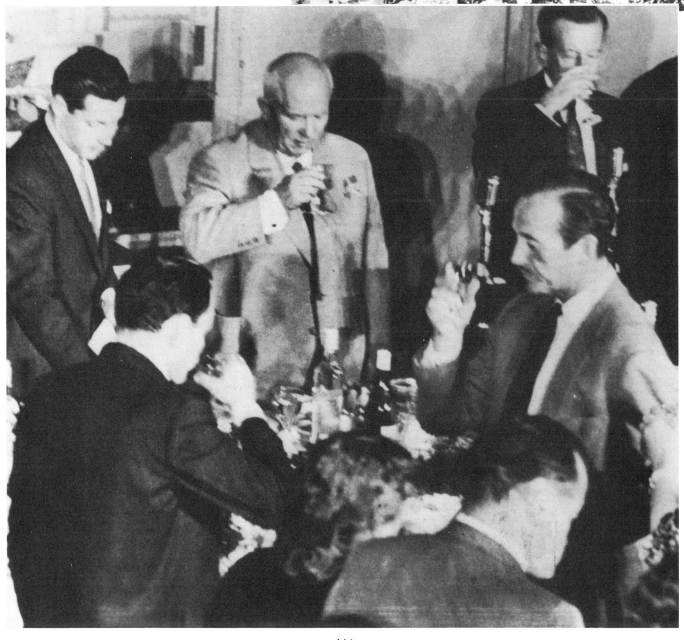

things. Most of her sad and whimsical love affairs in those last post-Miller years were conducted well away from the public eye, in a careful and secret reticence that Sinatra himself never mastered.

Certainly the other serious romance at this period of Sinatra's life became, almost from birth, the property of columnists and photographers. Sinatra first met and dated Juliet Prowse while they were both working on *Can-Can*. They continued to date seriously during the whole of the following year, with Miss Prowse often acting as Sinatra's hostess at parties. Her natural, unaffected and above all un-possessive manner seemed to be drawing Sinatra ever closer to her, though there was nothing as yet in the relationship to set her apart from any of his other girlfriends, past or present.

Then in October 1960 Sinatra's eldest daughter Nancy married rock 'n' roll singer Tommy Sands. A much-moved father officiated at the ceremony, giving away Nancy with Sammy Davis singing her theme song 'Nancy With The Laughing Face'. When Sinatra invited Juliet Prowse and her family to a party that Christmas even his cynical friends began to suspect he was himself thinking of marriage in the new year.

Instead 1961 would pass in a succession of other dates and affairs, most notably with Dorothy Provine and Princess Soraya. Juliet Prowse kept her distance and her demeanour, and for the second time in his life Sinatra found himself obsessed with a girl who refused to pursue him. At the end of 1961 Sinatra returned unhappy from a trip around the Far East

with Dorothy Provine and within a few days had proposed marriage to Juliet Prowse. After a period of thought Miss Prowse accepted the proposal, but without agreeing to Sinatra's demand that she give up her own career. It was on this point that the engagement floundered six weeks after its announcement. The break-up of the engagement, announced from his side, threw Sinatra into a period of what one friend later called 'agonizing loneliness'. For he was, as Sid Skolsky pointed out at the time, a man alone. 'On any night when the laughs get sleepy and there's no more booze and there are no more hours, Dean goes home to his wife, Lawford goes home to his, Sammy to his. But Frank just goes home.'

Perhaps that isolation is the secret of his incredible, often obsessive energy—the need to fill each hour of day and night with activity. There were many press features in 1960 covering the hectic rhythm of life in Las Vegas when Sinatra and his buddies moved in to shoot *Ocean's Eleven*, the first of the so-called Clan movies. Even *Playboy* ran a blow by blow account of the revelries on and off stage, though what amazes one now, beyond the clan clowning, is the amount of sheer hard work and action Sinatra was able to handle on his own. During a period of several days he was shooting on *Ocean's Eleven* from five in the morning to around midday; shooting again in the afternoon, a cameo part this time in *Pepe*; rehearsing in the

Far left: Sinatra and Juliet Prowse: they were engaged for six weeks in 1961. Centre: Sinatra and clan members Sammy Davis Jr and Peter Lawford. enjoying some airline hospitality. Below: Frank and daughter Nancy have always enjoyed a very close relationship.

evening for a forthcoming television show; and finally moving on stage with the Clan, Dean Martin, Sammy Davis Jr, Peter Lawford and Joey Bishop, to do two shows at the Sands night club, the last of which would not end until around two o'clock in the morning. And the whole day would be peppered with long-distance phone calls checking up on this or that aspect of this or that business activity.

Sinatra, the corporation man, had already put together a financial empire of some size: Essex Films with its various subsidiaries; four music publishing companies; Las Vegas and Lake Tahoe hotel and gambling interests (six per cent of Sands in Las Vegas, 25 per cent of the Cal-Neva on Lake Tahoe, Nevada); radio station partnerships with Danny Kaye; real estate just about everywhere. In the early 1960s his business interests were said to gross around twenty million dollars a year, and that in a period when his new-born record company, Reprise, was still losing money.

The combination of Clan and corporations proved irresistible to Sinatra's press enemies. Here, after all was a new and menacing figure of power, something of a Citizen Kane casting his shadow over the innocents down Sunset Boulevard. Their concern might have rung clearer and cleaner without the 'coincidence' of the Republican colours at every mast-head.

The Clan was assumed, mistakenly, to be some natural development of the Holmby Hills Rat Pack, as assumption that annoyed anyone intimately associated with Humphrey Bogart and the carefree anarchy of Lauren Bacall's original pack of rats. True rebellion and non-conformity fitted the members of the Sinatra clan less easily and the origins of Clan lay closer to the personal and professional retinue that Sinatra had

gathered round him like a screen over the years. For all the sleazy associations imparted to it in press reports, the Clan was primarily a working arrangement, an association of Sinatra's business partners—Sanicola, Jack Entratter, Peter Lawford, plus the various executives from Essex, Reprise and the publishing companies—with the men who shared Sinatra's performing life—Dean Martin, Sammy Davis Jr, Joey Bishop, songwriters Sammy Cahn and Jimmy Van Heusen, pianoman Bill Miller, make-up man Pondedell, and writer Don McGuire.

'Clan' traditions were first established, and publically recognized, in the night club routines, so hilariously shared by the central performing triumvirate of Sinatra, Martin and Davis. Their particular brand of indulgent, self-deprecating, incestuous humour became such a feature of the top Niter circuit that their innermost 'in-jokes' were accessible to audiences whether in New York, Miami, Las Vegas or Burbank. It was the third member of the triumvirate, Sammy Davis Jr, who the previous year had incurred the wrath of the King and demonstrated, inadvertently, the extent and possible abuse of Sinatra's power.

On the Jack Eigen show from Chicago early in 1959, Sammy Davis admitted about Sinatra '...there are many things he does that there is no excuse for. I don't care if you are the most talented man in the world, it does not give you the right to step on people and treat them rotten. That is what he does occasionally'. According to Earl Wilson this rebuke sent Sinatra off into a chair-throwing tantrum and the unfortunate Sammy was forthwith 'written out' of

Right: Sinatra and the Clan in their first joint movie, 'Ocean's 11'. L. to r.: Sinatra, Dean Martin, Sammy Davis Jr, Peter Lawford and Joey Bishop. Right top: On the set of 'Oceans 11' Sinatra discusses his cameo role in the film 'Pepe' with the director, George Sidney. Far right (left): Frank Sinatra's and Dean Martin's families appear together on Martin's Christmas television show and (right) Sinatra fools around with Bing Crosby and Dean Martin.

Sinatra's war movie *Never So Few*. His part, suitably reworked, ended up as Steve McQueen's first big break in a feature film—the one positive result of the outburst, for Sammy Davis repented and recanted, immediately withdrawing the criticism. But he still had to suffer months of torment while on the cold shoulder side of King Frank. The cold shoulder included the exercised prerogative of refusing him entry to hotels and clubs where Sinatra was staying or working. Eventually Sinatra and Davis made up, publicly, as was Sinatra's habit, at a Los Angeles charity show, falling into each other's arms in what Dean Martin described as 'a disgusting display'.

Dino's words were, of course, part of permissible clan banter. As was Sammy Davis's later definition of the Clan: 'It's just an ordinary bunch of guys who get together once a year and take over the whole world.'

Unfortunately Sinatra critics used such remarks at their face value. Al Aronowitz, in a series of articles for the *New York Post*, suggested that clan power had a lot to do with Sinatra's control over employment both on the night club circuit and the cinema. 'Sinatra is King and Dictator of Hollywood', he asserted, 'and everyone is afraid of him.'

This theme was taken up by a number of commentators in the national press and Sinatra suddenly found his many media enemies grouping and consolidating in a common camp as the nation prepared itself for another presidential campaign.

Sinatra denied the existence of the 'Clan' in spite of evidence to the contrary. Right: Clan members supported each other both publicly and privately—here Sinatra promotes Dean Martin's latest business venture during a Las Vegas shindig; l. to r.: Sinatra. Joey Bishop, Dean Martin. Sammy Davis Jr and Peter Lawford.

9 THE THOUSAND DAYS 1959-1962

Sinatra's association with the bright, young idealistic Kennedy age would begin sadly with his first and very significant ideological retreat, and end humiliatingly with cold shoulder and rebuff, treatment he had often handed out to others but was emotionally ill-equipped to assimilate himself.

It was already clear by the end of 1959 that Sinatra intended to involve himself in the election campaign and, given the Peter Lawford-Kennedy connection almost within the Clan, it was also predictable that he would back John Kennedy for the Democrat nomination. As a top entertainer he had instant access to unlimited publicity; as an influential figurehead he was a draw for the Italian vote; and as a millionaire in his own right he had the financial power to organize and contribute to party funds. Not surprising then, if the anti-Sinatra Republican press turned up their volume of criticism.

In March 1960 it became known that Sinatra had hired novelist Albert Maltz, one of the so-called 'Hollywood Ten', to adapt a screenplay from William Bradford Huie's documentary study, *The Execution Of Private Slovik.* Private Slovik had been the only American soldier executed by the army since the Civil War; Albert Maltz was one of the left-wing Hollywood writers fined $1000 and imprisoned for a year in 1950 for refusing to testify before the House Un-American Activities Committee. The combination of Maltz and Slovik offended American patriots, though there was nothing very ennobling to the American reputation in the howls of protest that greeted the news, the cries of a witch-hunt and a lynch-mob, from the not-so-silent majority.

'Dump Maltz and get yourself a true American' said a *Los Angeles Examiner* editorial. 'If Sinatra loves his country he won't do this,' Hedda Hopper wrote some days later in the *Los Angeles Times.* 'He has a fine family of which he's proud. Will he do this to them?'

Over and above his prison sentence and fine, Maltz had been black-listed in Hollywood ever since 1951 and while he, like Dalton Trumbo, had probably found work under assumed names, the studios took advantage of the subterfuge, paying them at much lower rates. It was an hypocrisy that Sinatra wanted to expose. Stanley Kramer and Otto Preminger had already set the precedent with writers Nedrich Young on *Inherit The Wind* and Dalton Trumbo on *Exodus,* but Sinatra was aware of the damage the Maltz hiring might do at this particular time to Kennedy's election chances and he had tried to keep the affair a secret until after the election in the autumn.

His fears were justified. As soon as the news broke John Wayne asked publicy what was Kennedy's attitude towards the signing up of this black-listed 'pinko' writer. Sinatra replied, as was his habit, with full-page advertisements in the Hollywood trade press: 'This type of partisan politics is hitting below the belt . . . it was not until I spoke to Albert Maltz that I found a writer who saw the screenplay in exactly the terms I wanted. This is, the Army was right. Under our Bill of Rights, I was taught that no one may prescribe what shall be orthodox in politics, relion or other matters of opinion.'

The advertisement mollified no one and the pressure on Sinatra increased. Actors Robert Taylor and Robert Lippert voiced their criticisms. Studios and banks made it quietly clear there would be no finance available for the film. Pontiac dropped Peter Lawford and other clan members from a TV programme they were sponsoring. Mike Connolly in the *Hollywood Reporter* turned on the venom in a daily campaign. On 23 March he noted in his column ' . . . some of our producers are signing up the scummies for MOST important task—screenwriting . . . Danger! Watch Out!' And on 24 March: 'My O My what a picnic "Tenner" Albert Maltz will have writing that un-American "Slovik" script . . . verrry interesting—the Hearst wire service story QUOTING Comrade Maltz's letter to a Russky rag in which this rabid red pledged his continued loyalty to Communism.' On 25 March Connolly dragged in a reference to the current dispute between the Writers Guild and the film industry: 'A "fink" in the parlance of Frank Sinatra and of Albert Maltz's pet propagandists *Pravda* and *The Daily Worker*, is a "capitalistic parasite" . . . In other words, a strikebreaker . . . Sinatra, who has always professed to despise finks, has switched his affections by signing the biggest fink in town, Albert Maltz, to script "Private Slovik" . . . Communist Maltz, y'see, is no longer a member of the striking Writers Guild of America . . . nevertheless he *is* a scripter . . . And since Sinatra hasn't signed a WGA contract it makes Maltz a sneaky, switchhitting, strikebreaking FINK . . . And not Sinatra nor any Commie apologist can wish this sick man Maltz out of his stinking kettle of fish.' On 29 March, after a weekend's pause, Connolly nudged a warning to the actor rumoured as probably cast for the film and resumed his political hysteria: 'Is TV star Steve

Right: President-Elect John F. Kennedy thanks Frank Sinatra for his support and loyalty during the 1960 Presidential Election Campaign.

Above: Sinatra and the President with opera singer Maria Callas celebrating Kennedy's triumph.

McQueen's career THAT secure—I mean that he can do "Private Slovik?" . . . Ben Hecht is adapting Commie playwright Bertolt Brecht's "Simone" for Broadway (he hopes!) . . . Apologists for the Redskis insist you can separate the man from his works . . . Bible says you can't ("By their works ye shall know them", Matthew VII, 16).'

On 30 March Connolly explained the reference: 'We meant the works of such non-Bible-believers as Picasso (the baleful "Peace Dove"), Chaplin ("King in New York"), Paul Robeson (rabble-rousing), Trumbo (specifically his "contributions" to "Spartacus"), Krushchev ("We'll bury you!") and Maltz (his pledge, to a red rag in East Germany, of eternal allegiance to the Hammer-and-Sickle).'

Eighteen days after the news first broke Sinatra caved in. The surrender was entirely out of character and one must assume that it was made in consideration of the political consequences for the Democrat campaign. It has often been reported, though never confirmed, that the elder Kennedy himself intervened. In his biography of Sinatra, Tony Scaduto quotes an unnamed Kennedy aide: 'The old man just put his foot down. Joe Kennedy called Sinatra and told him he'd either have to drop Maltz or disassociate himself from Jack Kennedy's campaign. Sinatra dropped Maltz.'

Sinatra issued a statement announcing his withdrawal 'Due to the reactions of my family, my friends and the American public, I have instructed my attorneys to make a settlement with Albert Maltz and

to inform him that he will not write the screenplay for *The Execution Of Private Slovik*. I had thought the major consideration was whether or not the resulting script would be in the best interests of the United States. Since my conversation with Mr Maltz had indicated that he had an affirmative, pro-American approach to the story and since I felt fully capable as producer of enforcing such standards, I have defended my hiring of Mr Maltz. But the American public has indicated that it feels the morality of hiring Mr Maltz is the more crucial matter and I will accept the majority opinion.'

A sad retreat, not without its own personal irony. Albert Maltz had been Sinatra's scriptwriter for *The House I Live In* which had won Sinatra a special Oscar for its liberal and humanitarian qualities back in 1945. Now, fifteen years later, the realities of power and Sinatra's own approach to them, had seemed more important.

The Maltz affair was not the only potential source of embarrassment to a Kennedy campaign adopted by King Frank and already in 1960 Bobby Kennedy had opened his own personal file on Sinatra's rumoured Mafia connections. The Kennedys were sponsoring a Constitutional Rights Conference in New York and it was in reference to Sinatra's possible appearance at the conference that Kennedy was told by his advisers not to meet Sinatra 'in public'. The advice was

120

modified when it was pointed out by campaign managers that Sinatra had always been considered something of a civil rights hero in the black ghettoes. He was subsequently used on a voter registration drive in Harlem.

The reluctance of one part of the Kennedy camp to accept Sinatra in the innermost circles might also have reflected a desire not to turn the campaign into too much of a show-biz razzamatazz. The intellectuals considered the use of Sinatra as a campaign weapon a lowering of the tone and a gimmick that could backfire on the already precariously youthful image of a possible president. But the irresistible attraction of Sinatra for the Democrats was his draw as a potential fund-raiser and apart from Bobby Kennedy's Mafia vetting Sinatra was pulled into the campaign without further reservations. Peter Lawford, Shirley MacLaine, Tony Curtis and Janet Leigh joined him in the Kennedy camp, while other members of the Sinatra Clan worked fund-raising dates under his generalship.

By mid-summer the Republican press had adopted the Clan as an anti-Kennedy weapon: 'Can a man whose brother-in-law is a member of the Clan be elected President of the United States?' Sinatra issued a statement denying the existence of the Clan. 'It's a figment of someone's imagination. Naturally people in Hollywood socialize with friends as they do in any community. But we do not get together in childish fraternities, as some people would like to think.' The Kennedys took their own precautions, sending an aide to Las Vegas to pick up the negatives of any photos showing Jack Kennedy in the company of the Clan (Kennedy had attended one of the Clan nights at the Sands Club in January 1960, this being the occasion when the future president first met Sinatra's ex-playmate Judith Campbell Exner).

Even more revealing of the campaign tactics was the attempted smear associated with the Sammy Davis-May Britt engagement. 'Politicos are giggling that the SDJr-May Britt nuptial is really secret Republican strategy.' The reference was of course racial, the suggestion being that a mixed marriage within the Clan would lose the Democrats a lot of votes. It is a sad reflection on American public opinion of the time that Sammy Davis felt obliged, for Frank's sake, to postpone the wedding until after the election. It is also illustrative of the loyalty that Sinatra can inspire in his closest friends. Sammy Davis made out that the ceremony had been postponed because of a legal hitch in May Britt's Mexican divorce. They eventually married on the Sunday after election day.

Smears or not, the very closeness of the election results might have persuaded Sinatra that his intervention had been decisive and his post-election gaiety had something of the King-maker about it. Whatever effect he may have had on the votes, his efforts on the fund-raising front certainly were decisive and it was no

surprise when Kennedy announced that Sinatra was to co-produce the inaugural gala with Peter Lawford.

A scornful article in *Time* magazine repeated the Hollywood story that Sinatra would now be appointed Ambassador to Italy; Sammy Davis Jr Ambassador to Israel or Kenya; Dean Martin Secretary of Liquor. The story had some basis in fact. Sinatra's political ambitions were well enough known and he might now have been hoping for some honorary post from which to launch himself into a future state or federal campaign.

For the moment Sinatra devoted himself to the organization of a gala to outlive all galas and the breadth and depth of talent he managed to collect was a reflection of his influence and stature inside show-business: Ella Fitzgerald (who had flown over with Nelson Riddle from an Australian tour); Gene Kelly (who had come from Switzerland); Ethel Merman (a battling Republican who nevertheless negotiated a release from her current show for the evening); Leonard Bernstein; Alan King; Nat 'King' Cole' Bette Davis; Harry Belafonte; Laurence Olivier; Milton Berle; Joey Bishop; Mahalia Jackson; Sidney Poitier; Juliet Prowse; Frederick March; Jimmy Durante; Helen Trauble; Tony Curtis and Janet Leigh; even Eleanor Roosevelt as special guest. Sinatra supervised every tiny detail of the show in the face of a continuous barrage of press ridicule.

On the evening of 19 January, 1961, Republican prayers seemed answered from above for Washington was suddenly blanketed in its worst-ever blizzard. The performers were delayed on their way to the theatre (The National Guard Armoury) and half the audience failed to turn up. But the tickets had all been pre-sold (over a million and a half dollars' worth) and even the show ended up as a triumph, notwithstanding the half-empty theatre. 'We are all indebted to a great friend, Frank Sinatra,' said President-elect Kennedy. 'Tonight we saw excellence.' Sinatra used Kennedy's words in a *Variety* advertisement thanking the performers, then eight days later, in the Carnegie Hall, repeated the success in an all-talent tribute show to mark Kennedy's release of Martin Luther King from a Georgia jail. Count Basie, Mahalia Jackson, Tony Bennet and the Clan entertained a packed house that had paid up to $100 per ticket and, at the emotional climax of the show, Harry Belafonte introduced Dr King himself. It was an evening to complete Sinatra's triumph and Republican discomfort.

Inauguration was the high point of Sinatra's affair with the Kennedys. On the night following the gala and in spite of five competing inaugural balls, the President still found time to make an appearance at Sinatra's own private party in the Statler Hilton and next morning, before flying south to Palm Beach with the elder Kennedy, Sinatra breakfasted with the Lawfords and Bobby Kennedy, then attended Bobby's swearing-in as Attorney General. It must have seemed to Sinatra in retrospect a strange and ironic breakfast party, for in Bobby Kennedy's eyes, Sinatra was already a marked man. The younger Kennedy was the first, and maybe the last, of post-war Attorney Generals to declare full frontal war on the Mafia world and as far as he was concerned, Sinatra had too many friends and contacts in that world. Within weeks of inauguration he was advising his brother to drop Sinatra from his circle of friends.

At Bobby's request the Narcotics Bureau and FBI agents re-opened old files on Sinatra's supposed connections with underworld figures, dating back to the earliest days with Willie Moretti in Jersey City and the Havana affair with Lucky Luciano. The FBI and to a lesser extent the CIA, also gathered contemporary evidence, keeping detailed logs on the movements of alleged Mafia associates. It is the complex web of relationships exposed in such files that now make the thousand days of Kennedy's presidency a happy hunting ground for the sensation-seekers and Sinatra is found somewhere near the centre of that web, connected with two girls who were at the time involved with Sam 'Momo' Giancana.

'Momo', one of the old-style Godfather figures, had been friendly for some time with Phyllis McGuire, of the McGuire singing sisters. 'Momo' Giancana was also an old buddy of Sinatra from early New York days and when Sinatra cast Phyllis McGuire for the Mrs Eckman role in *Come Blow Your Horn*, FBI agents suspected he was doing a favour for Giancana. Nothing was proved.

A more serious entanglement was created when Sinatra introduced one of his ex-mistresses to Giancana. Judith Campbell Exner, Las Vegas playgirl and mistress of President Kennedy, became through Sinatra's introductions, the girlfriend not only of Giancana, but of another Mafia suspect, John Roselli. At the time the knowledge of such politically explosive associations lay buried deep in Bureau files. It was only during the post-Watergate Senate investigation into the CIA that some of these facts came to light and that a further link was discovered between the White House (through the CIA), Sam Giancana (through Judith Exner) and an attempted assassination plot against Fidel Castro. But in 1975, before the Senate Committee could probe any further, Sam Giancana was murdered, shot in the back of the head while he cooked supper for a supposed friend. There are some underworld investigators in the middle of that maze who now believe themselves to be crossing trails that would ultimately lead to the secret of Kennedy's own assassination in Dallas.

Whatever the later implications, Bobby Kennedy was, by 1962, convinced of Sinatra's threat to White House prestige. He showed his brother a report compiled by his own department, part of which is quoted by Scaduto in his biography of Sinatra: 'Sinatra has had a long and wide association with hoodlums and racketeers which *seems* to be continuing. The nature of Sinatra's work *may*, on occasion, bring him into contact with underworld figures, but this cannot account for his friendship and/or financial involvement with people such as Joe and Rocco Fischetti, cousins of Al Capone, Paul Emilio D'Amato, John Formosa and Sam Giancana, all of whom are on our list of racketeers. No other entertainer *appears* to be mentioned nearly so frequently with racketeers.

'Available information indicates not only that Sinatra is associated with each of the above-named racketeers but that they *apparently* maintain contact with one another. This indicates a *possible* community of interest involving Sinatra and racketeers in Illinois, Indiana, New Jersey, Florida and Nevada.' [Author's italics]

The report proved nothing. But it was not intended to. Bobby Kennedy had not thought of attempting to implicate Sinatra legally. He just needed to know how potentially embarrassing the Sinatra friendship might be for the President during the next election campaign. President Kennedy was finally convinced by the political argument. The President had planned to stay with Sinatra on a visit to Palm Springs in March 1962 and Sinatra had built a special presidential wing to accommodate him. (Kennedy had already stayed at the house during the two days before his election in November 1960). At the last minute and ostensibly for security reasons, Kennedy's plans were changed. He stayed with Bing Crosby in Palm Desert instead, and Sinatra, shattered by the rebuff, left town for the duration of Kennedy's visit.

Already the previous summer a projected Clan visit to the elder Kennedy's villa at Cap d'Antibes had been cancelled, presumably for similar reasons. When Sinatra quarrelled with Peter Lawford later in that spring of 1962, the cooling off of relations seemed complete, though there are some who believe that Jack Kennedy's break with Sinatra was for public consumption only and that they continued to communicate with each other up until the time of Kennedy's assassination. Kennedy was certainly star-struck. His contact with the celebrities of Hollywood, especially the women, seemed to give him as much excitement as his meetings with world statesmen and King Frank was his *passe-partout* into that glittering parade.

Complete or incomplete, Sinatra's break with the White House was a humiliation and bitter disappointment. He had come close enough to feel the vibrations of true power and undoubtedly had his own ambitions for office of some sort. It was the pursuit of such ambitions that had seemed to dictate his political behaviour after that sad retreat in the Maltz affair — though it should be remembered in Sinatra's favour that as late as June 1962 the Ku Klux Klan were burning his effigy with the sign: 'Death to nigger-lover number one.'

Sinatra never forgave Bobby Kennedy his part in the break-up with brother Jack and in 1968 he was to campaign for Humphrey against Bobby in the battle for the Democrat nomination. To no avail. Frightened perhaps by the information the Bobby Kennedy camp could use against Sinatra, and no doubt prompted by an article in the *Wall Street Journal* listing Sinatra's underworld pals, Humphrey would quietly drop him from the campaign team.

Even after the initial break with the White House in 1961/62 Bobby Kennedy's anti-mafia campaign continued to embarrass Sinatra. In November 1962 he played, with other Clan members and Eddie Fisher, at a little-known and only recently re-opened night club in the suburbs of Chicago. This engagement at the Villa Venice puzzled most show-biz commentators, until *Variety* claimed to have discovered a big-money floating crap game in a nissen hut a few hundred yards away. The mysteries of the Villa Venice were never explained, though the general impression was that the engagement had resulted from Sinatra's links with the underworld—a favour asked or demanded by a friend.

But *Variety* also suggested that the entertainers at the night club had had no knowledge of the crap game round the corner.

By now, Bobby Kennedy, wholly unconvinced by the Hoover-FBI denials of large-scale organized crime, had stepped up surveillance of all known mafia racketeers, and it was the thoroughness of such surveillance that brought trouble to Sinatra's Cal-Neva Lodge at Lake Tahoe, Nevada. The Nevada State Gaming Board had circulated a 'black book' in 1960 naming eleven 'known gangsters' who were to be banned from any Nevada gambling premise (the list included Sam Giancana, Marshal Caifano, Trigger Mike Coppola and Joe Sica; but left out the mobsters who actually had financial stakes in Nevada casinos— Frank Costello, Meyer Lanksy and Carlo Gambino).

In 1962 the renovated gambling lodge was re-opened by Sinatra. Already that year the Lodge had caused a rift between Sinatra and his long-time manager, Hank Sanicola, and it could well be that Sanicola foresaw the complications that might arise

*Sinatra escorts Mrs Jacqueline
Kennedy to the Inaugural Gala.*

from that 'black book' of listed mobsters. Sure enough, the next summer, Sam Giancana, long-time buddy of Sinatra, visited the Cal-Neva with his girlfriend Phyllis McGuire. They stayed at one of the Lodge chalets under McGuire's name but Giancana's presence at the casino was harder to conceal. The State Gaming Authority told the Lodge manager to get rid of Giancana, but the manager ignored the request. Sinatra was not the man to throw a friend out of his own hotel at the behest of some authoritative body. The Authority then threatened to withdraw Sinatra's gaming licence.

Subsequently, without Sinatra's knowledge, one of the casino entourage, Skinny d'Amato (owner of the 500 Club in Atlantic City) approached the gaming board with the two casino heavies, known affectionately as Pucci East and Pucci West. A small bribe was offered and contemptuously refused. The chairman of the gaming board, Edward Olsen, now threatened to force Sinatra to testify. 'You subpoena me,' answered Sinatra, 'and you're going to get a big fat fucking surprise.'

Not surprisingly the board refused to withdraw. The issue had become too public. Olsen charged Sinatra with using 'obscene and indecent language which was menacing in the extreme and constituted a threat . . .'

Sinatra had predictably reacted against the hypocrisy of the situation, well aware himself of the selectivity of that infamous 'black book'. Even Sinatra's old press enemy, Robert Ruark, let off a blast against the Nevada authorities: 'For Nevada— by God, Nevada! —to go high and mighty . . . is the absolute Chinese end. There isn't enough real morality in Nevada to make a louse blink if it was all in his eye. Any state that lives off big gambling and its by-products—and I should not like to mention a high order of harlotry— and which has paid court to the likes of Bugsy and Mickey Cohen, is living in the glassiest of parlour houses.'

But the Gaming Authority persisted with its charges, citing Bobby Kennedy's condemnation of Giancana as a top mafia boss, and claiming that Sinatra intended to continue his association with Giancana in defiance of the Gaming Board's regulation.

Sinatra was given two weeks to answer these charges and found himself with a good deal of support from other Nevada Casinos. But to everyone's surprise Sinatra withdrew from the confrontation, selling his holdings in the Cal-Neva and Sands Casinos (worth, it was said, three and a half million dollars), but retaining his participation in the hotels. The reason he gave at the time was his premeditated decision to free himself from any investment and activity not associated with the world of entertainment. 'Since I have decided that I belong in the entertainment industry and not in the gaming industry, no useful purpose would be served by devoting my time and energies convincing the Nevada

Gaming officials that I should be part of their gaming industry.'

Whether there were other reasons for Sinatra's withdrawal has never been clear. He could have been apprehensive of a large-scale inquiry into his associations with Giancana and company. He might have been threatened—the legendary 'offers not to be refused'. But if so, by whom? There was no Mafia sub-chief at that time in a position to intimidate one of Momo's friends, unless Giancana himself told Sinatra to cool things off. A more likely explanation is that Sinatra, in that summer of 1963, was still trying to salvage something of his relationship with President Kennedy and that a public gambling/gangster row would not have helped his slim chances of reacceptance at the White House.

Three months later Kennedy was dead; and a little over two weeks after the Dallas tragedy Sinatra's own son, Frank Jr, was kidnapped. Again the sequence of events puzzled some people, for the kidnapping seemed almost like a warning—to be silent, to stay out of something? Was it possible in the after-shock of Kennedy's death that Sinatra had considered cooperating with Bobby Kennedy's anti-crime purge? Earl Wilson reports how Frank Jr had found his father curiously uneasy at the family Thanksgiving dinner: 'Frank Jr said it was the first time he'd remembered his father acting distant and he attributed it to his shock about the Kennedy death.'

Ten days later, on 8 December, 1963, the kidnapping took place. Frank Sinatra Jr was taken from a motel room across the road from Harah's Casino at Lake Tahoe where he was appearing as a singer (his professional singing career had started that summer, appropriately enough with the re-established remnants of what was still called the Tommy Dorsey Band). Sinatra Sr was at Palm Springs at the time and he flew up to Reno in a snow storm to take charge of operations. Kidnapping is a Federal offence and he was under the supervision of the FBI as he waited by the telephone for the kidnappers to make their first move.

$240,000 was the sum eventually demanded and the telephone contacts that led to the 'drop' took Sinatra from Reno to Carson City, to his ex-wife, Frankie Jr's mother in Bel-Air, to a gas station on Santa Monica Boulevard, to the Western Airlines at Los Angeles Airport, to another gas station in west Los Angeles, and finally to the 'drop' point between two parked school buses in an empty gas station by a cemetery on Sepulveda Boulevard. Frank Jr was released as promised an hour or so later in the Bel-Air area.

Whatever the tensions and unpleasantness of the kidnapping itself, the controversy that followed was almost as bad. The FBI cracked the case unusually quickly, when one of the kidnappers gave himself up. The three men who had taken part seemed to have been amateurs—one of them an ex-classmate of Nancy Jr at University High School in Beverly Hills and when the trial started in February 1964 the defence tried to suggest that the kidnapping had been rigged as a publicity stunt. It was a very subdued and quietly spoken Sinatra Sr who answered to such charges in the witness box and the jury believed him.

A British judge was later called to review factors in the case when Sinatra sued Independent Television for a panel show in which it was suggested that the kidnapping had been a stunt. The High Court judge awarded 'large' damages to Sinatra which Sinatra passed on to the Great Britain Sunshine Home for Blind Babies. There the matter seemed to rest, the only question mark left over the episode being not whether the Sinatras had fabricated the crime for their own purposes, but whether there was another, third party involved—in other words, that the kidnapping had been some kind of warning to Sinatra.

But then how much could Sinatra have known about mob activities? How much contact, active or coincidental, could he have had with the world of organized crime? In a sample pre-released page from her memoir, Judith Campbell Exner describes one of her meetings with Sinatra and the kind of company she found in his hotel room (the Claridge in Atlantic City): 'Joe Fish [Fischetti] and Skinny D'Amato, along with others of the entourage, the faceless ones, were in Frank's suite when I arrived.

'Frank was in his Dr Jekyll mood, although he couldn't have been too happy about appearing in Skinny's 500 Club, a booking that was as dubious as any he had in Chicago.

'I don't have any specifics, but from conversations between Sam [Giancana] and others, I have the impression that many top performers were forced to appear in certain clubs by underworld edict.

'In fact, Sam and Johnny Rosselli used to laugh about the things they made performers do. Their control over juke-boxes and night clubs, from the lowest to the plushest, is more pervasive than most people realize. This gives the underworld power over certain recording companies, radio, television and movie productions.'

Was Sinatra helped, or hindered, by the underworld? Did his association with racketeers benefit him more than the innuendos have harmed him? Impossible to say; just as it is impossible to answer or substantiate the general public assumption that Sinatra is himself connected with the Mafia. One organization executive, when asked whether Sinatra ranked in the hierarchy, laughed at the idea: 'A man like that? He's far too exposed, far too vulnerable.'

Perhaps the last Kennedy, in or near the White House, will one day dare to repeat the questions.

Sinatra and his ex-wife Nancy with Frank Jr
after his release from kidnapping.

10 THE SUMMIT 1962-1971

If 1962 proved to be the watershed for Sinatra the Politician—the shattering of a dream—it turned out to be something of a comeback year for Sinatra the Singer and the Actor, the first year of success for his new young record company and the year of *The Manchurian Candidate.*

The previous three years had been edgy. At times he had believed himself to be on the verge of another 'free fall' from the heights of success. The euphoria of the mid-fifties was fading. The films were not quite good enough. An expensive TV show had once again collapsed, the failure unquestionably his own inability to project either Jekyll-Sinatra or Hyde-Sinatra as a convincing image for the public. On that cruel, small screen he was uneasy, unnatural, unlikeable.

They were also unhappy recording years. Relations with Capitol were on the wane and the spark seemed to vanish from his singing. Had it not been for the successful run of *Pal Joey* (1957) on the big screens the situation might have begun to echo the bad years at the tail-end of the 1940s—as though the approach of each new decade demanded its own reassessment, a new Sinatra, re-born and revitalized.

In 1961 he had admitted some of his fears to Robin Douglas-Home: 'As a singer I'll only have a few more years to go—as an actor maybe a few more than that but not many. I've been performing out front for nearly thirty years now and frankly I'm getting a bit tired. Now I want to do more and more behind the scenes, using my head.'

Sinatra the Corporation Man had been growing since 1954 when independent film production had become one of his post-Oscar ambitions. After his deal with United Artists in 1955 there were not many Sinatra films in which he did not have some kind of a stake, operating under a variety of names: Essex, Kent Production, Dorchester, Sincap, Sam, P-C Productions, M.C. or Sinatra Enterprises.

His independence in film production reached something of a peak with the so-called Clan home

The early sixties saw a spate of 'Clan' movies. Left: Sinatra in 'Four for Texas'. Below: Sinatra with Bing Crosby (centre) and Dean Martin in 'Robin and the Seven Hoods'. Below left : With Peter Lawford (right) and Dean Martin in 'Sergeants Three'. Right: 1962 was a comeback year for Sinatra the Singer.

movies—*Ocean's Eleven* (1960), *Sergeants Three* (1962), *Four For Texas* (1963) and *Robin And The Seven Hoods* (1964). Made with the Sinatra, Sammy Davis Jr, Dean Martin trio plus assorted friends, there was an inevitable element of self-indulgence both in story-lines and acting. But well-drilled Niter team that they were, the trio never failed to entertain and contrary to popular belief, the films were also financially successful.

1961 had been Sinatra's first independent year as a recording star. He had set up Reprise Records and was at last free of his contract at Capitol. As he announced in a public statement, the public would be hearing a 'new, happier, emancipated Sinatra, untrammelled, unfettered, unconfined'. Capitol did not react kindly to the insinuation that they had been the cause of Sinatra's declining quality of output. But then battle

Melody Maker

July 27, 1963   Friday 6d

EXCLUSIVE! EXCLUSIVE! EXCLUSIVE!

SINATRA— HE'S KING, SAYS BING

Why he signed for Frank's disc label

By RAY COLEMAN

Sinatra—'proud moment'

Crosby—'How's Holliday?'

BING CROSBY told me from his Hollywood home this week why he had made the shock decision to sign with Frank Sinatra's Reprise record label.

"Let's face it—Sinatra is a king," said Bing. "He is a very sharp operator, a keen record chief, and has a keen appreciation of what the public wants.

"I'm happy to be associated with him after all these years. I hope our partnership will work out as a mutual benefit."

Crosby, aged 59, has been singing for 40 years and his disc sales are estimated to be around 200 million.

There has always been an atmosphere of intense rivalry between Sinatra and Crosby.

At 3 am on the MM's press day, after two days of chasing Bing around offices, cars, golf clubs and other places, I finally contacted him at his home.

It was 7 pm in Hollywood and Bing had just finished a four-hour game of golf. Told the time in Britain, he quipped: "A case of 'when the blue of the night meets the gold of the day' then?"

Many plans

Asked why he decided to sign with Reprise, Crosby replied: "Purely because it is a sensible thing for me to do. Frank is very progressive. He has so many plans for the company and really does know what he is doing."

How long did Bing plan to carry on singing? What about his recent statement that he planned to "ease up"?

"I'll sing for as long as the pipes hold out," Bing replied. "Of course, that can't be long—a few years yet, I guess. I've been taking things steadier for some time, you know.

"Right now I'm in line for four TV shows,

'I'd like to record with Duke'

a couple of films—they keep me busy most of the time."

Did he plan to team up with Sinatra on record? Did he plan to team up with Sinatra on record? "Guess so—it's early to say," Bing answered. "Guess so—they tell me we're doing a Christmas album together and the A&R men over there are working out a whole host of ideas. I am very pleased about the set-up.

"Nelson Riddle, who is with Frank, has a very fertile musical brain. He gives a singer wonderful backings—some of the best in the business."

Suggestion

"The chemistry is there to dispense some wonderful music."

Crosby said he looked forward, too, to the prospect of working with some of Reprise's jazz signings—including Duke Ellington. "That'd be good," he remarked.

He reacted promptly to a suggestion that in joining Sinatra he had teamed up with a rival.

"He's no rival of mine. I've recorded. I've known him for 25 years. I've recorded with many artists—the Boswell Sisters, Rosie Clooney, Louis Armstrong, the Mills Brothers. Nobody's rivals in this business."

Admiration

Asked if Sinatra had approached him personally to sign a disc contract, Crosby replied: "No. His representative called me. I haven't seen Frank about it yet but hope to discuss things with him soon."

Sinatra said in Hollywood that the capture of Crosby was "a proud moment for the whole organisation."

Crosby added: "Frank knows this business and Reprise is going places. I have respect and admiration for his work as a record chief."

BEFORE HANGING UP, BING SAID: "GIVE MY BEST REGARDS TO MICHAEL HOLLIDAY—HOW'S HE DOING?"

THEY'RE COMING!

JOHNNIE RAY— the man they called "The million dollar tear-drop" years ago—is heading back to Britain. Impresario Vic Lewis plans to tour Johnnie here in concerts this year.

ANDY WILLIAMS—America's stylish balladeer—is coming to Britain this year for a series of appearances. Andy had a smash hit disc recently with "Can't get used to losing you."

DELLA REESE, jazz-fringe disc star, flies into Britain soon for a tour. At presstime, no firm arrival date had been fixed. Although she has been here for TV appearances, this will be her first tour.

JIMMY RUSHING is an additional star name for the COUNT BASIE-SARAH VAUGHAN tour opening at Southend on September 7. It will be "Mr. five by five's" fourth British visit.

RUSHING TO TOUR WITH BASIE BAND

THE famous combination of Count Basie and singer Jimmy Rushing is being revived for British fans.

Rushing has been added to the Basie-Sarah Vaughan package which opens a three-week British tour at Southend Odeon on September 7.

Agent Harold Davison told the MM this week: "Rushing will be featured with the Basie Band. Sarah will be bringing her own regular backing group, the Kirk Stewart Trio, but I hope she will also do a number or two with Basie."

There have been a number of personnel changes in the Basie band since its last visit.

BEAT CRAZY—that's Britain

centre pages

lines were already drawn up as the big company planned to squeeze the young label out of the market place.

It was just the sort of fight Sinatra relished. He personally supervised each aspect of the new company, from the appointment of Morris Ostin (from MGM-Verve Records) as vice-president, to the details of marketing and publicity. Not surprisingly, that first year the recording schedule was geared to the production of Sinatra albums. Including the dates he still 'owed' under contract to Capitol, Sinatra managed seventeen full recording sessions that year, producing no less than sixty-seven songs. Reprise issued three albums: 'Ring-A-Ding-Ding', 'Swing Along With Me' and the Tommy Dorsey nostalgic LP 'I Remember Tommy'. The albums were successful in an unspectacular way during those early months, though gathered momentum with the free publicity whipped up when Capitol took Reprise to court over the second title, 'Swing Along With Me'. Capitol already had an album entitled 'Come Swing With Me' and they claimed, in the California Superior Court, that the Reprise album 'closely resembled' their own, 'in concept, type of repertoire, style, accompaniment and title'. The Court upheld their complaint and Reprise had to change the new title to 'Sinatra Swings'.

Capitol then offered dealers a fifteen per cent discount on their two 1961 Sinatra albums, 'Swingin' Session', and 'All The Way'. Sinatra countered the move by issuing his Reprise albums ahead of schedule, and by personally courting the disc jockeys in an expensive party at Romanoffs.

Even more significant was his close vetting of

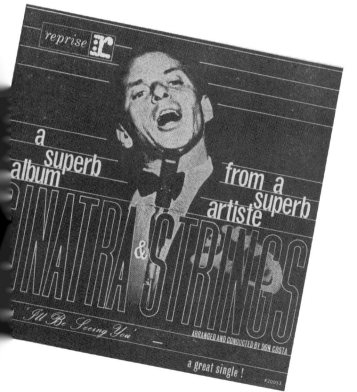

recording quality. He is said to have rejected more master-tapes during this first year at Reprise than in any other twelve-month period of his recording career. Deprived of his favourite arranger/conductor, Nelson Riddle, (still under contract to Capitol) Sinatra rang the changes through these early Reprise sessions between Johnny Mandel, Billy May, Sy Oliver, Don Costa, and, in 1962, Count Basie's former arranger Neal Hefti.

1962 was Reprise's year to sue in the legal and marketing battle with Capitol. In an attempt to overwhelm Reprise's three existing Sinatra LPs Capitol had advertised a collection of twenty-one Sinatra LPs at a bargain 'two-fer' rate. Sinatra took them to court in a million dollar lawsuit alleging restraint of trade and violation of a price discrimination act. He lost the case but counter-attacked, again through the retailers, by offering the shops discounts on Reprise records. Capitol responded with another marketing gimmick, coupling the most popular of the Sinatra songs onto a Rodgers and Hart album and a three-record anthology entitled 'The Great Years'.

This shop-window war backfired on Capitol. They had hoped to sink the new company, already in debt to the tune of $1½ million. They achieved instead a record volume of sales that not only helped boost the Reprise issues but also earned Sinatra enough in royalties to bail out that debt. In the summer of 1962 he had no fewer than fourteen LPs on the best-seller list and though Reprise could only claim two out of the fourteen, Sinatra's new selling strength was such that four new Reprise albums were all instant best-sellers. He had bounced back again, old Sinatra and new Sinatra, Capitol and Reprise, to outsell every other artist on the LP charts—including Elvis and the rock 'n' roll stars.

Reprise were quick to capitalize on success. Offering artists complete freedom to organize their own recording sessions, plus the ownership of their own master-tapes, the company had attracted a healthy and active list of talent: the Hi-Los, Joe E. Lewis, Ben Webster, Jimmy Witherspoon, Mort Sahl, Dean Martin, Sammy Davis Jr, Calvin Jackson. In 1963 Nelson Riddle's contract with Capitol expired and he rejoined the family in time to make 'The Concert Sinatra' and one of Reprise's most successful Sinatra albums, 'Sinatra's Sinatra'. Both of Riddle's 1963 collaborations with Sinatra duplicated many songs previously recorded on Capitol and critics remarked on a sense of detachment that had never been present in any but Sinatra's last sessions for Capitol. It was certainly no lack of commitment; perhaps the arrangements and singing were now so polished and organized that they came over more as performances than as deep felt moods and emotions.

A more original Reprise Sinatra was to emerge from his association with Count Basie that had started at a recording session in October 1962. Just as Nelson

Riddle had helped him create the swinging Capitol sound in the 1950s so now his work with the Basie band and Basie's arranger, Neal Hefti, completed the development of Sinatra as a great jazz singer. 'Sinatra-Basie' contained a good many of Sinatra's old favourites — 'The Tender Trap', 'My Kind Of Girl', 'Learnin' The Blues'—but that did not stop his public buying these new arrangements. When the album was released early in 1963 it became an instant bestseller.

The success of Reprise Records had by now attracted the attention of another king in Hollywood. Jack Warner stepped in where MGM and 20th Century Fox were hesitating and offered Sinatra a three-part $10 million deal: Reprise Records were to merge with Warner Bros Records in an arrangement that left Sinatra with one third ownership and the freedom to continue as an independent; Sinatra was to become a film and TV consultant producing package deals in cooperation with Jack Warner; and thirdly, Sinatra Enterprises were to produce features films with finance and distribution from Warners. The first two sections of the deal were finalized in August 1963, with Sinatra still impressionable enough to insist on carrying the multi-million dollar cheque around with him in his pocket for more than a week.

Only one month later Sinatra *père et fils* were featured together on a cover of *Life* magazine. Frank Jr was making his major singing debut in the Royal Box of the Americana Hotel, New York, backed appropriately enough by the orchestra of Tommy Dorsey. *Life* reported: 'The new Sinatra sound is an eerie, incredible exact echo of Frank Sr's singing', though *Variety* had one or two minor reservations: 'He may not have the tonal texture of his father; he may not now generate excitement; however he has the stuff that can build into another Sinatra legend . . .'

It was characteristic of both Sinatra father and Sinatra businessman that his son's debut was given the full corporate backing of the Sinatra empire. The flexibility of that empire had already been demonstrated during the charity tours Sinatra had undertaken, at his own expense, over the previous two years. Sinatra or the empire had spent over a quarter of a million dollars organizing and running two series of charity concerts in Mexico, and a two-month charity tour performing in Japan, Italy, Britain, Greece, France and Monaco. The total amount raised on this world-wide campaign exceeded one million dollars, and since Sinatra had paid all musicians and travel expenses himself the proceeds were net profit for the different charities concerned.

Not that the tour was universally applauded in the United States. Some people saw it as a cynical attempt by Sinatra to refurbish his image, and make himself once more acceptable to inner White House circles. *Time* magazine wrote of the trip as 'a winning confection of goodwill and grandeur—like a maharajah on a mahout outing', and the same magazine described

Melody Maker

June 2, 1962   Friday 6d

Exclusive!
Exclusive!
Exclusive!

60 LPs to
be won
SEE PAGE 8

Cliff &
Helen
SEE PAGE 9

Erroll
Garner
SEE PAGE 8

A streetcar in Tokyo

E WORLD — WITH SINATRA!
Now he swings into Britain

DOROTHY ENTRATTER CHILDRENS
NURSERY HOME

*...k takes a walk in the grounds of a
Nazareth nursery*

Tickets and discs for MM readers

Dean due

Every year

Above: Sinatra's world-wide concert tours
netted $1 million for children's charities.
With few exceptions, the public and press
were generous with their praise. Left: Sinatra
singing to thousands of young people in Hibiya
Park, Tokyo, as part of his fund-raising activities.

131

Sinatra, with an undisguised hollow laugh, as a 'prince of charity, prophet of peace and generous, sober, chaste diplomat'.

1962 was also the year when Sinatra's acting career, dormant in quality since *Pal Joey* (1957) and *Some Came Running* (1958), came briefly back to life under John Frankenheimer's direction in *The Manchurian Candidate* (1962). Sinatra's study of an ex-POW might not have the creativity and originality of *Pal Joey,* but as a straight, tough, deadpan performance it works and the relationship he builds through the film with Janet Leigh has a quality and life beyond mere good dialogue.

And Sinatra needed quality in his films, something that would draw from him another shade of talent, another stage of development. *Variety* wrote of *The Manchurian Candidate* '. . . Sinatra, who after several pix in which he appeared to be sleep-walking, is again a wide-awake pro creating a straight, quietly humorous character of some sensitivity.' He had his own companies, he could choose his own material. Unhappily he found neither the right material nor the talent to create it. He eased his way through *Come Blow Your Horn* (1963), played a rubber-mask cameo in *The List of Adrian Messenger* (1963), then reverted, notwithstanding Robert Aldrich, to the *déjà vu* of Clan spoofs in *Four for Texas* (1964). A renaissance in American cinema was still three or four years distant (*Bonnie and Clyde, Point Blank, Easy Rider*) and Sinatra was playing in stories and film language that dated back to the 1940s. His one and only attempt at directing *(None But The Brave,* 1965) was competent enough, but the anti-war story creaked with moral hindsight and though realism was bravely maintained with Japanese dialogue and sub-titles the overall effect was contrived. Raoul Walsh and Don Siegel had already made the

definitive films on America's Second World War with *The Naked And The Dead* and *Hell Is For Heroes.* There was nothing more to be said in the old Hollywood language.

Sinatra enjoyed the job of directing. There was, he said, no time to be bored—a remark that reflected his usual attitude to film making. 'I found out that it was in some ways tougher than I had thought. The director has so many things to worry about—pace, wardrobe, the performance . . . Next time I won't try to perform when I direct . . .' But the experience had apparently not enthused him enough. He would never return behind camera. His achievement as film maker in *None But The Brave* seemed merely a part of his fiftieth birthday celebration, another notch on the totem pole, one more achievement to confound his critics.

And that fiftieth anniversary, that 1965, was for a twice

Below: Sinatra in relaxed mood. Left : Directing 'None But the Brave'. Centre: With Lawrence Harvey.

Left:Sinatra likes to drink tea to ease his voice before concerts. Below centre: Sinatra in his fifties, with greying hair but the same lean look. Below right: Performing in his celebratory TV spectacular, 'Frank Sinatra: A Man and his Music'.

'has-been' a very remarkable year. He won a Grammy award for his introspective album 'September Of My Years'; he released a double autobiographical album 'A Man And His Music', tracing his singing career from its earliest days, with references to his performance in *From Here To Eternity* and to a Niter sequence with the Clan clowns Dean Martin and Sammy Davis Jr (both these albums made Gold); he cut a single, appropriately titled 'It Was A Very Good Year', that not only won two Grammy awards (Sinatra's vocal and Gordon Jenkins' arrangement), but put Sinatra back into the Top Ten for the first time since the 1950s. (He followed up with 'Strangers In The Night', 'That's Life' and 'Somethin' Stupid' all of which made number one spot in a then intensely competitive and youthful singles market). Finally, in July of 1965, he attended the Newport Jazz Festival with Count Basie and broke audience records for his, admittedly controversial, appearance there.

After their first bestselling record in 1962 Basie and Sinatra had collaborated again two years later, this time with the arrangements of Quincy Jones. The second album, 'It Might As Well Be Swing', was not as successful as their first attempt. Sinatra had recorded it in the evenings, after directing and acting in *None But The Brave* during the day. The singing is tired and the addition of strings to the Basie band seems to flatten out the sound.

The 1965 concerts were more successful. Their historic appearance at Newport came in the middle of a series of charity performances in St Louis, New York, Detroit, Baltimore and Chicago (total net proceeds over half a million dollars). The Newport purists decried what they called 'the Sinatra circus', but his Sunday night appearance was the best attended session Newport had ever seen. Arnold Shaw writes in his biography, *Sinatra:* 'I have attended these annual July 4th leviathan presentations since their inception in 1955. There have been many memorable moments like the "discovery" of trumpeter Miles Davis in 1955 and the first appearance of Dave Brubeck in 1958. No one individual so electrified and literally possessed the Festival as did Sinatra in 1965.'

Perhaps nothing in a memorable year satisfied Sinatra quite so much as that appearance, though he had plenty to cheer about. A CBS documentary, 'Sinatra', had topped the ratings notwithstanding a savage and adverse review from *Variety:* 'An unmitigated rave for Frankie Goodfellow, star performer, tycoon with heart of gold, family man ("yet") and all round ball-haver.' In an NBC Special—'Sinatra, A Man And His Music'—he had, by playing his natural and singing self, for once conquered the little screen in person. He had been featured on the covers of the big news magazines, *Life* (the first sell-out issue since Kennedy's assassination), *Newsweek* and *Look*. And in the Publimetrix Poll that measured printed mentions of celebrities he came out way ahead of anyone else at the end of the year. That December he celebrated his fiftieth birthday at a huge show-biz party organized by his first wife, Nancy Sr—a party whose guests were described by the *New York Journal American* as the 'veritable cream of Hollywood society . . . emphatically A and not B group people'.

Illusory though it was, even his personal life seemed to be coming together at last. He was in love with twenty-year-old Mia Farrow and she, apparently, in love with him.

Sinatra had been living as a bachelor for more than ten years now and while there had never been a shortage of girlfriends, affairs, or one-off ding-dongs, he was often enough a lonely man. There had been relationships that seemed to promise something more: Bacall; Lady Adele Beatty; Juliet Prowse, and latterly Jill St John who reached the pre-engagement ritual of dinner with Mama Dolly Sinatra, but no further.

Sinatra had met Mia on the Twentieth Century lot in October of 1964. He was shooting on yet another 'Cowboys and Indians' war movie, *Von Ryan's Express;* she was playing Allison Mackenzie in the TV serial of *Peyton Place.* Daughter of film director John Farrow and actress Maureen O'Sullivan (Tarzan's most beautiful Jane), Mia Farrow was quite unlike Sinatra's usual companions: sylph-like, slight of body, intellectually sophisticated and very much of a new and independent generation of young women. The two of them began dating; they spent evening together, an occasional weekend in Palm Springs. Then in the summer of 1965 Allison Mackenzie was written into a coma for six weeks and Mia Farrow left Hollywood for an East Coast cruise with Sinatra on a chartered and heavily chaperoned yacht, the *Southern Breeze.* The press followed the preparations for the cruise and reported the departure in headlines: 'Sinatra and Mia sailing to Altar?'

It was a traumatic cruise. Sinatra visited the elder Kennedy at Hyannis Port; newspapers reported that widow Jackie Kennedy had boarded the yacht on Sinatra's return—reports emphatically denied and eventually withdrawn; finally, one foggy night a crewman from the yacht was drowned as he rowed back from shore. In another blizzard of press headlines Sinatra called off the trip. 'It had been', suggested *Time,* 'the most closely observed cruise since Cleopatra floated down the Nile to meet Mark Antony.'

The disruption of their cruise did not seem to affect the romance. In September Mia Farrow was taken for her first dinner at home with Mama Dolly and it was noted that after his fiftieth birthday party with Nancy Sr and children in December Frank Sinatra celebrated alone with Mia at a different location. It was during that week of celebration that Mia Farrow clipped her hair to its more familiar *garçon* look. Her friend and mentor, Salvador Dali, called her act, 'mythical suicide'; columnists saw it as a gesture of protest at not being invited to Nancy Sr's party; Arnold Shaw observed that in so doing she had stolen herself a lot of publicity.

The romance fluctuated, much as the Ava affair had, but without its violent extremes. Eventually in July 1966 Sinatra announced he was off to London for two months. He flew instead to Las Vegas and married Mia in Jack Entratter's suite at the Sands Hotel, with no member of either family in attendance.

Sinatra had married for the third time and for the third time, from the beginning, the love affair turned sour. It was due more to a difference of attitudes than to the difference in ages. Sinatra could tolerate the occasional discotheque and did not seem too perturbed if his bride danced with boys of her own age. But he did expect, as always, the old-fashioned Latin style wife, obedient, self-effacing, subordinate. Mia Farrow had known him long enough to be aware of at least part of his life-style. She had already complained more than once about 'Frank's nasty little chums'. She told a friend, months before her marriage: 'All they know how to do is tell dirty stories, break furniture, pinch waitresses' asses and bet on the horses.' Now, as his wife, she would have to live with that entourage. Maybe she imagined that she could change the scenery, improve the quality of Sinatra's court; maybe she had over-estimated Sinatra's own qualities of companionship and humour. The courting Frank, even at fifty, was by unanimous opinion an overwhelming seducer. Perhaps Frank the husband was somehow less overwhelming and less flattering.

Four weeks after the wedding Sinatra opened in a night club engagement at the Sands, Las Vegas, with his wife in attendance at a prominent table. 'Maybe you wondered why I finally got married,' he asked his audience. 'Well I finally found a broad I can cheat on.'

The remark was apparently meant to be part of his jokesy Clan-style repartee, but it shocked and hurt his young bride like a slap in the face. She stayed at her table in tears, where 'Hurricane Ava' would have stormed out in fury.

Not surprising then that Mia Farrow withdrew—into moods and meditations. The inevitable separations as the two of them worked at opposite ends of the country and the world did not help understanding. Mia travelled to London and Berlin early in 1967, filming *A Dandy In Aspic.* Sinatra picked up press gossip about Mia and Laurence Harvey; they quarrelled by transatlantic telephone; she flew over for two days, breaking the terms of her film contract in so doing. But in the two days she stayed with him in Florida (he was working at the Fontainebleau in Miami) he apparently gave her only half an hour of his time alone. And during the half-hour all he did was lecture her.

The final break came that autumn when Sinatra was waiting to film *The Detective* (1968) in New York and Mia was working on Polanski's *Rosemary's Baby.* She was scheduled to join Sinatra on *The Detective* in which she was to play the Norma MacIver part. *Rosemary's Baby* ran over schedule and Sinatra told Mia to walk off the picture. She refused. Jacqueline Bisset was

Right: Frank and Mia on their wedding day.

136

given her part in *The Detective* and Sinatra issued the abrupt press release announcing the end of his marriage with Mia. There were some attempts to get them together again over Christmas, but in January Mia flew off to India for meditation with the Maharishi Mahesh Yogi (where she also coincided with John Lennon and George Harrison of the Beatles). Back from India she tried again with Sinatra. But there were more walk-outs and her own acting career was on the move after her performance in *Rosemary's Baby*: the marriage was officially terminated in August 1968.

Perhaps it was no coincidence that *The Detective* ended up the best of Sinatra's later film performances. He played a tough New York detective haunted by corruption on the job and the memories of a happy but doomed marriage. There was a commitment in his playing and a communication of true emotion that had been missing in his films since *The Manchurian Candidate*. We see real pain in Detective Joe Leland for the first time since Frankie Machine in *The Man With The Golden Arm;* and that peculiar, doomed, vulnerable unease for the first time since Angelo Maggio.

Top: Frank and Nancy Jr collaborating on their first joint recording. Left: A scene from 'The Naked Runner'.

The Detective was sandwiched between two private-eye films with Sinatra playing out what was apparently the last of his fantasies, having graduated from Clan hoodlum again in *Assault On A Queen* (1966), through cold war spy in *The Naked Runner* (1967), to the Humphrey Bogart-Philip Marlowe style shamus in *Tony Rome* (1967) and *Lady in Cement* (1968). *The Detective* and the two Tony Rome pictures were directed by Gordon Douglas (last used by Sinatra on *Robin And The Seven Hoods*) and there was a certain sameness about pace and general image which blunted their overall effect. But Sinatra conveyed the shamus with the right degrees of flip cynicism and, given better stories, he might have created something of a genre.

Instead the old boredom returned. He was restless on set, determined to work fast, always pushing and pulling at the schedule to cut corners. *Tony Rome,* budgeted for 45 days' shooting was completed in 28 days. A film director once watched Sinatra insist on a re-take of a song in the recording studios to eliminate an over-emphasized consonant. 'Just try and get him to re-do scenes before the camera,' said the director. 'He's a genius at thinking up ways of making cuts and insertions—anything to avoid a re-take.'

Perhaps film-making was the wrong time of Frank Sinatra's day. He was an evening and nights man. His recording sessions always took place after dark; his night club appearances often after midnight. Perhaps film-making did not excite him enough. Perhaps the money was just too easy—up to a million dollars plus a percentage on some of his last films.

He certainly disappointed his earlier fans. Bosley Crowther was moved to this lament in the *New York Times* after seeing him in *Tony Rome:* 'It has not escaped the attention of a few hundred million persons in the land that a gentleman named Frank Sinatra is one of the phenomena of our age. Certainly his range and vitality are phenomenal and his extra-curricular reputation is awesome, to say the least. That's why it is provoking—nay, disturbing and depressing beyond belief—to see this acute and awesome figure turning up time and time again in strangely tricky and trashy motion pictures . . . His *Von Ryan's Express* was an outrageous and totally disgusting display of romantic exhibitionism in a pseudo-wartime environment. *Marriage On The Rocks* was a tawdry and witless trifle about a bored married man and *Assault On A Queen* was another of Sinatra's projections of himself as the altogether knowledgeable leader of a gang of thieves.

'Now comes the latest selection, *Tony Rome* which has the master of several realms of contemporar. enterprise being cynical but sincere and valiant as beat-up Miami Beach private eye. The role is strictly one of non-commitment—a lone detective out fo himself—and it simply exposes its rugged protagonis in an assortment of corrupt and sleazy environment and incidents. . .

'The clue to Sinatra's sad shortcoming is that he wilfully or carelessly allows his film—and his film it is, beyond question—to be sprinkled with many globs of sheer bad taste that manifest a calculated pandering to

The mid-sixties saw a resurgence of Sinatra's acting career. Left: As Colonel Joseph Ryan in 'Von Ryan's Express'. Right: With Jill St John on the set of 'Tony Rome'.

those who are easily and crudely amused. What grieves a long-time moviegoer is to remember how bright and promising he used to be, beginning with his charming performance in *Anchors Aweigh* and moving on into his poignant performance in *From Here To Eternity.'*

Sinatra was not to be persuaded by either criticism or flattery. For his final film appearance he really slung the muck at the fan, as it were. *Dirty Dingus Magee* (1970), unfunny, vulgar, vacuous western spoof, was surely the most graceless farewell an actor has ever given, and from a man who professed to love 'class'.

Come back Angelo Maggio, that all might be forgiven.

Early in 1969 Sinatra's father, Marty, died after a period of illness. Frank Sinatra was in Earl Wilson's words, 'tight-lipped, tearful and grief-stricken' as he attended the New Jersey funeral, for which twelve hearses were needed to carry the many elaborate wreaths from Sinatra's Hollywood and Manhattan friends. A guard of honour was formed by firemen from the department where Marty Sinatra had worked for twenty-four years, each detail of the funeral service having been planned and supervised personally by Frank Sinatra.

That same year Sinatra began having medical trouble of his own. His right hand—his microphone hand—was often in acute pain with what was eventually diagnosed as Dupuyten's Contracture, a distortion of muscular tissue in the palm and fingers. An operation to loosen the hand was successful, though it was to remain partially distorted and painful. His attendance at hospitals led inevitably to rumours of heart disease or cancer. Columnists all over the world detected what could have been the signs of cortisone treatment in Sinatra's puffy heavy face, and talk of his imminent retirement only increased speculation.

But when that retirement was announced, in March 1971, there was no mention of ill-health in Sinatra's press statement. There had been in his career, he said, 'little room or opportunity for reflection, reading, self-examination and that need which every thinking man has for a fallow period, a long pause in which to seek a better understanding of changes occurring in the world.' He expressed 'love and affection' for his millions of fans who had given him 'so much more than I could possibly hope to give them in return'.

In his albums he had given them some golden sounds during those last five years. 'Strangers In The Night' had been a happy climax to his long association with Nelson Riddle, with that mixture of blue mood and self-parody which characterized his best night club

performances. Then in 1967 he had joined up with a Brazilian composer-guitarist for the soft and sensual Bossa Nova LP titled with their two names ('Francis Albert Sinatra And Antonio Carlos Jobim'). In 1968 and 1969 he produced three original albums with Don Costa ('Cycles', 'My Way' and 'A Man Alone'), this time returning to the introspective, autobiographical emotion that had always seemed to spark his best recordings. 'Cycles' and 'My Way' both made gold albums for him, as also the anthology, 'Frank Sinatra's Greatest Hits'. Until his retirement statement, everyone assumed he would go on singing forever.

The moment of 'retirement' had its own theatrical magic. His 'last appearance' was to be at a black tie concert organized by Gregory Peck, who had presented Sinatra with the Jean Hersholt Humanitarian Award at the Oscar ceremony for 1971—a recognition of the many charity concerts and tours Sinatra had worked on over the past decade, engagements always paid for out of his own pocket. Only one year previously Sinatra had conquered London at one such charity concert, the usually frugal *Financial Times* being inspired to a three-column review by Kevin Henriques: 'Rare is the entertainer who brings royalty voluntarily and spontaneously to its feet, but Sinatra . . . achieved that at 2.15 yesterday morning as the entire Festival Hall audience rose ecstatically to acclaim him after 85 minutes of the most immaculate singing and entertaining one could be fortunate to hear . . .

'Sinatra glided effortlessly from song to song, mood to mood, tempo to tempo with impeccable assurance and poise. His voice was in superb condition. He had it under firm but not taut control. He bent it round the lyrics with compelling variety and although practically every song was familiar, his unique phrasing imbued them with an almost alarming freshness . . .

'One admired the balance and pace—mostly urgent —of the programme, especially the way a cluster of ballads was effectively inserted amid the up-tempo tunes. 'Try A Little Tenderness', with only accoustic guitar accompaniment, the haunting tribute to Billie Holliday, 'Poor Lady Day', and the reflective, plaintive 'Angel Eyes' were unforgettable, but what will live longest in people's ears, minds and hearts will certainly be his agonisingly dramatic 'Ole Man River', sung half sitting on a stool, hunched, head bent low over the microphone, looking to the floor—an intense evocation by a white man of Negro slavery . . .

'His public came to worship, wanting a reinstatement of the Sinatra legend. They got it—defiantly— from the legend who didn't spare himself an iota. But there was no rabble-rousing climax. He left with the highly personal and meaningful 'My Way' and Sinatra's way, like that of every top class professional artist, is to leave the multitude clamouring for more—which he did. . . .'

His 'last concert' took place at the Los Angeles Music Center on 14 June, 1971 in front of an audience that had paid well over the ticket price of $250 to attend such an historic event. 'We still have the man,' said Roz Russell, announcing him on stage. 'We still have the blue eyes, those wonderful blue eyes, that smile. For one last time we have the man, the greatest entertainer of the twentieth century.'

'Angel Eyes' was Sinatra's final song that evening, sung under a single spotlight, his face wreathed in cigarette smoke. And on the last line—'Excuse me while I disappear'—the spot went out and Sinatra vanished.

Left: Frank Sinatra plays Himself in the climax of 'The Oscar'. Below centre: A real award this time as Sinatra accepts his Certificate of Honorary Membership from the U.C.L.A. Alumni Association, watched by Charles Young (centre) and Andy Williams. Below: Sinatra with Count Basie.

11 THE LONG GOODBYE

Retire when you're on top and stay retired, the old pros used to say and even Sinatra's closest friends questioned, and continue to question, the wisdom of his continued comebacks after 1973. Headlines followed the magic name into and out of retirement. Frank Sinatra could still pull in massive audiences, weave magic with his voice and attract the unanimous eulogies of even the most cynical critics. But the image was now vulnerable and would take something of a battering as he approached his sixtieth birthday. Unlike Bing Crosby, Sinatra had never established himself on an unassailable plateau of public recognition. The two men shared mass adulation but while the mellow Crosby mellowed further, Sinatra has remained to the end a fighter fighting. For every old adversary who left the fray there were always new enemies to take their place and an ill-timed switch to the Republican camp under the aegis of Spiro Agnew frustrated any ambition he might have had in politics or public life. Twenty-nine months after his 'last concert' Sinatra came voluntarily out of retirement as Spiro Agnew was forced involuntarily and prematurely to his own resignation and the two events might have had some connection, at least subconsciously, in Sinatra's mind. His first reaction to Agnew's first suggestions of resignation was vintage Maggio: 'Quit? Shit! That would be an admission of guilt.'

Sinatra's friendship with Spiro Agnew had developed during 1969 after Agnew's visit to Palm Springs for the Republican Governors Convention (Agnew being at the time Governor of Maryland). Agnew stayed as the house guest of Bob Hope on that occasion, but played tennis with Barbara Marx, the wife of one of Sinatra's close friends in Palm Springs, Zeppo of the Marx Brothers. The next time Agnew visited Palm Springs he stayed in Sinatra's million dollar hideaway near the Tamarisk Country Club, with Barbara Marx acting as hostess. Sinatra's attachment to Barbara Marx seemed to grow in parallel with his friendship for Spiro Agnew and there were those gossips who began to suggest that Barbara's apparent link with Frank was only a cover for a more serious attachment to Spiro Agnew.

But it seems unlikely that Mrs Marx had ever been anything more than a temporary companion for Agnew, whereas her relationship with Sinatra was to develop into a serious and long lasting love affair. She left Zeppo and for the next six years would share Sinatra's life, looking after his house, travelling with him, bearing the brunt of his frequent moods, ignoring his insults, waiting with infinite patience until he was ready to marry her.

Following his new friendship with Agnew, Sinatra emerged in the Republican camp during the Californian campaign of 1970, helping Ronald Reagan to the governorship. It must have hurt many old friends to watch Sinatra and Dean Martin sharing a political platform with the two Republican die-hards of the show-biz world, Bob Hope and John Wayne. There were those who still remembered Sinatra's bitter quarrel with 'Duke' Wayne at the height of the Maltz affair when the two actors nearly came to blows at a party. Somehow that anger was not focused any more. His reaction to Reagan's tough line against rebellious students at Berkeley was indicative of his new politics: 'Now we must all work together to end the turmoil on the campuses and improve the communication between the students and what they refer to as the establishment.'

Notwithstanding friendships with Agnew and Reagan, Sinatra's total commitment to the Republican

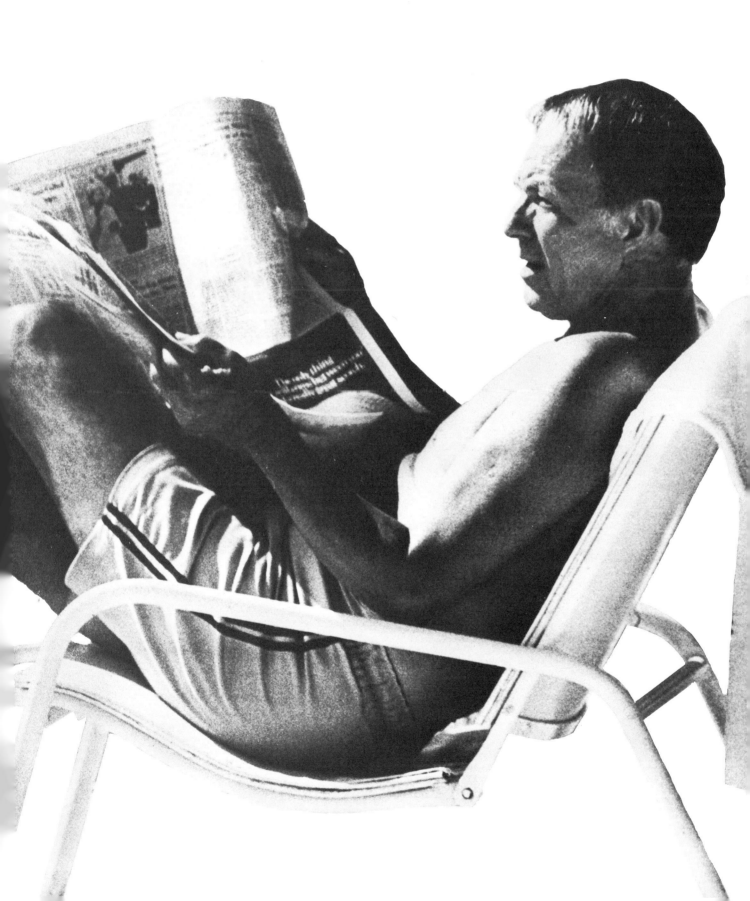

Party was not clear until Nixon's campaign of 1972. Early that year Sinatra was still reported talking of his intended support for McGovern and the Democrats, though a running battle that early summer with a Congress Committee over alleged Mafia connections made him once again an ambiguous bonus for anyone's campaign team.

The questions that surround Sinatra and his alleged mobster connections will go on being asked forever; and equally eternal will be the lack of evidence and answers. In terms of public debate, Sinatra had reserved his most spectacular show-down for the House Select Committee on Crime in 1972 and the showdown came after eight years of comparative peace and quiet in that long-running saga. A confrontation with the New Jersey State Commission of inquiry into organized crime had ended in Sinatra's favour. After months of delay in 1969 and 1970 Sinatra's appearance before the Commission resulted in the dropping of all charges against him.

But in 1972 the location switched to Washington where a Select Committee in Congress was probing mobster influence in commercial sport. There was talk of gambling coups at the Massachusetts race-course of Berkshire Downs in Hancock. Good horses were run under assumed names and at long odds and Mafia money was apparently invested in bets. Joseph 'The Baron' Barboza told the committee that Sinatra was vice-president and director of the by-then defunct Berkshire Downs course and that he held interests in two hotels as a front for Raymond Patriarca, a New England Mafia boss—the two hotels being the Fontainebleau on Miami Beach and the Sands at Las Vegas. Patriarca was then serving a five-year sentence in Atlanta and the witness, Barboza, was a self-confessed Mafia hit-man with twenty-seven admitted murders on his record.

The dubious origins of such testimony did not seem to worry either the committee or the newspapers. Pressure was applied from within the Committee to allow Sinatra to appear at an executive session, but the Committee insisted that Sinatra be treated like anyone else. Sinatra insisted in turn that he attend the Committee on 'invitation' not 'demand'. With the story nicely bubbling in the national press, a US Marshal attempted to present Sinatra with a subpoena as he arrived to sing at a gala for Spiro Agnew.

Sinatra disappeared. His next appearance in public was a visit to the English Derby on the Epsom Downs race course in June. He was in London for talks about an impending film—a musical based on Saint-Exupery's fairy tale *The Little Prince*. He had booked into an hotel under an assumed name; had had a night out on

Left: In more jocular mood, Sinatra entertains the crowd on the Fairway.

the town; then disappeared again. The newspapers reported him 'dodging the House crime probe'. He was said to be gambling in Monte Carlo.

The Committee took the hint and backed down. They had already allowed too much of the Barboza testimony to be publicized and they now withdrew their subpoenas. At which point Sinatra graciously agreed to accept the invitation to appear in open session on 18 July, 1972.

He could not have stage-managed the scene better himself. The room was crowded out with people expecting to see him embarrassed or humbled. Instead, to the joy of the pro-Sinatra faction in the crowd, Sinatra attacked the Commission: 'This bum went running off at the mouth. I resent it. I won't have it. I'm not a second class citizen and let's get that clear right now.'

Sinatra held up a newspaper in court with the headline reading 'Witness links Sinatra to reputed Mafia figure.'

'That's charming, isn't it? Isn't that charming. That's all hearsay evidence, isn't it?'

Sinatra's point was conceded and from then on it was Sinatra himself who virtually ran his own interrogation. He explained that his interest in the Berkshire Downs race course had been a mere $55,000 investment which he subsequently withdrew.

The committee than asked him about his alleged friendship with the Brooklyn and Manhattan racketeer, the late Tommy 'Three Fingers' Brown Luchese.

'Let's dispense with that kind of question,' was Sinatra's answer and the committee backed off.

The *Village Voice* reported Sinatra's answer to one of the Committee's last questions, 'Does organized crime, or as it is variously called, the Cosa Nostra, the Mafia, exist?':

'Sinatra's blue eyes cut into his inquisitor's face with a look to curdle a sloe gin fizz. "From the standpoint of reading about it," he answers, "I suppose it does exist. But I am not aware of a tremendous amount of crime".'

Sinatra walked out of the courtroom in triumph. Two of the Congressmen had even shaken him by the hand. But, as he pointed out through a featured letter in the *New York Times,* the whole process had still been damaging to him, especially, he might have added, in an election year:

'In practice,' he wrote, 'as we learned during the ugly era of Joe McCarthy, they (House or Senate Committees) can become star chambers in which "facts" are confused with rumor, gossip and innuendo, and where reputations and character can be demolished in front of the largest possible audiences.

'In my case a convicted murderer was allowed to throw my name around with abandon, while the TV cameras rolled on. His vicious little fantasy was sent into millions of American homes, including my own. Sure, I was given a chance to refute it, but as we have

all come to know, the accusation often remains longer in the public mind than the defence.'

A couple of years later Congressman and friend of Sinatra, Hugh Carey, indicated that the Committee had been in the wrong: 'There was no real question of Sinatra's implication in anything, except that he was a big personality . . . Seldom did Congress look, frankly, more ludicrous. I watched the proceedings for a while and saw that he [Sinatra] had the show well in hand. I almost waited for him to do a choreograph job on the Committee and tell 'em how to dance out of the room.'

The debate had been reported in great detail all round the world and certainly in the short-term did Sinatra more good than harm. His public appearance had been a triumph—a vindication. One London

Left: 'Ol' Blue Eyes' comes back: Sinatra proved he could still produce the old magic even approaching sixty.

newspaper, *The Daily Mail*, reported that Nixon himself had made a private call to Sinatra congratulating him, and it seemed that the affair had not after all jeopardized Sinatra's position in that election year.

Whether or not Sinatra had seriously considered the Democrat cause for the 1972 campaign, he was by the summer firmly established in the Republican camp, and one of Agnew's most ardent sponsors. 'I'm going to make him Vice-President,' Sinatra declared. Sinatra's influence may not have counted for much in inner Republican circles—they were certainly not in such need of his money as the Democrats had been—but he committed himself whole-heartedly to the 1972 campaign, among other things singing at a Young Voters-for-Nixon Rally in Chicago, and receiving a Medallion of Valor after helping Agnew at a State of Israel Bonds fund-raising (and vote catching) dinner in Los Angeles a few days before the election.

But Sinatra was still regarded by many Republicans as an old and hated enemy and it was hardly wise of him to reserve his most unpleasant and undignified confrontation with a journalist for one of their post-election celebrations—a private party given by Louise Gore at the Washington Jockey Club at which Sinatra was to officiate as MC. He was already in a foul mood that night after a friend of his, the comedian Pat Henry, had been refused admittance for lack of a security clearance. He had frightened off one woman journalist who attempted to ask him some questions with 'Who the hell do you think you are? If you want to see me write me a letter.' Then Maxine Cheshire of the *Washington Post*, probably unaware of his mood, came up and spoke to Sinatra's partner, Barbara Marx. Sinatra lost control. 'Get away from me, you scum! Go home and take a bath. I don't want to talk to you.' He was shouting now. 'I'm getting out of here, to get rid of the stench of Mrs Cheshire. You know Mrs Cheshire, don't you? That stench you smell is from her. You're nothing but a two dollar broad. Here's two dollars, baby, that's what you're used to.' Sinatra stuffed two dollar bills into her drink and according to some onlookers called her a 'two dollar cunt'.

The incident, not unnaturally, was gleefully reported by all journalists present and harmed Sinatra as much as the Lee Mortimer fracas of 1947, though it should be said that Sinatra's anger, ready for anyone that evening, had picked out the columnist who had been sniping continuously at Sinatra's relations with Spiro Agnew and the Republican camp and there were not a few journalists who felt Maxine Cheshire's injured innocence was out of place.

Sinatra must have felt he had blown his last chances of acceptance at the White House. After all, King Frank and the Clan had been merciless in their ridicule of Nixon during the 1960 Presidential campaign. For all his pre-election courtesy Nixon would not need much encouragement to keep him at arm's length and out in the cold. Instead, two factors worked in Sinatra's favour: Spiro Agnew; and the fact that Maxine Cheshire was a correspondent of the *Washington Post*. Nixon was no friend, then or later, of the *Post* and only three months after the incident at the Jockey Club party, on 17 April, 1973, Nixon, at Agnew's instigation, invited Sinatra to sing at a White House party in honour of the Italian Prime Minister, Giulio Andreotti.

'Once in a while,' said Nixon that evening, 'there is a moment when there is magic in this room, when a singer is able to move us and capture us all, and Frank Sinatra has done that and we thank him . . . this house is honoured to have a man whose parents were born in Italy, but yet from humble beginnings went to the very top in entertainment.' Sinatra was moved to tears by his reception and later that same evening Nixon personally asked him to come out of retirement.

Was Nixon's invitation a hint towards possible future office—an ambassadorship, or an honorary post in some corner of the U.N. empire? To no avail if it was. Within weeks the Watergate scandal had broken wide open. Not long after, Spiro Agnew was discredited on his own account for financial skulduggery during his governorship of Maryland, and eventually forced to resign. Sinatra, it seemed, had picked the wrong team.

That mid-summer of 1973 John Dean in his Watergate evidence made allegations that Nixon had tried to obtain tax favours for certain friends. Prominent in this list of favoured friends were Ronald Reagan, Jerry Lewis, Fred MacMurray, Lucille Ball, Peter Lawford, Sammy Davis Jr and Frank Sinatra. But for all the eager press anticipation this was Sinatra's only direct link with Watergate revelations and, apart from his tangential connection with the CIA mystery surrounding Sam Giancana, Judith Campbell Exner, President Kennedy and the Castro assassination plot, Sinatra has not been involved in any of the post-Watergate scandal.

'Did you ever think you would see a time when Frank Sinatra would be ashamed to be seen with a President of the United States?' Ethel Kennedy's barbed question may have summed up Democrat feelings about Sinatra's new choice of political companions, but whatever Sinatra's personal opinion of Nixon and the Watergate debacle his own high standards of loyalty would not permit him to desert the one disgraced Republican who had become his friend. Sinatra was conspicuously alone in his campaign for the reinstatement of Spiro Agnew, circulating friends for funds to help the ex-Vice-President and inviting him often and openly to his home in Palm Springs.

Sinatra's defiance might also have reflected his own frustrations. Politically he had run himself into a dead-end. Absolute retirement from public life had never been his intention and he needed to make his mark again.

Two years and five months after his 'retirement' the inevitable took place. Sinatra's unretirement was marked by a one-hour TV special on NBC in front of a black tie audience, the concert caption being 'Ol' Blues Eyes Is Back'. The date was November 1973, exactly five weeks after Spiro Agnew's eventual resignation.

The 'retirement from retirement' show was built up in trade and national press and heralded by the release of a new album under the same title, 'Ol' Blue Eyes Is Back'. Apparently to no avail. His black tie TV show was competing with a Dinah Shore special and the George C. Scott movie *Hospital* on the two other networks and he finished third and last in the race. Not that the notices failed to congratulate what many felt was a triumphant return. 'Well, Ol' Blues Eyes did it,' wrote John J. O'Connor. 'Frank Sinatra took an hour of television and turned it into the best popular music special of the year.' *Daily News* critic Kay Gardella wrote, 'We thought we were through writing love letters to Frank Sinatra. Here we go again!'

Sinatra followed up the TV comeback early the next year with a successful re-entry into concert cabaret at Caesar's Palace in Las Vegas. He played eight one hour shows between 25 and 31 January.

Back in Hollywood he played host to the American Film Institute's salute to James Cagney (March 1974), and the following month had a sell-out concert in the Carnegie Hall, New York, for the Variety Clubs International. He played thirteen concerts on tour that April in aid of the Variety Clubs, all of them pre-sold weeks in advance. His itinerary took him from New York to Providence, Detroit, Philadelphia, Washington and Chicago, a heavy enough programme for a man just out of retirement. And he still found the time and energy to record. Two new albums marked his return that year ('Ol' Blues Eyes Is Back' and 'Some Nice Things I've Missed') both albums reflecting the blend of old and new numbers prevalent in his come-back concert programmes.

In June he played another short season at Caesar's Palace, Las Vegas, and in July set off for the Far East, giving three concerts in Tokyo and one on the USS Midway at the Yokosuka naval base. But this was the trip that ended with his ill-fated return to Australia when, after so much acclaim in his come-back at home, the hoodlum image re-emerged to make bad headlines all round the world.

'The only man in town I'd be afraid to fight is Sinatra,' Bob Mitchum said once. 'I might knock him down but he'd keep getting up until one of us was dead.' Words to remind us again of Angelo Maggio—'that boy, he's about the toughest nut in the woods. He just keeps spittin' in Fatso's eye'.

The catalogue of Sinatra's fights is long and not always very heroic. It is easy to understand how many of the fights started, especially in the early years when the thin young crooner was so quick to take offence at a heckler or at a joke in bad taste. Nor is it difficult to understand how Sinatra's bad relations with the press escalated. He had a lot of provocation whether from politically motivated columnists, or from photographers prying into his private life. What are hard to justify are the extremes to which Sinatra would go in his pursuit of a vendetta and the bully-boy situations in which so many of his fights ended up.

'Frank Sinatra saved my life one night,' said a comedian to a night club audience. 'Five guys were beating me up in front of the Fontainebleau. After a while Frank said, "Okay, fellas, that's enough".'

And after an earthquake in Nevada, another comedian quipped: 'That'll teach them to fool around with Frank Sinatra.'

'Ol' Blue Eyes' seemed to have saved up a lot of his mean streak for these later years. There had been the mysterious fight with businessman Frederick Weisman at the Beverly Hills Hotel in 1966. Weisman had complained about the noise at Sinatra's table and the verbals led to a brawl which Weisman was thought to have started. Whoever started it, Sinatra's heavy mob allegedly finished it and a half-hour later Weisman was in the Mount Sinai Hospital having an emergency brain operation. But there were no charges after his recovery. Weisman had apparently injured his head falling.

A year later Sinatra broke his front teeth in a fight with the manager of his own Casino in the Sands at Las Vegas. Sinatra in a tearaway mood was $200,000 down on one night's gambling. The Casino refused him any more credit and Sinatra exploded. He had started up the Sands when it was little more than a sand pile; he'd tear it down to the sand again; he'd made Las Vegas what it was; he'd brought in the money and the entertainment and the big gamblers; he'd take them all out again. Sinatra returned to Los Angeles that night in his private plane, but was back again looking for trouble only a few hours later. The Las Vegas *Review-Journal* reported the battle: 'It was Carl Cohen, vice-president of the Sands, who finally halted Sinatra's wild weekend. The Sands executive bloodied the singer's nose and knocked his teeth out after Sinatra tipped a table over on him . . .

'Said a waiter: ". . . Sinatra had been going wild at the hotel all morning. I am told that he even set fire to his room. The next thing I knew Sinatra jumped up and threw a table right on Carl. Cohen then jumped up and punched Sinatra . . ."

'Said a security guard: ". . . Sinatra was yelling at Cohen because Carl had cut his credit off. The next thing I knew, a table was flying in the air and Cohen was pushing a table off his lap. He then hit Sinatra and Frank started yelling at Cohen for punching him. It

Above: Sinatra entrances an audience of 20,000 at New York's Madison Square Garden.

was terrible, somehow a chair, tossed by Sinatra, split a security guard's head."

'Said a floorman at the Sands: "You would have had to see Sinatra Monday morning to believe it. He went to the second floor of the hotel, went into the room where the switchboard is and yanked all the telephone jacks out. He was yelling at the top of his voice and everyone in the place was jittery . . ."

'Said a bellman: "Sinatra even took one of the baggage carts and drove it through a plate glass window".'

Like a good scene from a bad Sinatra movie.

A friend once told Sinatra: 'You've become the modern day gunslinger. When you're in town there will always be someone who will have to come up to you and prove that he is faster on the draw, so to speak, than you are . . .' The image, albeit romantic, could certainly apply to many of the Sinatra 'incidents', especially in the early years, but maybe the anonymous friend should have extended the analogy to portray the trigger-happy paranoia of a gunslinger always waiting for a challenge and sometimes anticipating the threat when it is not even there.

Sinatra in retirement and unretirement was no less unpredictable and a sour, battling image collided head-on with press and public on the disastrous come-

back tour of Australia in the summer of 1974. Trouble started almost as soon as the entourage arrived from Japan. A woman reporter asked for an interview; there was the usual exchange of verbals; then a fight between Sinatra's bodyguard and a group of reporters and photographers.

'Bums, parasites, hookers and pimps,' were the words Sinatra later used to describe Australian journalists and he was particularly vehement about the women. 'They are the hookers of the press . . . I might offer them a buck and a half. I once paid a broad in Washington two dollars [a reference to the Maxine Cheshire incident]. I overpaid her, I found out. She didn't even bathe. Most of them don't.'

It was Sinatra at his worst, out of control and using juvenile language. In America such an outburst might have passed by without too much drama, but in Australia it caused a furore. The newspapers carried pictures of Sinatra's security guards fighting with a photographer. The Transport Workers' Union demanded an apology for Sinatra's insulting remarks and when he in turn demanded apologies from the Australian Journalists' Association, the Transport Workers' Union announced a boycott on Sinatra. The boycott meant in effect that Sinatra's private plane was grounded for lack of fuel and servicing and that he could not use public transport. A lot of people besides Sinatra stood to lose investments made in the tour and eventually Bob Hawke, head of the Australian Council of Trade Unions and himself a Sinatra fan, intervened to negotiate a compromise statement—a kind of defiant semi-apology from Sinatra.

The row smouldered on. Sinatra continued to snipe at journalists during his shows and the newspapers replied in kind. The tour came to an end, uneasily, but without further explosions, but the hoodlum image was in ascendancy.

Almost as soon as he was back from the Australian disaster, Sinatra had to face a court case referring back to a 1973 brawl, this time a fight in the men's room of the Trinidad Hotel in Palm Springs. A young businessman, Frank Weinstock, alleged that a member of Sinatra's entourage had been eyeing his wife in the Hotel lounge and that the man had told Weinstock to 'beat it' next time his wife went to the ladies' room. When Mrs Weinstock eventually did visit the toilet her husband accompanied her, but found himself surrounded in the men's room where Frank Sinatra accused him of eyeing his own partner, Barbara Marx. Weinstock said Sinatra hit him in the chest with the palm of his hand, while the other men pushed him around saying, 'Respect the man, respect the man.' Weinstock then protested that there had been a mistake and Sinatra 'took a step back, snapped his fingers and said, "Okay boys, get him".' According to Weinstock, he was pummelled around and finally hit in the head three times by Jilly Rizzo.

In the end Jilly Rizzo, denying vehemently that he was Sinatra's bodyguard, admitted that he had knocked Weinstock down, but only because Weinstock had raised his hands at him. Weinstock's brother-in-law, who had witnessed the scene, could not substantiate that Sinatra had actually said 'Okay boys, get him'. Jilly Rizzo was found guilty of assault and battery and heavily fined. Sinatra and his other friends were cleared, but coming on top of the Australian fracas, the trial had lost Sinatra sympathy with the public. The out-of-retirement honeymoon was over.

Seven weeks after his return from Australia, Sinatra played a 'family' show with Frank Jr and Nancy at Harrah's, Lake Tahoe, and Caesar's Palace, Las Vegas. At the end of September he gave a benefit concert in Los Angeles for the Cedars Mount Sinai Hospital, then almost immediately embarked on a nine-city tour with Woody Herman's Young Thundering Herd. The 'comeback' novelty had worn off. *Variety* reported him 'pricing himself out of the market', presumably in reference to falling audience figures, and his 13 October concert at Madison Square Gardens, New York, televised under the title 'The Main Event', was far from the critical success his original come-back show had been the previous year.

'The Main Event' was also the title for a new album amalgamating the best numbers from these autumn concerts. Sinatra's tour ended back in New York when he sang nine songs in a Hugh Carey Rally at Madison Square Gardens. Little wonder if he took life easy over the next two months. In the year since his 'retirement from retirement' Sinatra had produced three new albums and taken part in nearly a hundred concerts.

But that vulnerable image stayed with him. This was an America already plunging with Watergate into bitter self-examination. George Frazier wrote in the *Boston Globe*: 'The trouble with you, Frankie, is you got no style. All your life you wanted to be a big man but the wrong kind of big man. Look, Sinatra, Momo Giancana is just another version of Haldeman, and Agnew makes three. You're a sad case, Frankie. I think you're the best male vocalist who ever lived, but I also think you're a miserable failure as a human being.'

Sinatra was associated irrevocably with that particular area of American life now so closely under scrutiny. Even his physical appearance was used by one commentator to symbolize disgust — Ralph Gleason in *Rolling Stone*:

'It is simply weird now to see him all glossed up like a wax dummy, with that rug on his head looking silly and the onstage movement, which used to be panther-tense, now a self-conscious hoodlum bustle. It's even odder to see him with the bodyguards and hear all the gossip about his côterie of friends and their careers in this club or that hotel or that gambling joint ...

'Today he's swopped Charlie Lucky and the other mobsters for Spiro Agnew and Ronald Reagan ... All I know is that what seemed a youthful bravado 25 years ago seems like angry perversity now. You used to think of him as a guy who could be Robin Hood, who would help some poor cat who was in real need. Today the guys he helps are millionaires and he behaves, even if only half the print is true, like an arrogant despot with a court of sycophants Uncle Tomming their asses off ...

'The voice is good today but I don't believe, anymore, that he is one of us. He's one of *them* now, singing from the other side of the street and I guess he doesn't have a whiff of how power-mad and totalitarian it all seems, those bodyguards and the Rat Pack and all that egocentric trivia that has nothing to do with music. And he was once a thorough musician, right down to his toes. But then he didn't wear a rug and I have a feeling he wouldn't have. All that came later when, in truth, he had lost more than his hair.'

And the other Sinatra, the Robin Hood, Hyde's Dr. Jekyll, the man known in show-biz as the world's softest touch, the benefactor, often anonymous, of practically anyone in need or in trouble? Just another side of the ego trip, say his critics; part of the power complex, the God or Godfather complex. Perhaps—but it doesn't really seem quite that simple. He is a shy man when he gives and he hates to be thanked. Columnist Hendis Rocklin commented once: 'Sinatra rarely speaks of the generous things he does. He's too busy alienating reporters, hating cops ...'

When former World Heavyweight Champion Joe

Louis was taken ill in 1977 it was Sinatra who flew him from Las Vegas to Texas and paid for the heart operation that saved his life. Lee J. Cobb, Sylvia Sims, Sammy Davis Jr, Jack E. Leonard, Buddy Rich, have all spoken of Sinatra's kindness and generosity when they were at various times ill or in trouble. He converted his plane into a hospital transport and flew it to the aid of Claudette Colbert's husband, Dr Joel Pressman,when he was taken ill in the Bahamas. He had helped and encouraged Bela Lugosi when Lugosi admitted himself into a clinic as a drug addict. He gave Buddy Rich (drummer and ex-room mate of Sinatra with the Dorsey band) 'twenty five grand and no strings attached' when Rich told him of his ambition to start up his own band. He sent George Raft a signed blank cheque unlimited up to a million dollars when Raft was in trouble with the Federal tax authorities. He flew coast-to-coast in the slow-flying days of the 1940s just to back up Phil Silvers at a Copacabana opening night after Silvers' scheduled partner, Rags Ragland, had died suddenly in hospital. And when Charlie Morrison of the Mocambo night club died penniless and near to bankruptcy, Sinatra moved into the club with Nelson Riddle to play two weeks of packed houses until Mrs Charlie Morrison had made enough to pay the bills and keep the club afloat. Toots Shor confided once to Earl Wilson that over the years Sinatra had given him $150,000. 'One time he'd been gambling and he won ten grand. He turned to me and said, "Here, you need this more than I do".' Father Bob Perrella wrote in his book, *They Call Me The Showbiz Priest,* 'When tragedy struck the lives of the Judy Garlands, the Ethel Barrymores, the unlucky ones never knew the identity of the man who paid their rents and bought their food.'

In 1976 Sinatra received the Scopus Award from the American Friends of the Hebrew University for 'humanitarian accomplishment', and was awarded an Honorary Doctorate of Humane Letters by the University of Nevada in Las Vegas. In 1965 he had been given the De Gaulle Peace Award; in 1971 City of Los Angeles and Jean Hersholt Humanitarian Awards; in 1972 the Beverly Hills Friars Humanitarian Award. Each of these honours had been conferred on him primarily for his work and contributions for charity, but they might equally reflect his many acts of kindness to individuals—friends and strangers alike.

Sinatra the *Padrone;* Sinatra the romantic; or Sinatra the sentimental? All dangerous men, we are told, are sentimental. One day in a London home for blind children Sinatra had been talking to the kids and listening to their singing. A little girl came up to him and asked: 'Mr Sinatra, please sir, what colour is the wind?'

'You see, sweetheart,' he told her, 'the wind blows so fast you can't see the colour'.

Sinatra had finished 1974 voted 'Sour Apple of the

Year' by the Lady Journalists of Hollywood. He began his sixtieth year more quietly, apparently intent on making it, like his fiftieth year in 1965, 'a very good year'. He soothed his audiences at Harrah's and Caesar's Palace through January, February and March; talked a lot about his grand-daughter, Angela Jennifer, Nancy's first child; he left the press alone; cut out the haranguing; even ignored the occasional heckler.

In April he set out on another long tour—San Francisco, Portland, Seattle, Denver, Chicago, Minneapolis, Indianapolis, St Louis, Montreal, Toronto, Providence and New York. His orchestra was conducted by Don Costa and it was Costa who left with him the day after the New York concert to take charge of an English orchestra on Sinatra's European tour, another arduous programme with concerts scheduled in Monte Carlo, Paris, Vienna, Munich, Frankfurt, Berlin, London, Brussels and Amsterdam.

Sinatra had had his share of trouble in Toronto where a photographer alleged he had been punched by a Sinatra bodyguard. Sinatra offered the man a million dollars if he could prove the allegation. The photographer did not even try. In Germany the press were not so easily put off. They taunted him with his half-empty concert halls and ridiculed him when he cancelled his Berlin show after a kidnap threat: German newspapers told him, perhaps with justification, that he was scared of the empty rows of seats. They condemned his ticket prices and criticized his performances and dubbed him 'super gangster'. Sinatra kept his cool and continued to refuse interviews. He said later to his London audience, *à propos* that 'super gangster' jibe: 'I could have started mentioning something about the sins of their fathers—like Dachau and a few places like that.'

London offered him, not for the first or last time, refuge, relaxation and crowded, happy audiences. He gave two concerts in the Albert Hall, the first to an audience that included two of his former wives (Ava Gardner and Mia Farrow), and three princesses (Princess Margaret, Princess Anne and Princess Grace of Monaco). He was King again and his reception from both audience and critics was rapturous.

Returning to the States he played as a last minute substitute for Diana Ross at Caesar's Palace in mid-June, then sang in a week of highly successful back-to-back evenings with John Denver at Harrah's, Lake Tahoe, Sinatra in a DJ, Denver in denims (a combination repeated the following year in a TV spectacular, 'John Denver and Friend'). The week's engagement at Lake Tahoe was a sell-out, with 'Ol' Grandad' in introspective mood talking a lot between his songs. 'You got to love living, baby,' he said one night. 'Dying's a pain in the ass.'

He followed Harrah's with another short tour—Washington, Toronto, New Jersey and Saratoga—before taking up perhaps the most significant and challenging engagement since his come-back, a two week season at the Uris Theatre, New York, sharing the programme with Count Basie and Ella Fitzgerald. The sixteen shows grossed over a million dollars and on one of his last evenings Jackie Onassis arrived at the theatre as Sinatra's date for the evening. It was said later she was there to sign up his autobiography for a New York publisher. But whatever the reason, her presence told everybody that the King was back on his throne, respectable and loved, going but not quite all gone with that colourless wind.

In November Sinatra played an equally successful week of concerts at the London Palladium, his first return to that Mecca of showbiz since 1953. He was programmed again with Count Basie's orchestra and shared some of his singing this time with Sarah Vaughan. Spiro Agnew joined him in London and after the Palladium engagement Sinatra travelled with the ex-Vice-President to give a concert in Tehran and two charity shows in Israel for the Jerusalem Foundation for Arab and Jewish Children.

Full page advertisements in the trade press to mark Sinatra's busy sixtieth year that December boasted with justifiable pride of 140 performances in 105 days and audiences of half a million. It had been, as intended, 'a very good year'.

Sinatra's private life during and after retirement was centred on his luxurious retreat in Palm Springs. He was still surrounded by the male entourage but for the last five years the domestic scene had at least been softened by the presence of Barbara Marx. Sinatra's romantic attachments, real or imagined, were now harder to find in the gossip columns. The traditionalists, among them his own mother, continued to hope for a fairy-tale return to first wife Nancy. Others chronicled his public or semi-public appearances with Hope Lange and Pamela Hayward—wife of producer Leland Hayward and mother of Winston Churchill Jr. Barbara Marx survived the gossip or reality of these 'dates' and continued to act as hostess in Sinatra's household and accompany him on his tours. The on-off game of wedding bells between them was more of a press invention than a reflection of the real situation between them, Barbara Marx being well aware of the result of previous attempts to hurry Sinatra into marriage. According to the columnists it was the re-appearance of Lauren Bacall on Sinatra's arm that finally provoked Barbara to an ultimatum.

Whatever the truth of this story, Frank married Barbara on 25 May, 1976, two months after the birth of his second grandchild, Amanda Catharine. Children and grandchildren were present as bride and bride-groom exchanged luxury cars (a Jaguar XJS from Barbara and a Rolls-Royce from Frank) in front of a gathering of distinguished guests led by Gregory Peck, Kirk Douglas, Sammy Davis Jr, Ronald Reagan and Spiro Agnew. It was Sinatra's fourth wedding and, by

all accounts, his most relaxed. When Barbara was asked if she would take her husband 'for richer or poorer', Frank interjected with a grin; 'Richer, richer'.

The couple denied themselves an immediate honey-moon. Sinatra was due back on stage only two days after the wedding to complete an earlier engagement at the Latin Casino, Philadelphia, cut short due to illness. Voted Entertainer of the Year by the Friars Club, the Voice had nevertheless eased his schedule during 1976. He played the inevitable Caesar's Palace, the Premier Theatre, Tarrytown, New York, briefly the Pacific Coliseum in Vancouver and Harrah's at Lake Tahoe for another week of shows with John Denver. He sang, as in 1975, for Jerry Lewis's September Telethon, 21½ hours of continuous TV entertainment on behalf of the Muscular Dystrophy Association and this year Sinatra used the occasion to stage a reunion between Jerry Lewis and Dean Martin. The two old comedy partners had not been on speaking terms for 20 years, and Sinatra the Fighter had turned Peacemaker.

The evident happiness and serenity of his marriage had come just in time to help Sinatra through one of the most difficult emotional moments in his life.

Early in January 1977 a private jet carrying Sinatra's mother, Dolly, disappeared shortly after take-off from Palm Springs. Dolly had been on her way to see her son perform in Las Vegas. Frank was told that the plane had probably crashed in the San Bernadino mountains but two days of desperate waiting passed before the wreckage and bodies were found in that snow-bound wilderness. On 13 January, while Hollywood attended a simultaneous memorial service in Beverly Hills, Dolly Sinatra was buried beside her husband in Palm Springs after a quiet family ceremony. Frank Sinatra left the church overcome with grief, leaning on his wife's arm.

It is difficult not to see Dolly Sinatra as the dominant figure in her son's life—though perhaps equally difficult to imagine any figure exactly dominating the life of such an extraordinary man. Certainly Sinatra had remained in awe of his mother to the very end of her life. She was insistently proud of his success and he, according to close friends, always in need or in search of her approval and praise. The strong but often absent mother of his childhood had remained for ever part of his ceaseless and obsessive drive to succeed and dominate in his own right.

The death of Dolly Sinatra was to be a direct cause of Sinatra's return to the screen, a come-back in the most unexpected manner imaginable. Laying aside his previous vow never to make TV movies he now agreed to take the part of an anti-Mafia cop in a TV dramatization of Philip Rosenberg's *Contract On Cherry Street*. The novel had been Dolly Sinatra's favourite book and her son's decision to make the film was a direct tribute to his dead mother. The end result

Below: Sinatra with his mother Dolly. Left: Frank with Barbara Marx on their wedding day.

Was shown on NBC in November 1977. It was well received by *Variety* and the intensity of Sinatra's acting has been compared with his performances in *From Here to Eternity* and *The Man With The Golden Arm.*

The sudden and unexpected death of his mother is said to have changed Sinatra. He is, we are told, sobered, less impetuous, more reflective. It was certainly a muted Sinatra who flew in to London a month and a half after Dolly's death for a long-standing engagement at the Albert Hall. Apart from a press row over his arrival—Sinatra had taken over the whole of Luton Airport and demanded absolute privacy—his reception in London was once again rapturous. He had already named them 'his most loyal fans' and attempted to reward them by keeping ticket prices as low as possible, a move sabotaged by black market touts who were re-selling tickets at twenty times their face value. His opening night (the full engagement ran for a week) was dedicated to a National Advisory Centre on the Battered Child, run by the National Society for the Prevention of Cruelty to Children, and a black tie audience, including Princess Margaret and Ava Gardner, raised £60,000 for the NSPCC project.

'Once again the simple mastery of Francis Albert Sinatra triumphed', said James Johnson in the *Evening Standard.* 'In just under two hours the years of experience mesmerized a breathlessly faithful and devoted audience.'

'The voice is mostly still there', wrote Tom Sutcliffe in the *Guardian.* 'Sinatra always cruised along on that tangy, jaded image and, as age wreaks its gentle revenge on the instrument, he ripens into what he always pretended to be, a bit croaky, a bit short on legato, but effortlessly and often perversely characterized . . . He's above hoarseness. It's the opposite of a look-no-strings approach, especially with orchestral arrangements like this. More a case of this is how it's done, and you love it.'

In a decade that has seen the deaths of so many entertainment giants, Sinatra's continuity seems all the more unique and valuable, though not extraordinary. For the many faithful and devoted 'original' members of his audiences there are equal numbers of younger listeners who still go to hear 'the Master'. On disc and on stage Sinatra has survived the onslaught of rock with its many modern pop derivatives. He can sing a Paul Anka song ('My Way') or an Elton John number ('Sorry Seems To Be The Hardest Word') with a defiance or a melancholy all his own. Neil Diamond, John Denver, George Harrison, Lennon and McCartney, Neil Sedaka, Stevie Wonder—he has interpreted them all with his inimitable analysis of lyric and mood.

It was the young writer and film director Ray Connolly in a profile on Sinatra for the London *Evening Standard,* who gave the retrospective of a younger generation on this epic American idol: 'He's been a giant hero of my lifetime—yet in no way has he been part of my generation's life-style. Even when he was at his peak in the mid-fifties he was singing about a society already obsolete—a pre-war society upon which social issues never seemed to impinge; a wonderful era of light-hearted de-sexed romanticism . . . Nelson Riddle may have added a new swinging style to his songs but the message was the same as ever. He sang and has always sung, about love. Lust was never mentioned. His music is stylized and contrived. They'd probably call it *kitsch* now were he not such a revered figure . . . But he has a sense of theatre, which comes over on record too, to make the lyrics of what may sometimes seem the most clichéd of songs an achingly meaningful experience in poetry . . . He sings as he moves, gently fox-trotting from side to side, snapping his white cuffs to add interpretation, briskness and style, then slooping down his shoulders into that thin man look of lost love and instant vulnerability.

'From a lesser performer such theatricals might have been embarrassing, but he's so subtle that one cannot fail to join in the mood . . . Behind him he leaves three decades of beautifully sung songs, three decades of nostalgia and bucketfuls of maidenly tears. While Sinatra records are still being played around the world we'll all be romantics from time to time.'

Roderick Mann, in search of the true Sinatra for the *Sunday Express* was told by a Hollywood producer: 'You've got to decide which Sinatra you're looking for. The one who knocks people down—or the one who lifts people up . . .'

'Public arrogance and private kindness' was the theme of one *Life* profile on Sinatra, but then his life and personality are full of such contradictions. He defies analysis. Each controversial theme is hedged with reservations. Did he—didn't he; is he—isn't he? He will tell the story himself one day, or part of the story—maybe. For the moment autobiography is in his songs—not through the words, but through the emotion he feels and engenders. And the spine-tingling is usually accompanied by pain—loss, loneliness, fear, regret. They live in him somewhere. He does not inspire serenity.

Perhaps, the fourth Mrs Sinatra will draw the sting from this solitary man, the King who for all his fame and success cannot bear to be alone until he sleeps, who from his earliest days bought courtiers with money or affection or favours and has kept them around him, only their names and faces changing, ever since.

His life tells us; the emotion in his songs express it; Prewitt said it in *Eternity:* 'No-one ever lies about being lonely.'

FILMOGRAPHY

LAS VEGAS NIGHTS (1941)

Director: Ralph Murphy
Producer: William LeBaron
Original screenplay by Ernest Pagano and Harry Clork
Musical Director: Victor Young
Musical Advisor: Arthur Franklin
Musical numbers staged by LeRoy Prinz
Incidental score by Phil Boutelje and Walter Scharf
Musical arrangements by Axel Stordahl, Victor Young, Charles
Bradshaw, Leo Shuken and Max Terr
Director of photography: William C. Mellor
Paramount

Cast: Constance Moore (*Norma Jennings*), Bert Wheeler (*Stu Grant*), Phil
Regan (*Bill Stevens*), Lillian Cornell (*Mildred Jennings*), Virginia Dale
(*Patsy Lynch*)

SHIP AHOY (1942)

Director: Edward Buzzell
Producer: Jack Cummings
Screenplay by Harry Clork
Music supervised and conducted by George Stoll
Musical arrangements by Axel Stordahl, Sy Oliver, Leo Arnaud, George
Bassman and Basil Adlam
Incidental score by George Bassman, George Stoll and Henry Russell
Directors of photography: Leonard Smith and Robert Planck
Metro-Goldwyn-Mayer

Cast: Eleanor Powell (*Tallulah Winters*), Red Skelton (*Merton K.
Kibble*), Bert Lahr (*Skip Owens*), Virginia O'Brien (*Fran Evans*), William
Post (*H. U. Bennett*)

REVEILLE WITH BEVERLY (1943)

Director: Charles Barton
Producer: Sam White
Original screenplay by Howard J. Green, Jack Henley and Albert Duffy
Musical Director: Morris Stoloff
Director of photography: Philip Tannura
Columbia

Cast: Ann Miller (*Beverly Ross*), William Wright (*Barry Lang*), Dick
Purcell (*Andy Adams*), Franklin Pangborn (*Vernon Lewis*), Tim Ryan
(*Mr. Kennedy*), Larry Parks (*Eddie Ross*)

HIGHER AND HIGHER (1942)

Producer and Director: Tim Whelan
Associate Producer: George Arthur
Screenplay by Jay Dratler and Ralph Spence
Based on the play by Gladys Hurlbut and Joshua Logan
Musical director: Constantin Bakaleinikoff
Orchestral arrangements: Gene Rose
Musical arrangements for Frank Sinatra by Axel Stordahl
Incidental score by Roy Webb
Orchestrated by Maurice de Packh
Vocal arrangements by Ken Darby
Musical numbers staged by Ernst Matray
Director of photography: Robert DeGrasse
RKO

Cast: Michele Morgan (*Millie*), Jack Haley (*Mike*), Frank Sinatra (*Frank*),
Leon Errol (*Drake*), Marcy McGuire (*Mickey*), Victor Borge (*Fitzroy
Wilson*)

STEP LIVELY (1944)

Director: Tim Whelan
Producer: Robert Fellows
Screenplay by Warren Duff and Peter Milne
Based on the play *Room Service* by John Murray and Allen Boretz
Musical Director: Constantin Bakaleinikoff
Orchestral arrangements: Gene Rose
Musical arrangements for Frank Sinatra by Axel Stordahl
Vocal arrangements: Ken Darby
Musical numbers created and staged by Ernst Matray
Director of photography: Robert DeGrasse
RKO

Cast: Frank Sinatra (*Glen*), George Murphy (*Miller*), Adolphe Menjou (*Wagner*), Gloria de Haven (*Christine*), Walter Slezak (*Gribble*), Eugene Pallette (*Jenkins*)

ANCHORS AWEIGH (1945)

Director: George Sidney
Producer: Joe Pasternak
Screenplay by Isobel Lennart
Music supervised and conducted by George Stoll
Frank Sinatra's vocal arrangements by Axel Stordahl
Kathryn Grayson's vocal arrangements by Earl Brent
Incidental score by George Stoll and Calvin Jackson
Orchestrations: Ted Duncan, Joseph Nussbaum, Robert Franklyn and Wally Heglin
Dance sequences created by Gene Kelly
Directors of photography: Robert Planck and Charles Boyle
Metro-Goldwyn-Mayer. Technicolor

Cast: Frank Sinatra (*Clarence Doolittle*), Kathryn Grayson (*Susan Abbott*), Gene Kelly (*Joseph Brady*), Jose Iturbi (*Himself*), Dean Stockwell (*Donald Martin*)

THE HOUSE I LIVE IN (1945)

Director: Mervyn Le Roy
Producer: Frank Ross
Original screenplay by Albert Maltz
Musical Director: Axel Stordahl
Incidental score by Roy Webb
Film Editor: Philip Martin Jr.
RKO Radio

TILL THE CLOUDS ROLL BY (1946)

Director: Richard Whorf
Producer: Arthur Freed
Screenplay by Myles Connolly and Jean Holloway
Based on the life and music of Jerome Kern
Music supervised and conducted by Lennie Hayton
Orchestrations by Conrad Salinger
Incidental score by Conrad Salinger, Lennie Hayton and Roger Edens
Additional orchestrations by Robert Franklyn, Wally Heglin, Leo Shuken, Sidney Cutner and Ted Duncan
Vocal arrangements: Kay Thompson
Musical numbers staged and directed by Robert Alton
Judy Garland's numbers directed by Vincente Minnelli
Directors of photography: Harry Stradling and George Folsey
Metro-Goldwyn-Mayer. Technicolor

Cast: June Allyson (*Star*), Lucille Bremer (*Sally*), Judy Garland (*Marilyn Miller*), Kathryn Grayson (*Magnolia*), Van Heflin (*James I. Hessler*), Lena Horne (*Julie*), Van Johnson (*Band Leader*), Angela Lansbury (*Guest Star*), Tony Martin (*Gaylord Ravenal*), Virginia O'Brien (*Ellie*), Dinah Shore (*Julie Sanderson*), Frank Sinatra (*Guest Star*), Robert Walker (*Jerome Kern*)

IT HAPPENED IN BROOKLYN (1947)

Director: Richard Whorf
Producer: Jack Cummings
Screenplay by Isobel Lennart
Musical supervision, direction and incidental score by Johnny Green
Orchestrations by Ted Duncan
Frank Sinatra's vocal orchestrations by Axel Stordahl
Musical numbers staged and directed by Jack Donohue
Piano solos arranged and played by Andre Previn
Director of photography: Robert Planck
Metro-Goldwyn-Mayer

Cast: Frank Sinatra (*Danny Webson Miller*), Kathryn Grayson (*Anne Fielding*), Peter Lawford (*Jamie Shellgrove*), Jimmy Durante (*Nick Lombardi*), Gloria Grahame (*Nurse*)

Left: 'Step Lively'. Below left: Sinatra and Gene Kelly in 'Anchors Aweigh'. Below: 'Till The Clouds Roll By'.

THE MIRACLE OF THE BELLS (1948)

Director: Irving Pichel
Producer: Jesse L. Lasky and Walter MacEwen
Screenplay by Ben Hecht and Quentin Reynolds
Based on the novel by Russell Janney
Additional material for Frank Sinatra's sequences by De Witt Bodeen
Music: Leigh Harline
Director of photography: Robert de Grasse
RKO Radio

Cast: Fred MacMurray (*Bill Dunnigan*), Alida Valli (*Olga Treskovna*), Frank Sinatra (*Father Paul*), Lee J. Cobb (*Marcus Harris*), Harold Vermilye (*Orloff*)

THE KISSING BANDIT (1948)

Director: Laslo Benedek
Producer: Joe Pasternak
Original screenplay by Isobel Lennart and John Briard Harding
Music supervised and conducted by George Stoll
Musical arrangements by Leo Arnaud
Incidental score by George Stoll, Albert Sendrey, Scott Bradley and Andre Previn
Additional orchestrations by Albert Sendrey, Calvin Jackson, Conrad Salinger, Robert Van Eps, Paul Marquardt and Earl Brent
Dance director: Stanley Donen
Director of photography: Robert Surtees
Metro-Goldwyn-Mayer. Technicolor

Cast: Frank Sinatra (*Ricardo*), Kathryn Grayson (*Teresa*), J. Carrol Naish (*Chico*), Mildred Natwick (*Isabella*)

TAKE ME OUT TO THE BALL GAME (1949)

Director: Busby Berkeley
Producer: Arthur Freed
Screenplay by Harry Tugend and George Wells
Based on a story by Gene Kelly and Stanley Donen

Below: A wild scene from 'On The Town'. Right: With Shelley Winters in 'Meet Danny Wilson'. Far right: With Montgomery Clift in 'From Here To Eternity'.

Music supervised and conducted by Adolph Deutsch
Incidental score by Roger Edens
Orchestral arrangements by Adolph Deutsch, Conrad Salinger, Robert Franklyn, Paul Marquardt, Alexander Courage, Axel Stordahl and Leo Arnaud
Vocal arrangements by Robert Tucker
Dance Directors: Gene Kelly and Stanley Donen
Director of photography: George Folsey
Metro-Goldwyn-Mayer. Technicolor

Cast: Frank Sinatra (*Dennis Ryan*), Esther Williams (*K. C. Higgins*), Gene Kelly (*Eddie O'Brien*), Betty Garrett (*Shirley Delwyn*), Edward Arnold (*Joe Lorgan*), Jules Munshin (*Nat Goldberg*)

ON THE TOWN (1949)

Directors: Gene Kelly and Stanley Donen
Producer: Arthur Freed
Screenplay by Adolph Green and Betty Comden, from their musical play based on an idea by Jerome Robbins
Music supervised and conducted by Lennie Hayton
Orchestral arrangements by Conrad Salinger, Robert Franklyn and Wally Heglin
Vocal arrangements by Saul Chaplin
Incidental score by Roger Edens, Saul Chaplin and Conrad Salinger
Music for 'Miss Turnstiles' Dance and 'A Day in New York' Ballet by Leonard Bernstein
Director of photography: Harold Rosson
Metro-Goldwyn-Mayer. Technicolor

Cast: Gene Kelly (*Gabey*), Frank Sinatra (*Chip*), Betty Garrett (*Brunhilde Esterhazy*), Ann Miller (*Claire Huddesen*), Jules Munshin (*Ozzie*)

DOUBLE DYNAMITE (1951)

Director: Irving Cummings
Producer: Irving Cummings Jr.
Screenplay by Melville Shavelson
Additional dialogue by Harry Crane
From an original story by Leo Rosten, based on a character created by
Manni Manheim
Music by Leigh Harline
Director of photography: Robert de Grasse
RKO Radio

Cast: Jane Russell (*Mildred (Mibs) Goodhug*), Groucho Marx (*Emile J. Keck*), Frank Sinatra (*Johnny Dalton*), Don McGuire (*Bob Pulsifer Jr*), Howard Freeman (*R. B. Pulsifer Sr.*), Nestor Paiva (*Bookie*)

MEET DANNY WILSON (1951)

Director: Joseph Pevney
Producer: Leonard Goldstein
Associate Producer and original screenplay by Don McGuire
Musical Director: Joseph Gershenson
Musical numbers staged by Hal Belfer
Director of photography: Maury Gertsman
Universal-International

Cast: Frank Sinatra (*Danny Wilson*), Shelley Winters (*Joy Carroll*), Alex Nicol (*Mike Ryan*), Raymond Burr (*Nick Driscoll*), Tommy Farrell (*Tommy Wells*)

FROM HERE TO ETERNITY (1953)

Director: Fred Zinnemann
Producer: Buddy Adler
Screenplay by Daniel Taradash
Based on the novel by James Jones
Music supervised and conducted by Morris Stoloff
Background music by George Duning
Orchestrations by Arthur Morton
Song 'Re-enlistment Blues' by James Jones, Fred Karger and Robert Wells
Director of photography: Burnett Guffey
Columbia

Cast: Burt Lancaster (*Sgt. Milton Warden*), Montgomery Clift (*Robert E. Lee Prewitt*), Deborah Kerr (*Karen Holmes*), Donna Reed (*Lorene*), Frank Sinatra (*Angelo Maggio*), Philip Ober (*Capt. Dana Holmes*), Mickey Shaughnessy (*Sgt. Leva*)

SUDDENLY (1954)

Director: Lewis Allen
Producer: Robert Bassler
Original screenplay by Richard Sale
Music: David Raksin
Director of photography: Charles G. Clarke
A Libra Production. Released by United Artists

Cast: Frank Sinatra (*John Baron*), Sterling Hayden (*Tod Shaw*), James Gleason (*Pop Benson*), Nancy Gates (*Ellen Benson*), Willis Bouchey (*Dan Carney*)

YOUNG AT HEART (1955)

Director: Gordon Douglas
Producer: Henry Blanke
Adaptation by Liam O'Brien from the screenplay *Four Daughters* by Julius J. Epstein and Lenore Coffee
Music supervised, arranged and conducted by Ray Heindorf
Piano solos played by Andre Previn
Director of photography: Ted McCord
An Arwin Production. Released by Warner Bros. Warner Color; print by Technicolor

Cast: Doris Day (*Laurie Tuttle*), Frank Sinatra (*Barney Sloan*), Gig Young (*Alex Burke*), Ethel Barrymore (*Aunt Jessie*), Dorothy Malone (*Fran Tuttle*), Robert Keith (*Gregory Tuttle*)

NOT AS A STRANGER (1955)

Producer and Director: Stanley Kramer
Screenplay by Edna and Edward Anhalt
Based on the novel by Morton Thompson
Music composed and conducted by George Antheil
Orchestrations by Ernest Gold
Director of photography: Franz Planer
A Stanley Kramer Production. Released by United Artists

Cast: Olivia de Havilland (*Kristina Hedvigson*), Robert Mitchum (*Lucas Marsh*), Frank Sinatra (*Alfred Boone*), Gloria Grahame (*Harriet Lang*), Broderick Crawford (*Dr. Aarons*), Charles Bickford (*Dr. Runkleman*)

THE TENDER TRAP (1955)

Director: Charles Walters
Producer: Lawrence Weingarten
Screenplay by Julius J. Epstein
Based on the play by Max Shulman and Robert Paul Smith
Music composed and conducted by Jeff Alexander
Orchestrations: Will Beittel
Director of photography: Paul C. Vogel
Metro-Goldwyn-Mayer. Eastman Color; CinemaScope

Cast: Frank Sinatra (*Charlie Y. Reader*), Debbie Reynolds (*Julie Gillis*), David Wayne (*Joe McCall*), Celeste Holm (*Sylvia Crewes*), Jarma Lewis (*Jessica Collins*), Lola Albright (*Poppy Matson*)

GUYS AND DOLLS (1955)

Director: Joseph L. Mankiewicz
Producer: Samuel Goldwyn
Screenplay by Joseph L. Mankiewicz
From the musical play, book by Jo Swerling and Abe Burrows, music and lyrics by Frank Loesser
Based on the story *The Idyll of Miss Sarah Brown* by Damon Runyon
Music supervised and conducted by Jay Blackton
Orchestral arrangements by Skip Martin, Nelson Riddle (for Sinatra), Alexander Courage and Albert Sendrey
Background music adapted by Cyril J. Mockridge, assisted by Herbert Spencer
Director of photography: Harry Stradling
A Samuel Goldwyn Production. Released by Metro-Goldwyn-Mayer.

Left: Marlon Brando and Frank Sinatra in 'Guys And Dolls'.
Above: With Kim Novak in 'The Man With The Golden Arm'.
Right: Grace Kelly with Sinatra in 'High Society'.

Eastman Color

Cast: Marlon Brando (*Sky Masterson*), Jean Simmons (*Sarah Brown*), Frank Sinatra (*Nathan Detroit*), Vivian Blaine (*Miss Adelaide*), Robert Keith (*Lt. Brannigan*)

THE MAN WITH THE GOLDEN ARM (1955)

Producer and Director: Otto Preminger
Screenplay by Walter Newman and Lewis Meltzer
Based on the novel by Nelson Algren
Music composed and conducted by Elmer Bernstein
Orchestrations by Frederick Steiner
Director of photography: Sam Leavitt
A Carlyle Production. Released by United Artists

Cast: Frank Sinatra (*Frankie Machine*), Eleanor Parker (*Zosh*), Kim Novak (*Molly*), Arnold Stang (*Sparrow*)

MEET ME IN LAS VEGAS (1956)

Director: Roy Rowland
Producer: Joe Pasternak
Original screenplay by Isobel Lennart
Music supervised and conducted by George Stoll
Music for 'Frankie and Johnny' ballet adapted by Johnny Green
Lena Horne's number arranged and conducted by Lennie Hayton
Orchestrations by Albert Sendrey and Skip Martin
Songs by Nicholas Brodszky and Sammy Cahn
Dances and musical numbers created and staged by Hermes Pan
'Rehearsal Ballet' and 'Sleeping Beauty Ballet' created and staged by
Eugene Loring
Music co-ordinator: Irving Aaronson
Director of Photography: Robert Bronner
Metro-Goldwyn-Mayer. Eastman Color; CinemaScope

Cast: Dan Dailey (*Chuck Rodwell*), Cyd Charisse (*Maria Corvier*), Jerry Colonna (*MC at Silver Slipper*), Paul Henried (*Maria's Manager*), Frankie Laine (*Guest Star at Sands*), Mitsuko Sawamura (*Japanese Girl*)

JOHNNY CONCHO (1956)

Director: Don McGuire
Producer: Frank Sinatra
Associate Producer: Henry Sanicola
Screenplay by David P. Harmon and Don McGuire
Based on the story *The Man Who Owned the Town* by David P. Harmon
Music composed and conducted by Nelson Riddle
Orchestrations by Arthur Morton
Director of photography: William Mellor
A Kent Production. Released by United Artists

Cast: Frank Sinatra (*Johnny Concho*), Keenan Wynn (*Barney Clark*), William Conrad (*Tallman*), Phyllis Kirk (*Mary Dark*), Wallace Ford (*Albert Dark*)

HIGH SOCIETY (1956)

Director: Charles Walters
Producer: Sol C. Siegel
Screenplay by John Patrick
Based on the play *The Philadelphia Story* by Philip Barry
Music supervised and adapted by Johnny Green and Saul Chaplin
Orchestra conducted by Johnny Green
Orchestral arrangements by Conrad Salinger and Nelson Riddle
Additional orchestrations by Robert Franklyn and Albert Sendrey
Musical numbers staged by Charles Walters
Director of photography: Paul C. Vogel
Metro-Goldwyn-Mayer. Technicolor; Vista-Vision

Cast: Bing Crosby (*C. K. Dexter-Haven*), Grace Kelly (*Tracy Lord*), Frank Sinatra (*Mike Connor*), Celeste Holm (*Liz Imbrie*), John Lund (*George Kittredge*), Louis Calhern (*Uncle Willie*), Sidney Blackmer (*Seth Lord*), Louis Armstrong (*Himself*)

AROUND THE WORLD IN 80 DAYS (1956)

Director: Michael Anderson
Producer: Michael Todd
Screenplay by James Poe, John Farrow and S. J. Perelman
Based on the novel by Jules Verne
Music by Victor Yound
Associate Producer: William Cameron Menzies
Second unit Director: Kevin O'Donovan McClory
Director of photography: Lionel Lindon

162

A *Michael Todd Production. Released by United Artists. Eastman Color; Print by Technicolor; Todd-AO*

Cast includes: David Niven (*Phileas Fogg*), Cantinflas (*Passepartout*), Shirley MacLaine (*Princess Aouda*), Robert Newton (*Inspector Fix*), Frankie Sinatra (*Barbary Coast saloon drunk*)

THE PRIDE AND THE PASSION (1957)

Producer and Director: Stanley Kramer
Screenplay by Edna and Edward Anhalt
Based on the novel *The Gun* by C. S. Forester
Music by George Antheil
Orchestrated and conducted by Ernest Gold
Director of photography: Franz Planer
A Stanley Kramer Production. Released by United Artists. Technicolor; Vista-Vision

Cast: Cary Grant (*Captain Anthony Trumbull*), Frank Sinatra (*Miguel*), Sophia Loren (*Juana*), Theodore Bikel (*General Jouvet*)

THE JOKER IS WILD (1957)

Director: Charles Vidor
Producer: Samuel J. Briskin
Screenplay by Oscar Saul
Based on the book by Art Cohn
Music composed and conducted by Walter Scharf
Orchestrations by Leo Shuken and Jack Hayes
Orchestral arrangements of songs by Nelson Riddle
Speciality songs and parodies by Harry Harris
Dances staged by Josephine Earl
Director of photography: Daniel L. Fapp
An A.M.B.L. Production. Released by Paramount. Vista-Vision

Cast: Frank Sinatra (*Joe E. Lewis*), Mitzi Gaynor (*Martha Stewart*), Jeanne Crain (*Letty Page*), Eddie Albert (*Austin Mack*), Beverly Garland (*Cassie Mack*)

PAL JOEY (1957)

Director: George Sidney
Producer: Fred Kohlmar
Screenplay by Dorothy Kingsley
Based on the musical play by John O'Hara (book), Richard Rodgers (music), and Lorenz Hart (lyrics)
Music supervised and conducted by Morris Stoloff
Musical arrangements by Nelson Riddle
Music adaptation by George Duning and Nelson Riddle
Orchestrations by Arthur Morton
Director of photography: Harold Lipstein
An Essex-George Sidney Production. Released by Columbia. Technicolor

Cast: Rita Hayworth (*Vera Simpson*), Frank Sinatra (*Joey Evans*), Kim Novak (*Linda English*), Barbara Nichols (*Gladys*), Bobby Sherwood (*Ned Galvin*)

KINGS GO FORTH (1958)

Director: Delmer Daves
Producer: Frank Ross
Screenplay by Merle Miller
Based on the novel by Joe David Brown
Music composed and conducted by Elmer Bernstein
Orchestrations by Leo Shuken and Jack Hayes
Director of photography: Daniel L. Fapp
A Frank Ross-Eton Production. Released by United Artists

Cast: Frank Sinatra (*Lt. Sam Loggins*), Tony Curtis (*Sgt. Britt Harris*), Natalie Wood (*Monique Blair*), Leora Dana (*Mrs. Blair*), Karl Swenson (*Colonel*)

SOME CAME RUNNING (1958)

Director: Vincente Minnelli
Producer: Sol C. Siegel
Screenplay by John Patrick and Arthur Sheekman
Based on the novel by James Jones
Music composed and conducted by Elmer Bernstein
Orchestrations by Leo Shuken and Jack Hayes
Director of photography: William H. Daniels
Metro-Goldwyn-Mayer. MetroColor; CinemaScope

Cast: Frank Sinatra (*Dave Hirsh*), Dean Martin (*Bama Dillert*), Shirley MacLaine (*Ginny Moorehead*), Martha Hyer (*Gwen French*), Arthur Kennedy (*Frank Hirsh*)

A HOLE IN THE HEAD (1959)

Producer and Director: Frank Capra
Screenplay by Arnold Schulman, based on his play
Music by Nelson Riddle
Director of photography: William H. Daniels
A Sincap Production. Released by United Artists. Color by DeLuxe. CinemaScope

Cast: Frank Sinatra (*Tony Manetta*), Edward G. Robinson (*Mario Manetta*), Eleanor Parker (*Mrs. Rogers*), Carolyn Jones (*Shirl*), Thelma Ritter (*Sophie Manetta*), Keenan Wynn (*Jerry Marks*)

NEVER SO FEW (1959)

Director: John Sturges
Producer: Edmund Grainger
Screenplay by Millard Kaufman
Based on the novel by Tom T. Chamales
Music by Hugo Friedhofer; orchestrated by Robert Franklyn; conducted by Charles Wolcott
Director of photography: William H. Daniels
A Canterbury Production. Released by Metro-Goldwyn-Mayer. Metrocolor; CinemaScope

Cast: Frank Sinatra (*Capt. Tom C. Reynolds*), Gina Lollobrigida (*Carla Vesari*), Peter Lawford (*Capt. Grey Travis*), Steve McQueen (*Bill Ringa*), Richard Johnson (*Capt. Danny De Mortimer*), Paul Henried (*Nikko Regas*), Brian Donlevy (*General Sloan*)

CAN-CAN (1960)

Director: Walter Lang
Producer: Jack Cummings
Screenplay by Dorothy Kingsley and Charles Lederer
Based on the musical play by Abe Burrow
Songs by Cole Porter
Music arranged and conducted by Nelson Riddle
Vocal supervision by Bobby Tucker
Associate Producer: Saul Chaplin
Director of photography: William H. Daniels
A Suffolk-Cummings Production. Released by 20th Century-Fox. Technicolor; Todd-AO

Cast: Frank Sinatra (*François Durnais*), Shirley MacLaine (*Simone Pistacho*), Maurice Chevalier (*Paul Barriere*), Louis Jourdan (*Philippe Forrestier*), Juliet Prowse (*Claudine*)

OCEAN'S ELEVEN (1960)

Producer and Director: Lewis Milestone
Screenplay by Harry Brown and Charles Lederer
Music composed and conducted by Nelson Riddle
Orchestrations by Arthur Morton
Director of photography: William H. Daniels
A Dorchester Production. Released by Warner Bros. Technicolor; Panavision

Cast: Frank Sinatra (*Danny Ocean*), Dean Martin (*Sam Harmon*), Sammy Davis Jr. (*Josh Howard*), Peter Lawford (*Jimmy Foster*), Angie Dickinson (*Beatrice Ocean*), Richard Conte (*Anthony Bergdorf*), Cesar Romero (*Duke Santos*), Patrice Wymore (*Adele Ekstrom*), Joey Bishop ('*Mushy*' *O'Conners*), Akim Tamiroff (*Spyros Acebos*), Henry Silva (*Roger Corneal*)

PEPE (1960)

Producer and Director: George Sidney
Screenplay by Dorothy Kingsley and Claude Binyon
Based on the play *Broadway Magic* by Ladislas Bush-Fekete
Music supervision and background score by Johnny Green
Associate Producer: Jacques Gelman
Director of photography: Joe MacDonald
A G.S. Posa Films International Production. Released by Columbia. Print by Technicolor; Panavision and CinemaScope

Cast: Cantinflas (*Pepe*), Dan Dailcy (*Ted Holt*), Shirley Jones (*Suzie Murphy*), Carlos Montalban (*Auctioneer*), Vickie Trickett (*Lupita*)

THE DEVIL AT FOUR O'CLOCK (1961)

Director: Mervyn LeRoy
Producer: Fred Kohlmar
Screenplay by Liam O'Brien
Based on the novel by Max Catto
Music by George Duning; orchestrated by Arthur Morton
Director of photography: Joseph Biroc
Columbia. Eastman Color

Cast: Spencer Tracy (*Father Matthew Doonan*), Frank Sinatra (*Harry*), Kerwin Mathews (*Father Joseph Perreau*), Jean Pierre Aumont (*Jacques*), Gregoire Aslan (*Marcel*)

SERGEANTS THREE (1962)

Director: John Sturges
Producer: Frank Sinatra
Executive Producer: Howard W. Koch
Original screenplay by W. R. Burnett
Music: Billy May

Director of photography: Winton C. Hoch
*An Essex-Claude Production. Released by United Artists. Technicolor;
Panavision*

Cast: Frank Sinatra (*1st Sgt. Mike Merry*), Dean Martin (*Sgt. Chip Deal*),
Sammy Davis Jr. (*Jonah Williams*), Peter Lawford (*Sgt. Larry Barrett*),
Joey Bishop (*Sgt. Major Roger Boswell*), Henry Silva (*Mountain Hawk*),
Ruta Lee (*Amelia Parent*), Buddy Lester (*Willie Sharpknife*)

THE ROAD TO HONG KONG (1962)

Director: Norman Panama
Producer: Melvin Frank
Original screenplay by Norman Panama and Melvin Frank
Music composed and conducted by Robert Farnon
Musical associates: Douglas Gamley and Bill McGuffie
Musical numbers staged by Jack Baker and Sheila Meyers
Songs by James Van Heusen and Sammy Cahn
Director of photography: Jack Hildyard
A Melnor Films Production. Released by United Artists.

Cast: Bing Crosby (*Harry Turner*), Bob Hope (*Chester Babcock*), Joan
Collins (*Diane*), Dorothy Lamour (*Herself*), Robert Morley (*The Leader*),
Walter Gotell (*Dr. Zorbb*)

THE MANCHURIAN CANDIDATE (1962)

Director: John Frankenheimer
Producer: George Axelrod and John Frankenheimer
Executive Producer: Howard W. Koch
Screenplay by George Axelrod
Based on the novel by Richard Condon
Music composed and conducted by David Amram
Director of photography: Lionel Lindon
An M.C. Production. Released by United Artists

Cast: Frank Sinatra (*Bennett Marco*), Laurence Harvey (*Raymond Shaw*),
Janet Leigh (*Rosie*), Angela Lansbury (*Raymond's Mother*), Henry Silva
(*Chunjin*), James Gregory (*Senator John Iselin*), Leslie Parrish (*Jocie
Jordan*)

*Far left: 'Never So Few' with Gina Lollobrigida.
Below: 'The Manchurian Candidate'.*

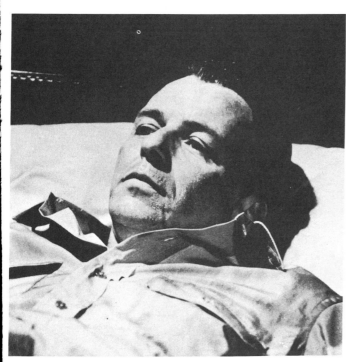

COME BLOW YOUR HORN (1963)

Director: Bud Yorkin
Producer: Norman Lear and Bud Yorkin
Executive Producer: Howard W. Koch
Screenplay by Norman Lear
Based on the play by Neil Simon
Music composed and conducted by Nelson Riddle
Orchestrations by Gil Grau
Directors of photography: William H. Daniels
*An Essex-Tandem Production. Released by Paramount. Technicolor;
Panavision*

Cast: Frank Sinatra (*Alan Baker*), Lee J. Cobb (*Papa Baker*), Molly Picon
(*Mama Baker*), Barbara Rush (*Connie*), Jill St. John (*Peggy*), Tony Bill
(*Buddy Baker*)

THE LIST OF ADRIAN MESSENGER (1963)

Director: John Juston
Producer: Edward Lewis
Screenplay by Anthony Veiller
Based on the novel by Philip MacDonald
Music by Jerry Goldsmith
Director of photography: Joe MacDonald
A Joel Production. Released by Universal

Cast: George C. Scott (*Anthony Gethryn*), Dana Wynter (*Lady Jocelyn
Bruttenholm*), Clive Brook (*Marquis of Gleneyre*), Gladys Cooper (*Mrs.
Karoudjian*), Herbert Marshall (*Sir Wilfred Lucas*), Jacques Roux (*Raoul
Le Borg*)

FOUR FOR TEXAS (1964)

Producer and Director: Robert Aldrich
Executive Producer: Howard W. Koch
Original screenplay by Teddi Sherman and Robert Aldrich
Music composed and conducted by Nelson Riddle
Orchestrations by Gil Grau
Director of photography: Ernest Laszlo
A Sam Company Production. Released by Warner Bros. Technicolor.

Cast: Frank Sinatra (*Zack Thomas*), Dean Martin (*Joe Jarrett*), Anita
Ekberg (*Elya Carlson*), Ursula Andress (*Maxine Richter*), Charles
Bronson (*Matson*), Victor Buono (*Harvey Burden*)

ROBIN AND THE SEVEN HOODS (1964)

Director: Gordon Douglas
Producer: Frank Sinatra
Executive Producer: Howard W. Koch
Original screenplay by David R. Schwartz
Music composed and conducted by Nelson Riddle
Orchestrations by Gil Grau
Associate Producer and Director of Photography: William H. Daniels
*A P.C. Productions Picture. Released by Warner Bros. Technicolor;
Panavision*

Cast: Frank Sinatra (*Robbo*), Dean Martin (*John*), Sammy Davis Jr. (*Will*),
Peter Falk (*Guy Gisborne*), Barbara Rush (*Marian*), Victor Buono (*Sheriff
Potts*), Hank Henry (*Six Seconds*)

NONE BUT THE BRAVE (1965)

Producer and Director: Frank Sinatra
Executive Producer: Howard W. Koch
Associate Producer: William H. Daniels
Producer for Tokyo Eiga Company and original story by Kikumaru
Okuda
Screenplay by John Twist and Katsuya Susaki
Music composed by Johnny Williams
Music supervised and conducted by Morris Stoloff
Japanese music advisor: K. Hirose

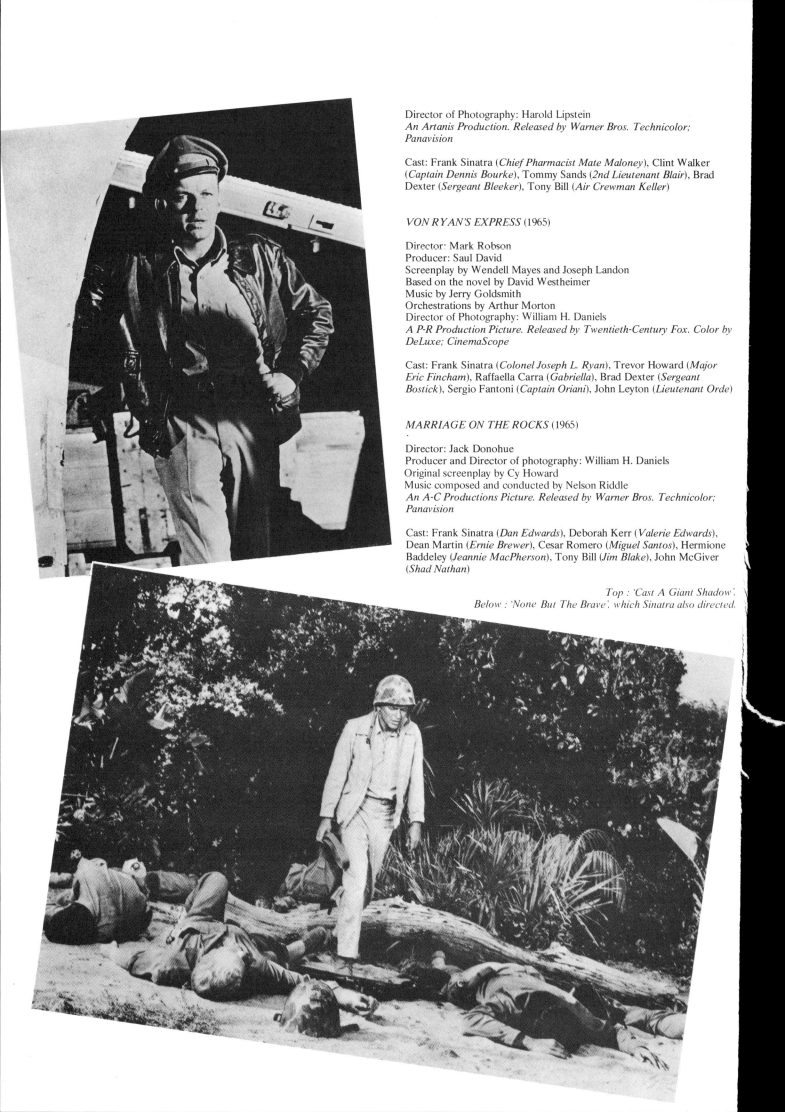

Director of Photography: Harold Lipstein
An Artanis Production. Released by Warner Bros. Technicolor; Panavision

Cast: Frank Sinatra (*Chief Pharmacist Mate Maloney*), Clint Walker (*Captain Dennis Bourke*), Tommy Sands (*2nd Lieutenant Blair*), Brad Dexter (*Sergeant Bleeker*), Tony Bill (*Air Crewman Keller*)

VON RYAN'S EXPRESS (1965)

Director: Mark Robson
Producer: Saul David
Screenplay by Wendell Mayes and Joseph Landon
Based on the novel by David Westheimer
Music by Jerry Goldsmith
Orchestrations by Arthur Morton
Director of Photography: William H. Daniels
A P-R Production Picture. Released by Twentieth-Century Fox. Color by DeLuxe; CinemaScope

Cast: Frank Sinatra (*Colonel Joseph L. Ryan*), Trevor Howard (*Major Eric Fincham*), Raffaella Carra (*Gabriella*), Brad Dexter (*Sergeant Bostick*), Sergio Fantoni (*Captain Oriani*), John Leyton (*Lieutenant Orde*)

MARRIAGE ON THE ROCKS (1965)

Director: Jack Donohue
Producer and Director of photography: William H. Daniels
Original screenplay by Cy Howard
Music composed and conducted by Nelson Riddle
An A-C Productions Picture. Released by Warner Bros. Technicolor; Panavision

Cast: Frank Sinatra (*Dan Edwards*), Deborah Kerr (*Valerie Edwards*), Dean Martin (*Ernie Brewer*), Cesar Romero (*Miguel Santos*), Hermione Baddeley (*Jeannie MacPherson*), Tony Bill (*Jim Blake*), John McGiver (*Shad Nathan*)

Top : 'Cast A Giant Shadow'.
Below : 'None But The Brave', which Sinatra also directed.

CAST A GIANT SHADOW (1966)

Producer and Director: Melville Shavelson
Co-producer: Michael Wayne
Screenplay by Melville Shavelson
Based on the book by Ted Berkman
Music composed and conducted by Elmer Bernstein
Orchestrations by Leo Shuken and Jack Hayes
Director of Photography: Aldo Tonti
A Mirisch-Llenroc-Batjac Production. Released by United Artists. Color by DeLuxe; Panavision

Cast: Kirk Douglas (*Col. David 'Mickey' Marcus*), Senta Berger (*Magda Simon*), Angie Dickinson (*Emma Marcus*), James Donald (*Major Safir*), Stathis Giallelis (*Ram Oren*), Luther Adler (*Jacob Zion*), Gary Merrill (*Pentagon Chief of Staff*), Haym Topol (*Abou Ibn Kader*)

THE OSCAR (1966)

Director: Russell Rouse
Producer: Clarence Greene
Executive Producer: Joseph E. Levine
Screenplay by Harlan Ellison, Russell Rouse and Clarence Greene
Based on the novel by Richard Sale
Music by Percy Faith
Orchestrations by Leo Shuken and Jack Hayes
Director of Photography: Joseph Ruttenberg
A Greene-Rouse Production. Released by Embassy Pictures. Pathe Color

Cast: Stephen Boyd (*Frank Lane*), Elke Sommer (*Kay Bergdahl*), Milton Berle (*Kappy Kapstetter*), Eleanor Parker (*Sophie Cantaro*), Joseph Cotten (*Kenneth H. Regan*), Jill St. John (*Laurel Scott*), Tony Bennett (*Hymie Kelly*), Edie Adams (*Trina Yale*), Ernest Borgnine (*Barney Yale*), Ed Begley (*Grobard*), Walter Brennan (*Orrin C. Quentin*), Broderick Crawford (*Sheriff*), James Dunn (*Network Executive*), Edith Head (*Herself*), Hedda Hopper (*Herself*), Peter Lawford (*Steve Marks*), Merle Oberon (*Herself*), Nancy Sinatra (*Herself*)

ASSAULT ON A QUEEN (1966)

Director: Jack Donohue
Producer: William Goetz
Screenplay by Rod Serling
Based on the novel by Jack Finney
Music by Duke Ellington
Orchestral arrangements by Van Cleave and Frank Comstock
Associate Producer and Director of Photography: William H. Daniels
A Sinatra Enterprises-Seven Arts Production. Released by Paramount. Technicolor; Panavision

Cast: Frank Sinatra (*Mark Brittain*), Virna Lisi (*Rosa Lucchesi*), Tony Franciosa (*Vic Rossiter*), Richard Conte (*Tony Moreno*), Alf Kjellin (*Eric Lauffnauer*), Errol John (*Linc Langley*), Murray Matheson (*Captain, Queen Mary*)

THE NAKED RUNNER (1967)

Director: Sidney J. Furie
Producer: Brad Dexter
Screenplay by Stanley Mann
Based on the novel by Francis Clifford
Music by Harry Sukman
Orchestrations by Herbert Spencer
Director of Photography: Otto Heller
A Sinatra Enterprises Production. Released by Warner Bros. Technicolor; Techniscope

Cast: Frank Sinatra (*Sam Laker*), Peter Vaughan (*Slattery*), Derren Nesbitt (*Colonel Hartmann*), Nadia Gray (*Karen*), Toby Robins (*Ruth*), Inger Stratton (*Anna*)

TONY ROME (1967)

Director: Gordon Douglas
Producer: Aaron Rosenberg

Screenplay by Richard L. Breen
Based on the novel *Miami Mayhem* by Marvin H. Albert
Music by Billy May
Director of Photography: Joseph Biroc
An Arcola-Millfield Production. Released by 20th Century-Fox. Color by DeLuxe; Panavision

Cast: Frank Sinatra (*Tony Rome*), Jill St. John (*Ann Archer*), Richard Conte (*Lieutenant Santini*), Gena Rowlands (*Rita Kosterman*), Simon Oakland (*Rudolph Kosterman*), Jeffrey Lynn (*Adam Boyd*), Lloyd Bochner (*Vic Rood*)

THE DETECTIVE (1968)

Director: Gordon Douglas
Producer: Aaron Rosenberg
Screenplay by Abby Mann
Based on the novel by Roderick Thorp
Music by Jerry Goldsmith
Orchestration by Warren Barker
Director of Photography: Joseph Biroc
An Arcola-Millfield Production. Released by 20th Century-Fox. Color by DeLuxe; Panavision

Cast: Frank Sinatra (*Joe Leland*), Lee Remick (*Karen Leland*), Ralph Meeker (*Lt. Curran*), Jack Klugman (*Lt. Dave Schoenstein*), Horace McMahon (*Chief Tom Farrell*), Lloyd Bochner (*Dr. Wendell Roberts*), William Windom (*Colin MacIver*), Tony Musante (*Felix Tesla*), Al Freeman Jr. (*Det. Robbie Loughren*), Robert Duvall (*Det. Mickey Nestor*), Jacqueline Bisset (*Norma MacIver*)

LADY IN CEMENT (1968)

Director: Gordon Douglas
Producer: Aaron Rosenberg
Screenplay by Marvin H. Albert and Jack Guss
Based on the novel by Marvin H. Albert
Music composed and conducted by Jugo Montenegro
Orchestration by Billy May
Director of Photography: Joseph Biroc
An Arcola-Millfield Production. Released by 20th Century-Fox. Color by DeLuxe; Panavision

Cast: Frank Sinatra (*Tony Rome*), Raquel Welch (*Kit Forrest*), Dan Blocker (*Earl Gronsky*), Richard Conte (*Lieutenant Santini*), Martin Gabel (*Al Mungar*), Lainie Kazan (*Maria Baretto*), Pat Henry (*Hal Rubin*)

DIRTY DINGUS MAGEE (1970)

Producer and Director: Burt Kennedy
Screenplay by Tom and Frank Waldman and Joseph Heller
Based on the novel *The Ballad of Dingus Magee* by David Markson
Music by Jeff Alexander; additional music by Billy Strange
Title song by Mack David, sung by The Mike Curb Congregation
Director of Photography: Harry Stradling
Released by Metro-Goldwyn-Mayer. MetroColor; Panavision

Cast: Frank Sinatra (*Dingus Magee*), George Kennedy (*Hoke Birdsill*), Anne Jackson (*Belle Knops*), Lois Nettleton (*Prudence Frost*), Jack Elam (*John Wesley Hardin*)

CONTRACT ON CHERRY STREET (1977)

Director: William A. Grahame
Producer: Hugh Benson
Screenplay by Edward Anhalt
Based on the novel by Phillip Rosenberg
Music by Jenny Goldsmith
Director of photography: Jack Priestley

Cast: Frank Sinatra (*Frank Hovannes*), Martin Balsam (*Ernie Weinberg*), Jay Black (*Tommy Sinardos*), Verna Bloom (*Emily Hovannes*), Joe de Santis (*Vin Seruto*), Harry Guardino (*Ron Polito*).

DISCOGRAPHY

Note: For this representative discography, Frank Sinatra's major album releases with RCA Victor, Columbia, Capitol and Reprise have been included, with their U.S. catalogue numbers, years of recording and track listings. Some less important albums released in the United States and in Britain by the major labels have also been listed.

With RCA Victor

Title and US Catalogue Number	Recording dates

WE THREE   1942
Dig Down Deep/The Lamplighter's Serenade/Night And Day/The Night We Called It A Day/The Song Is You/Tell Me At Midnight/We Three/I'll Be Seeing You/It Started All Over Again/Fools Rush In/This Is The Beginning Of The End/Whispering

THE DORSEY/SINATRA SESSIONS   1940-42
(Set of 6 Albums)
The Sky Fell Down/Too Romantic/Shake Down The Stars/Moments In The Moonlight/I'll Be Seeing You/Say It/Polka Dots And Moonbeams/The Fable Of The Rose/This Is The Beginning Of The End/Hear My Song Violetta/Fools Rush In/Devil May Care/April Played The Fiddle/I Haven't Time To Be A Millionaire/Imagination/Yours Is My Heart Alone/You're Lonely And I'm Lonely/East Of The Sun/Head On My Pillow/It's A Lovely Day Tomorrow/I'll Never Smile Again/All This And Heaven Too/Where Do You Keep Your Heart/Whispering/Trade Winds/The One I Love/The Call Of The Canyon/Love Lies/I Could Make You Care/The World Is In My Arms/Our Love Affair/Looking For Yesterday/Tell Me At Midnight/We Three/When You Awake/Anything/Shadows On The Sand/You're Breaking My Heart All Over Again/I'd Know You Anywhere/Do You Know Why/Not So Long Ago/Stardust/Oh Look At Me Now/You Might Have Belonged To Another/You Lucky People You/It's Always You/I Tried/Dolores/Without A Song/Do I Worry/Everything Happens To Me/Let's Get Away From It All/I'll Never Let A Day Pass By/Love Me As I Am/This Love Of Mine/I Guess I'll Have To Dream The Rest/You And I/Neiani/Free For All/Blue Skies/Two In Love/Pale Moon/I Think Of You/How Do You Do Without Me/A Sinner Kissed An Angel/Violets For Your Furs/The Sunshine Of Your Smile/How About You/Snooty Little Cutie/Poor You/I'll Take Tallulah/The Last Call For Love/Somewhere A Voice Is Calling/Just As Though You Were Here/Street Of Dreams/Take Me/Be Careful It's My Heart/In The Blue Of The Evening/Dig Down Deep/There Are Such Things/Daybreak/It Started All Over Again/Light A Candle In The Chapel

With Columbia Records

Title and US Catalogue Number	Recording dates

FRANKIE/CL 606   1943-51
Hello Young Lovers/I Only Have Eyes For You/Falling In Love With Love/You'll Never Know/It All Depends On You/S'posin'/All Of Me/Time After Time/How Cute Can You Be/Almost Like Being In Love/Nancy/Oh What It Seemed To Be

THE VOICE/CL 743   1944-50
I Don't Know Why/Try A Little Tenderness/A Ghost Of A Chance/Paradise/These Foolish Things/Laura/

She's Funny That Way/Fools Rush In/Over The Rainbow/That Old Black Magic/Spring Is Here/Lover

THAT OLD FEELING/CL 902   1945-49
That Old Feeling/Blue Skies/Autumn In New York/Don't Cry Joe/The Nearness Of You/That Lucky Old Sun/Full Moon And Empty Arms/Once In Love With Amy/A Fellow Needs A Girl/Poinciana/For Every Man There's A Woman/Mean To Me

ADVENTURES OF THE HEART/CL 953   1945-49
I Guess I'll Have To Dream The Rest/If Only She'd Look My Way/Love Me/Nevertheless/We Kiss In A Shadow/I Am Loved/Take My Love/I Could Write A Book/Mad About You/Sorry/Stromboli/It's Only A Paper Moon

CHRISTMAS DREAMING/CL 1032   1945-50
(Arranged and conducted by Axel Stordahl) White Christmas/Jingle Bells/O Little Town Of Bethlehem/Have Yourself A Merry Little Christmas/Christmas Dreaming/Silent Night/It Came Upon The Midnight Clear/Adeste Fideles/Santa Claus Is Comin' To Town/Let It Snow Let It Snow Let It Snow

THE FRANK SINATRA STORY IN MUSIC/
CL 1130   1945-52
Ciribiribin/All Or Nothing At All/You'll Never Know/If You Are But A Dream/Nancy/You Go To My Head/Stormy Weather/The House I Live In/If I Loved You/Soliloquy/How Deep Is The Ocean/Ol' Man River

THE FRANK SINATRA STORY IN MUSIC/
CL 1131   1945-52
You'll Never Walk Alone/I Concentrate On You/Castle Rock/Why Was I Born/I've Got A Crush On You/Begin The Beguine/The Birth Of The Blues/April In Paris/I'm Glad There Is You/Laura/One For My Baby/Put Your Dreams Away
(Two 'Frank Sinatra Story' Albums also available as a set, C2L6)

PUT YOUR DREAMS AWAY/CL 1136   1944-47
(Arranged and conducted by Axel Stordahl) I Dream Of You/Dream/I Have But One Heart/The Girl That I Marry/The Things We Did Last Summer/Lost In The Stars/If I Forget You/Mam'selle/The Song Is You/It Never Entered My Mind/Ain'tcha Ever Comin' Back/Put Your Dreams Away

LOVE IS A KICK/CL 1241 1944-52
You Do Something To Me/Bim Bam Baby/My Blue
Heaven/When You're Smiling/Saturday Night/Bye Bye
Baby/The Continental/Deep Night/Should I/American
Beauty Rose/Five Minutes More/Farewell Farewell To
Love

THE BROADWAY KICK/CL 1297 1946-51
There's No Business Like Show Business/They Say It's
Wonderful/Some Enchanted Evening/You're My Girl/
Lost In The Stars/Why Can't You Behave/I Whistle A
Happy Tune/The Girl That I Marry/Can't You Just See
Yourself/There But For You Go I/Bali Ha'i/Bess Oh
Where's My Bess

COME BACK TO SORRENTO/CL 1359 1944-52
(Arranged and conducted by Axel Stordahl) When The
Sun Goes Down/None But The Lonely Heart/Luna
Rossa/My Melancholy Baby/Embraceable You/Day By
Day/Come Back To Sorrento/I Hear A Rhapsody/
Someone To Watch Over Me/September Song/Among
My Souvenirs/Always

REFLECTIONS/CL 1448 1944-50
Stella By Starlight/But Beautiful/Body And Soul/
Where Or When/When Your Lover Has Gone/Strange
Music/Goodnight Irene/Dear Little Boy Of Mine/
Mighty Lak' A Rose/The Cradle Song/Nature Boy/All
The Things You Are

*GREATEST HITS, THE EARLY YEARS
VOLUME 1*/CL 2474 1943-47
I've Got A Crush On You/If You Are But A Dream/
Nancy/The Girl That I Marry/The House I Live In/
Dream/Saturday Night/Five Minutes More/The Coffee
Song/Sunday Monday Or Always/Put Your Dreams
Away

*GREATEST HITS, THE EARLY YEARS
VOLUME 2*/CL 2572 1943-51
Mean To Me/I Have But One Heart/The Moon Was
Yellow/Full Moon And Empty Arms/Time After
Time/I'm A Fool To Want You/Day By Day/I
Couldn't Sleep A Wink Last Night/Ol' Man River/
People Will Say We're In Love/September Song

*THE ESSENTIAL FRANK SINATRA
VOLUME 1*/CL 2739/Stereo CS 9539 1939-46
From The Bottom Of My Heart/Melancholy Mood/My
Buddy/Here Come The Night/Close To You/There's
No You/The Charm Of You/When Your Lover Has
Gone/I Should Care/A Friend of Yours/My Shawl/
Nancy/You Are Too Beautiful/Why Shouldn't I/One
Love/Something Old Something New

*THE ESSENTIAL FRANK SINATRA
VOLUME 2*/CL 2740/Stereo CS 9540 1946-49
Blue Skies/Guess I'll Hang My Tears Out To Dry/Why
Shouldn't It Happen To Us/It's The Same Old Dream/
You Can Take My Word For It Baby/Sweet Lorraine/
My Romance/One For My Baby/It All Came True/
Poinciana/Body And Soul/I Went Down To Virginia/If
I Only Had A Match/Everybody Loves Somebody/
Comme Ci Comme Ca/If You Stub Your Toe On The
Moon

*THE ESSENTIAL FRANK SINATRA
VOLUME 3*/CL 2741/CS 9541 1949-52
The Right Girl For Me/The Hucklebuck/If I Ever Love
Again/Why Remind Me/Sunshine Cake/Sure Thing/
It's Only A Paper Moon/My Blue Heaven/Nevertheless/
You're The One/Love Me/I'm A Fool To Want You/
The Birth Of The Blues/Walkin' In The Sunshine/
Azure-Te/Why Try To Change Me Now
(Boxed set of 3 albums S3L42/Stereo S3S42)

IN HOLLYWOOD/CL 2913 1943-49
I Couldn't Sleep A Wink Last Night/The Music
Stopped/A Lovely Way To Spend An Evening/I
Begged Her/What Makes The Sunset/I Fall In Love
Too Easily/The Charm Of You/The House I Live In/
Time After Time/It's The Same Old Dream/The
Brooklyn Bridge/I Believe/Ever Homeward/Senorita/
If I Steal A Kiss/The Right Girl For Me

SINATRA RARITIES VOLUME 1/MM 1 1943-51
Old School Teacher/Home On The Range/You'll
Know When It Happens/So They Tell Me/It's All Up
To You/My Love For You/Catana/Help Yourself To
My Heart/Kisses and Tears/There's Something
Missing/Meet Me At The Copa/A Good Man Is Hard
To Find/If You Please/Lily Belle/Don't Forget Tonight
Tomorrow/All Through The Day

SINGS EVERGREENS/Avenue AV INT 1004 1945-52
I've Got A Crush On You/They Say It's Wonderful/
The Girl That I Marry/I Hear A Rhapsody/If I Loved
You/You Do Something To Me/Laura/Why Was I
Born/A Ghost Of A Chance/The Music Stopped/I
Love You/Strange Music

THE MASTER OF SONG/Avenue AV INT 1012 1947-50
While The Angelus Was Ringing/When Is Sometime/
Bop Goes My Heart/Just For Now/My Cousin Louella/
Life Is So Peculiar/Chattanoogie Shoe Shine Boy/The
Old Master Painter/A Fella With An Umbrella/It Only
Happens When I Dance With You/If You Stub Your
Toe On The Moon/Sunflower

THE ROMANTIC SINATRA/Avenue AV INT 1012 1944-50
One Finger Melody/It Happens Every Spring/If I Ever
Love Again/London By Night/If Only She's Look My
Way/The Stars Will Remember/I'm Sorry I Made You
Cry/All Of Me/My Girl/My Love For You/Kiss Me
Again/Somewhere In The Night

More Columbia Releases

American releases

Songs By Sinatra/C 124; Frank Sinatra/C; Get
Happy/CL 2521; I've Got A Crush On You/CL 2539;
Christmas With Sinatra/CL 2542; The Voice Of Frank
Sinatra/CL 6001; Christmas Songs By Sinatra/CL 6019;
Frankly Sentimental/CL 6059; Songs By Sinatra
Volume 1/CL 6087; Dedicated To You/CL 6096; Sing
and Dance With Frank Sinatra/CL 6143; I've Got A
Crush On You/CL 6290; Young At Heart (with Doris
Day)/CL 6339; Romantic Songs From The Early Years/
HL 7405; Someone To Watch Over Me/HS 11277;
Frank Sinatra/HS 11390; Greatest Hits The Early

Years/KH 30318; In The Beginning/KG 31358; The
Frank Sinatra Story In Music/C2L6 (Double album set)

British Releases

Sing And Dance With Frank Sinatra/BBR 8003;
Fabulous Frank/BBR 8038; Young At Heart/BBR 8040;
Christmas Dreaming/BBR 8114; The Frank Sinatra
Story/TFL 5030; Doris And Frank/BBL7137; Sinatra
Souvenir/TFL 5138; Sinatra Plus/SET 303; The Early
Years/SIIM 500; IIave Yourself A Merry Little
Christmas/SHM 521; Someone To Watch Over Me/
SHM 592; Frank Sinatra/SHM 676; Greatest Hits/SHM
736; The Early Days/AV INT 1001; Stars Of
Hollywood/AV INT 1011

With Capitol Records

Title and US Catalogue Number   Recording Dates

*FRANK SINATRA CONDUCTS TONE POEMS
OF COLOUR*/W 735

THE MAN I LOVE/T 864
Vocals by Peggy Lee, arranged by Nelson Riddle,
conducted by Frank Sinatra

SLEEP WARM/ST 1150
Vocals by Dean Martin, arranged by Pete King,
conducted by Frank Sinatra

IN THE WEE SMALL HOURS/W 581   1954-55
(Arranged and conducted by Nelson Riddle) In The
Wee Small Hours Of The Morning/Mood Indigo/Glad
To Be Unhappy/I Get Along Without You Very Well/
Deep In A Dream/I See Your Face Before Me/Can't
We Be Friends/When Your Lover Has Gone/What Is
This Thing Called Love/Last Night When We Were
Young/I'll Be Around/Ill Wind/It Never Entered My
Mind/Dancing On The Ceiling/I'll Never Be The
Same/This Love Of Mine

SONGS FOR SWINGIN' LOVERS/W 653   1956
(Arranged and conducted by Nelson Riddle) You Make
Me Feel So Young/It Happened In Monterey/You're
Getting To Be A Habit With Me/You Brought A New
Kind Of Love To Me/Too Marvellous For Words/Old
Devil Moon/Pennies From Heaven/Love Is Here To
Stay/I've Got You Under My Skin/I Thought About
You/We'll Be Together Again/Makin' Whoopee/
Swingin' Down The Lane/Anything Goes/How About
You

HIGH SOCIETY/SW 750   1956
(Conducted by Johnny Green) Overture/Calypso (Louis
Armstrong)/Little One (Bing Crosby)/Who Wants To
Be A Millionaire/True Love (Bing Crosby and Grace
Kelly)/You're Sensational/I Love You Samantha (Bing
Crosby)/Now You Has Jazz (Crosby and Armstrong)/
Well Did You Evah (with Crosby)/Mind If I Make Love
To You

THIS IS SINATRA/T 768   1953-54
(Arranged and conducted by Nelson Riddle) I've Got
The World On A String/Three Coins In The
Fountain/Love And Marriage/From Here To Eternity/
South Of The Border/Rain/The Gal That Got Away/
Young At Heart/Learnin' The Blues/My One And Only
Love/The Tender Trap/Don't Worry 'Bout Me

CLOSE TO YOU/W 789   1956
(Arranged and conducted by Nelson Riddle) Close To
You/P.S. I Love You/Love Locked Out/Everything
Happens To You/I've Had My Moments/I Couldn't
Sleep A Wink Last Night/The End Of A Love Affair/
It's Easy To Remember/Don't Like Goodbyes/With

Every Breath I Take/Blame It On My Youth/It Could
Happen To You

A SWINGIN' AFFAIR/W 803   1956
(Arranged and conducted by Nelson Riddle) Night And
Day/I Wish I Were In Love Again/I Got Plenty Of
Nuttin'/I Guess I'll Have To Change My Plan/Nice
Work If You Can Get It/Stars Fell On Alabama/No
One Ever Tells You/I Won't Dance/The Lonesome
Road/At Long Last Love/You'd Be So Nice To Come
Home To/I Got It Bad And That Ain't Good/From
This Moment On/If I Had You/Oh Look At Me Now

WHERE ARE YOU?/SW 855   1957
(Arranged and conducted by Gordon Jenkins) Where
Are You?/The Night We Called It A Day/I Cover The
Waterfront/Maybe You'll Be There/Laura/Lonely
Town/Autumn Leaves/I'm A Fool To Want You/I
Think Of You/Where Is The One/There's No
You/Baby Won't You Please Come Home

A JOLLY CHRISTMAS FROM FRANK SINATRA/
W 894   1957
(Arranged and conducted by Gordon Jenkins, with the
Ralph Brewster Singers) Jingle Bells/The Christmas
Song/Mistletoe And Holly/I'll Be Home For Christmas/
The First Noel/The Christmas Waltz/Have Yourself A
Merry Little Christmas/Hark The Herald Angels Sing/
O Little Town Of Bethlehem/Adeste Fideles/It Came
Upon A Midnight Clear/Silent Night

PAL JOEY/W 912   1957
(Arranged by Nelson Riddle, conducted by Morris
Stoloff and Nelson Riddle) Overture/That Terrific
Rainbow (Kim Novak)/I Didn't Know What Time It
Was/Do It The Hard Way/Great Big Town/There's A

Small Hotel/Zip (Rita Hayworth)/I Could Write A Book/Bewitched (Rita Hayworth)/The Lady Is A Tramp/Plant You Now Dig You Later/My Funny Valentine (Kim Novak)/You Mustn't Kick It Around/Bewitched/Strip Number/What Do I Care For A Dame

COME FLY WITH ME/SW 920   1957
(Arranged and conducted by Billy May) Come Fly With Me/Around The World/Isle Of Capri/Moonlight In Vermont/Autumn In New York/On The Road To Mandalay/Let's Get Away From It All/April In Paris/London By Night/Brazil/Blue Hawaii/It's Nice To Go Trav'ling

THIS IS SINATRA VOLUME 2/W 982   1954-57
(Arranged and conducted by Nelson Riddle) Hey Jealous Lover/Everybody Loves Somebody/Something Wonderful Happens In Summer/Half As Lovely/You're Cheatin' Yourself/You'll Always Be The One I Love/You Forgot All The Words/How Little We Know/Time After Time/Crazy Love/Wait For Me/If You Are But A Dream/So Long My Love/It's The Same Old Dream/I Believe/Put Your Dreams Away

FRANK SINATRA SINGS FOR ONLY THE LONELY/SW 1053   1958
(Arranged and conducted by Nelson Riddle) Only The Lonely/Angel Eyes/What's New/It's A Lonesome Old Town/Willow Weep For Me/Goodbye/Blues In The Night/Guess I'll Hang My Tears Out To Dry/Ebb Tide/Spring Is Here/Gone With The Wind/One For My Baby

COME DANCE WITH ME/SW 1069   1958
(Arranged and conducted by Billy May) Come Dance With Me/Something's Gotta Give/Just In Time/Dancing In The Dark/Too Close For Comfort/I Could Have Danced All Night/Saturday Night/Day In Day Out/Cheek To Cheek/Baubles Bangles And Beads/The Song Is You/The Last Dance

LOOK TO YOUR HEART/W 1164   1953-55
(Arranged and conducted by Nelson Riddle, except one track) Look To Your Heart/Anytime Anywhere/Not As A Stranger/Our Town/You My Love/Same Old Saturday Night/Fairy Tale/The Impatient Years/I Could Have Told You/When I Stop Loving You/If I Had Three Wishes/I'm Gonna Live Till I Die

NO ONE CARES/SW 1221   1959
(Arranged and conducted by Gordon Jenkins) When No One Cares/A Cottage For Sale/Stormy Weather/Where Do You Go/A Ghost Of A Chance/Here's That Rainy Day/I Can't Get Started/Why Try To Change Me Now/Just Friends/I'll Never Smile Again/None But The Lonely Heart

CAN-CAN/SW 1301   1960
(Arranged and conducted by Nelson Riddle) Entr'acte/It's All Right With Me/Come Along With Me/(Shirley MacLaine)/Live And Let Live (Maurice Chevalier and Louis Jourdan)/You Do Something To Me (Louis Jourdan)/Let's Do It (Shirley MacLaine)/Main Title/Montmart' (with Maurice Chevalier)/C'est Magnifique/Maidens Typical Of France/Just One Of Those Things (Maurice Chevalier)/I Love Paris (with Maurice Chevalier)/Can-Can

NICE 'N' EASY/SW 1417   1960
(Arranged and conducted by Nelson Riddle) Nice 'N' Easy/That Old Feeling/How Deep Is The Ocean/I've Got A Crush On You/You Go To My Head/Fools Rush In/Nevertheless/She's Funny That Way/Try A Little Tenderness/Embraceable You/Mamselle/Dream

SWING EASY/W 1429   1953-54
(Arranged and conducted by Nelson Riddle, except one track) Jeepers Creepers/Taking A Chance On Love/Wrap Your Troubles In Dreams/Lean Baby/I Love You/I'm Gonna Sit Right Down And Write Myself A Letter/Get Happy/All Of Me/How Could You Do A Thing Like That To Me/Why Should I Cry Over You/Sunday/Just One Of Those Things

SONGS FOR YOUNG LOVERS/W 1432   1953-54
(Arranged and conducted by Nelson Riddle) The Girl Next Door/They Can't Take That Away From Me/Violets For Your Furs/Someone To Watch Over Me/My One And Only Love/Little Girl Blue/Like Someone In Love/A Foggy Day/It Worries Me/I Can Read Between The Lines/I Get A Kick Out Of You/My Funny Valentine

SINATRA'S SWINGING SESSION!/SW 1491   1960
(Arranged and conducted by Nelson Riddle) When You're Smiling/Blue Moon/S'posin'/It All Depends On You/It's Only A Paper Moon/My Blue Heaven/Should I/September In The Rain/Always/I Can't Believe That You're In Love With Me/I Concentrate On You/You Do Something To Me.

ALL THE WAY/SW 1538   1957-60
(Arranged and conducted by Nelson Riddle) High Hopes/Talk To Me/French Foreign Legion/To Love And Be Loved/River Stay 'Way From My Door/All The Way/It's Over It's Over It's Over/Ol' MacDonald/This Was My Love/All My Tomorrows/Sleep Warm/Witchcraft

COME SWING WITH ME!/SW 1594   1961
(Arranged by Heinie Beau and Billy May, conducted by Billy May) Day By Day/Sentimental Journey/Almost Like Being In Love/Five Minutes More/American

Beauty Rose/Yes Indeed/On The Sunny Side Of The
Street/Don't Take Your Love From Me/That Old
Black Magic/Lover/Paper Doll/I've Heard That Song
Before

POINT OF NO RETURN/SW 1676   1961
(Arranged by Heinie Beau and Axel Stordahl,
conducted by Axel Stordahl) When The World Was
Young/I'll Remember April/September Song/A Million
Dreams Ago/I'll See You Again/There Will Never Be
Another You/Somewhere Along The Way/It's A Blue
World/These Foolish Things/As Time Goes By/I'll Be
Seeing You/Memories Of You

SINATRA SINGS . . . OF LOVE AND THINGS/
SW 1729   1957-62
The Nearness Of You/Hidden Persuasion/The Moon
Was Yellow/I Love Paris/Monique/Chicago/Love
Looks So Well On You/Sentimental Baby/Mr
Success/They Came To Cordura/I Gotta Right To Sing
The Blues/Something Wonderful Happens In Summer

*FRANK SINATRA SINGS RODGERS AND
HART*/W 1825   1953-61
The Lady Is A Tramp/Little Girl Blue/Spring Is Here/
Dancing On The Ceiling/Wait Till You See Her/I Wish
I Were In Love Again/Lover/It Never Entered My
Mind/My Funny Valentine/It's Easy To Remember/
Glad To Be Unhappy/Blue Moon

TELL HER YOU LOVE HER/T 1919   1955-57
(Arranged and conducted by Nelson Riddle) Tell Her
You Love Her/Ill Wind/Love Is Here To Stay/It Never
Entered My Mind/Can't We Be Friends/I've Got It Bad
And That Ain't Good/Makin' Whoopee/Weep They
Will/Pennies From Heaven/When Your Love Has
Gone/I Guess I'll Have To Change My Plan/Night And
Day

FOREVER FRANK/T 2602   1953-58
Can I Steal A Little Love/Your Love For Me/Chicago/
Melody Of Love/Two Hearts Two Kisses/Flowers
Mean Forgiveness/Same Old Song And Dance/It It's
The Last Thing I Do/From The Bottom To The Top/
Don't Make A Beggar Of Me/You'll Get Yours

SINATRA LIKE NEVER BEFORE/Longines
SYS 5637   1953-60
The One I Love Belongs To Somebody Else/I Couldn't
Care Less/Five Hundred Guys/There's A Flaw In My
Flue/Take A Chance/Day In Day Out/I'm Walking
Behind You/It All Depends On You/Memories Of
You/Don't Change Your Mind About Me

More Capitol Releases

American Releases

Songs For Young Lovers/H 488; Swing Easy/H 528;
Swing Easy/Songs For Young Lovers/W 587; The
Great Years/W 1726 (3 album set); Sinatra Sings The
Select Johnny Mercer/W 1984; The Great Hits Of
Frank Sinatra/T 2036; Sinatra Sings The Select Harold
Arlen/W 2123; Sinatra Sings The Select Cole Porter/W
2301; The Frank Sinatra De-Luxe Set/STFL 2814 (6
album set); The Best Of Frank Sinatra/DKAO 2950;
The Sinatra Touch/DNFR 7630 (6 album set); Close
Up/DWBB 254 (Double album); Cole Porter Song
Book/94408; Sentimental Journey/90986; Round
1/SABB 11357 (Double album); What Is This Thing
Called Love/DF 530; The Night We Called It A Day/
SF 531; My One And Only Love/DF 725; Sentimental
Journey/SF 726; The Nearness Of You/SPC 3450; Try
A Little Tenderness/SPC 3452; Nevertheless/SPC 3456;
Just One Of Those Things/SPC 3457; This Love Of
Mine/SPC 3458; My Cole Porter/SPC 3463; Sinatra
The Works/LS 308A (10 album set); One More For
The Road/ST 11309

British Releases

Songs For Young Lovers/LC 6654; Swing Easy/LC
6689; In The Wee Small Hours Part 1/LC 6702; In The
Wee Small Hours Part 2/LC 6705; London By Night/T
20389; My Funny Valentine/T 20577; Singing and
Swinging/W 20652; The Connoisseur's Sinatra/T 20734;
Sinatra For The Sophisticated/T 20757; The Best Of
Frank Sinatra/ST 21140; The Very Best Of Frank
Sinatra/EST 23256; Look Over Your Shoulder/TP 81;
September Song/T 635; Sinatra Sings The Select Cole
Porter/SRS 5009; Sinatra Sings Mercer/SRS 5167;
Swingin' Sinatra/DUO 102; Sinatra Sings Cahn And Van
Heusen/OU 2044; When Your Lover Has Gone/101;
Sinatra Sings Music For Pleasure/MFP 1120; Sunday
And Every Day/MFP 1324; Close To You/MFP 1415;
Nice 'N' Easy/MFP 5258; One For My Baby/MFP
50089; Sinatra Swings/MFP 50320; Love/SPR 90039;
Pal Joey/VMP 1005; The Rare Sinatra/EST 24311.

With Reprise Records

Title and US Catalogue Number	Recording dates
RING-A-DING DING!/FS 1001	1960

(Arranged and conducted by Johnny Mandel) Ring-A-
Ding Ding/Let's Fall In Love/Be Careful It's My
Heart/A Foggy Day/A Fine Romance/In The Still Of
The Night/The Coffee Song/When I Take My Sugar
To Tea/Let's Face The Music And Dance/You'd Be So

Easy To Love/You And The Night And The Music/I've Got My Love to Keep Me Warm

SINATRA SWINGS . . ./FS 1002   1961
(Arranged and conducted by Billy May) Falling In Love With Love/The Curse Of An Aching Heart/Don't Cry Joe/Please Don't Talk About Me When I'm Gone/Love Walked In/Granada/I Never Knew/Don't Be That Way/Moonlight On The Ganges/It's A Wonderful World/Have You Met Miss Jones/You're Nobody Till Somebody Loves You

I REMEMBER TOMMY . . ./FS 1003   1961
(Arranged and conducted by Sy Oliver) I'm Getting Sentimental Over You/Imagination/There Are Such Things/East Of The Sun/Daybreak/Without A Song/I'll Be Seeing You/Take Me/It's Always You/Polka Dolts And Moonbeams/It Started All Over Again/The One I Love Belongs To Somebody Else (with Sy Oliver)/I'm Getting Sentimental Over You (edited)

SINATRA AND STRINGS/FS 1004   1961
(Arranged and conducted by Don Costa) I Hadn't Anyone Till You/Night And Day/Misty/Stardust/Come Rain Or Come Shine/It Might As Well Be Spring/Prisoner Of Love/That's All/All Or Nothing At All/Yesterdays

SINATRA AND SWINGIN' BRASS/FS 1005   1962
(Arranged and conducted by Neal Hefti) Goody Goody/They Can't Take That Away From Me/At Long Last Love/I'm Beginning To See The Light/Don'cha Go 'Way Mad/I Get A Kick Out Of You/Tangerine/Love Is Just Around The Corner/Ain't She Sweet/Serenade In Blue/I Love You/Pick Yourself Up

*SINATRA SINGS GREAT SONGS
FROM GREAT BRITAIN/R9 1006*   1962
(Arranged and conducted by Robert Farnon) The Very Thought Of You/We'll Gather Lilacs/If I Had You/Now Is The Hour/The Gypsy/A Nightingale Sang In Berkeley Square/A Garden In The Rain/London By Night/We'll Meet Again/I'll Follow My Secret Heart

ALL ALONE/FS 1007   1962
(Arranged and conducted by Gordon Jenkins) All Alone/The Girl Next Door/Are You Lonesome Tonight/Charmaine/What'll I Do/When I Lost You/Oh How I Miss You Tonight/Indiscreet/Remember/Together/The Song Is Ended

SINATRA-BASIE/FS 1008   1962
(Arranged and conducted by Neal Hefti) Pennies From Heaven/Please Be Kind/The Tender Trap/Looking At The World Through Rose Coloured Glasses/My Kind Of Girl/I Only Have Eyes For You/Nice Work If You Can Get It/Learnin' The Blues/I'm Gonna Sit Right Down And Write Myself A Letter/I Won't Dance

THE CONCERT SINATRA/FS 1009   1963
(Arranged and conducted by Nelson Riddle) I Have Dreamed/My Heart Stood Still/Lost In The Stars/Ol' Man River/You'll Never Walk Alone/Bewitched/This Nearly Was Mine/Soliloquy

SINATRA'S SINATRA/FS 1010   1963
(Arranged and conducted by Nelson Riddle) I've Got You Under My Skin/In The Wee Small Hours Of The Morning/The Second Time Around/Nancy/Witchcraft/Young At Heart/All The Way/How Little We Know/Pocketful Of Miracles/Oh What It Seemed To Be/Call Me Irresponsible/Put Your Dreams Away

*FRANK SINATRA SINGS DAYS OF
WINE AND ROSES/FS 1011*   1963-64

(Arranged and conducted by Nelson Riddle) Days Of Wine And Roses/Moon River/The Way You Look Tonight/Three Coins In The Fountain/In The Cool Cool Cool Of The Evening/Secret Love/Swinging on A Star/It Might As Well Be Spring/The Continental/Love Is A Many Splendoured Thing/All The Way

IT MIGHT AS WELL BE SWING/FS 1012   1964
(Arranged and conducted by Quincy Jones) Fly Me To The Moon/I Wish You Love/I Believe In You/More/I Can't Stop Loving You/Hello Dolly/I Wanna Be Around/The Best Is Yet To Come/The Good Life/Wives And Lovers

SOFTLY AS I LEAVE YOU/FS 1013   1962-64
Emily/Here's To The Losers/Dear Heart/Come Blow Your Horn/Love Isn't Just For The Young/I Can't Believe I'm Losing You/Pass Me By/Softly As I Leave You/Then Suddenly Love/Available/Talk To Me Baby/The Look Of Love

SEPTEMBER OF MY YEARS/FS 1014   1965
(Arranged and conducted by Gordon Jenkins) The September Of My Years/How Old Am I/Don't Wait Too Long/It Gets Lonely Early/This Is All I Ask/Last Night When We Were Young/The Man In The Looking Glass/It Was A Very Good Year/When The Wind Was Green/Hello Young Lovers/I See It Now/Once Upon A Time/September Song

MY KIND OF BROADWAY/FS 1015   1961-65
Ev'rybody Has The Right To Be Wrong/Golden Moment/Luck Be A Lady/Lost In The Stars/Hello Dolly/I'll Only Miss Her When I Think Of Her/They Can't Take That Away From Me/Yesterdays/Nice Work If You Can Get It/Have You Met Miss Jones/Without A Song

SINATRA: A MAN AND HIS MUSIC/2FS 1016   1960-65
(set of 2 albums)
Put Your Dreams Away/All Or Nothing At All/I'll Never Smile Again/There Are Such Things/I'll Be Seeing You/The One I Love Belongs To Somebody Else/Polka Dots And Moonbeams/Night And Day/Oh What It Seemed To Be/Soliloquy/Nancy/The House I Live In/Extract From Film 'From Here To Eternity'/Come Fly With Me/How Little We Know/Learnin' The Blues/In The Wee Small Hours Of The Morning/Young At Heart/Witchcraft/All The Way/Love And Marriage/I've Got You Under My Skin/Ring-A-Ding Ding/The Second Time Around/The Summit (with Dean Martin et al)/The Oldest Established (with Bing Crosby et al)/Luck Be A Lady/Call Me Irresponsible/Fly Me To The Moon/Softly As I Leave You/My Kind Of Town/The September Of My Years

STRANGERS IN THE NIGHT/FS 1017   1966
(Arranged and conducted by Nelson Riddle—except for title track) Strangers In The Night/Summer Wind/All Or Nothing At All/Call Me/You're Driving Me Crazy/On A Clear Day/My Baby Just Cares For Me/Downtown/Yes Sir That's My Baby/The Most Beautiful Girl In The World

MOONLIGHT SINATRA/FS 1018   1965
(Arranged and conducted by Nelson Riddle) Moonlight Becomes You/Moon Song/Moonlight Serenade/Reaching For The Moon/I Wished On The Moon/Oh You Crazy Moon/The Moon Got In My Eyes/Moonlight Mood/Moon Love/The Moon Was Yellow

SINATRA AT THE SANDS/2FS 1019   1966
(In concert with Count Basie and his Orchestra) Come Fly With Me/I've Got A Crush On You/I've Got You Under My Skin/The Shadow Of Your Smile/Street Of Dreams/One For My Baby/Fly Me To The Moon/One

O'Clock Jump (Instrumental)/Monologue/You Make Me Feel So Young/All Of Me (Instrumental)/The September Of My Years/Get Me To The Church On Time/It Was A Very Good Year/Don't Worry 'Bout Me/Makin' Whoopee (Instrumental)/Where Or When/Angel Eyes/My Kind Of Town/Monologue/My Kind Of Town

THAT'S LIFE/FS 1020   1965-66
(Arranged and conducted by Ernie Freeman) That's Life/I Will Wait For You/Somewhere My Love/Sand And Sea/What Now My Love/Winchester Cathedral/Give Her Love/Tell Her You Love Her Each Day/The Impossible Dream/You're Gonna Hear From Me

FRANCIS ALBERT SINATRA & ANTONIO CARLOS JOBIM/FS 1021   1967
(Arranged and conducted by Claus Ogerman) The Girl From Ipanema (with Antonio Carlos Jobim)/Dindi/Change Partners/Quiet Nights Of Quiet Stars/Meditation/If You Never Come To Me/How Insensitive (with Antonio Carlos Jobim)/I Concentrate On you (with Antonio Carlos Jobim)/Baubles Bangles And Beads (with Antonio Carlos Jobim)/Once I Loved

FRANK SINATRA AND THE WORLD WE KNEW/FS 1022   1967
The World We Knew/Somethin' Stupid (with Nancy Sinatra)/This Is My Love/Born Free/Don't Sleep In The Subway/This Town/This Is My Song/You Are There/Drinking Again/Some Enchanted Evening

FRANCIS A. AND EDWARD K./FS 1024   1967
(With the Duke Ellington Orchestra, arranged by Billy May) Follow Me/Sunny/All I Need Is The Girl/Indian Summer/I Like The Sunrise/Yellow Days/Poor Butterfly/Come Back To Me

FRANK SINATRA'S GREATEST HITS!/FS 1025   1964-67
Strangers In The Night/Summer Wind/It Was A Very Good Year/Somewhere In Your Heart/Forget Domani/Somethin' Stupid (with Nancy Sinatra)/That's Life/Tell Her You Love Her Each Day/The World We Knew/When Somebody Loves You/This Town/Softly As I Leave You

THE SINATRA FAMILY WISH YOU A HAPPY CHRISTMAS/FS 1026   1968
(Arranged and conducted by Nelson Riddle, except one track) I Wouldn't Trade Christmas/It's Such A Lonely Time Of Year/Some Children See Him/O Bambino/The Bells Of Christmas/Whatever Happened To Christmas/Santa Claus Is Coming To Town/Kids/The Christmas Waltz/The Twelve Days of Christmas

CYCLES/FS 1027   1968
(Arranged by Don Costa and conducted by Bill Miller) Rain In My Heart/From Both Sides Now/Little Green

Apples/Pretty Colours/Cycles/Wandering/By The Time I Get To Phoenix/Moody River/My Way Of Life/Gentle On My Mind

MY WAY/FS 1029   1968-69
(Arranged and conducted by Don Costa) Watch What Happens/Didn't We/Hallelujah I Love Her So/Yesterday/All My Tomorrows/My Way/A Day In The Life Of A Fool/For Once In My Life/If You Go Away/Mrs. Robinson

A MAN ALONE/FS 1030   1969
(Arranged and conducted by Don Costa) A Man Alone/Night/I've Been To Town/From Promise To Promise/The Single Man/The Beautiful Strangers/Lonesome Cities/Love's Been Good To Me/Empty Is/Out Beyond The Window/Some Travelling Music/A Man Alone

WATERTOWN/FS 1031   1969
Watertown/Goodbye/For A While/Michael And Peter/I Would Be In Love Anyway/Elizabeth/What A Funny Girl You Used To Be/What's Now Is Now/She Says/The Train

FRANK SINATRA'S GREATEST HITS VOLUME 2/RSLP 1032 (Not released in the USA)   1963-69
The Shadow Of Your Smile/Yesterday/Blue Lace/For Once In My Life/Born Free/My Way/Little Green Apples/From Both Sides Now/Mrs. Robinson/Call Me Irresponsible/Gentle On My Mind/Love's Been Good To Me

SINATRA AND COMPANY/FS 1033   1969-70
Drinking Water (with Antonio Carlos Jobim)/Someone To Light Up My Life/Triste/Don't Ever Go Away/This Happy Madness (with Antonio Carlos Jobim)/Wave/One Note Samba (with Antonio Carlos Jobim)/I Will Drink The Wine/Close To You/Sunrise In The Morning/Bein' Green/My Sweet Lady/Leaving On A Jet Plane/Lady Day

FRANK SINATRA'S GREATEST HITS VOLUME 2/FS 1034   1968-70
My Way/A Man Alone/Cycles/Bein' Green/Love's Been Good To Me/I'm Not Afraid/Goin' Out Of My Head/Something/What's Now Is Now/Star/The September Of My Years
SINATRA '65/R9 6167   1963-65
Tell Her You Love Her Each Day/Anytime At All/Stay With Me/I Like To Lead When I Dance/You Brought A New Kind Of Love To Me/My Kind Of Town/When Somebody Loves You/Somewhere In Your Heart/I've Never Been In Love Before/When I'm Not Near The Girl I Love/Luck Be A Lady

THE VOICE VOLUME 1/FS 5238   1960-68
The Second Time Around/Tina/Moment To Moment/

I Left My Heart In San Francisco/The Look Of Love/
Little Green Apples/Me And My Shadow (with Sammy
Davis Jr.)/Name It And It's Yours/Nothing But The
Best/Everybody's Twistin'/Forget Domani/Star

THE VOICE VOLUME 2/FS 5240   1962-69
Please Be Kind/My Way/Love's Been Good To Me/
All The Way/The Tender Trap/Out Beyond The
Window/A Man Alone/Didn't We/Forget To
Remember/Fly Me To The Moon/Goin' Out Of My
Head/My Kind Of Town

THE VOICE VOLUME 3/FS 5250   1961-70
Younger Than Springtime/I'm Not Afraid/Life's A
Trippy Thing (with Nancy Sinatra)/Song Of The Sabia/
Feelin' Kinda Sunday (with Nancy Sinatra)/Something/
I Can't Believe I'm Losing You/Somethin' Stupid (with
Nancy Sinatra)/Luck Be A Lady/How Old Am I/
Granada/You're A Lucky Fellow Mr. Smith

THE VOICE VOLUME 4/FS 5283   1962-69
Early American/The House I Live In/Let Us Break
Bread Together (with Bing Crosby)/You Never Had It
So Good (with Bing Crosby)/By The Time I Get To
Phoenix/A Day In The Life Of A Fool/We Open In
Venice (with Dean Martin and Sammy Davis Jr.)/
Charmaine/When I Lost You/Here's To The Losers/
Golden Moment/Shadow Of The Moon

AMERICA I HEAR YOU SINGING/FS 2020   1964
(With Bing Crosby, conducted by Fred Waring)
America I Hear You Singing (Fred Waring)/This Is A
Great Country (Bing Crosby)/The House I Live In/The
Hills Of Home (Fred Waring)/This Is Your Land (Bing
Crosby)/Give Me Your Tired Your Poor (Fred
Waring)/You're A Lucky Fellow Mr. Smith/A Home In
The Meadow (Bing Crosby)/Early American/You
Never Had It So Good (with Bing Crosby)/Let Us
Break Bread Together (with Bing Crosby)/The Stars
And Stripes Forever (Fred Waring)

ROBIN AND THE SEVEN HOODS/FS 2021   1964
(Arranged and conducted by Nelson Riddle) Overture/
My Kind Of Town/All For One And One For All (Peter
Falk)/Don't Be A Do-Badder (Bing Crosby)/Any Man
Who Loves His Mother (Dean Martin)/Style (with Bing
Crosby and Dean Martin)/Mister Booze (with Bing
Crosby, Dean Martin and Sammy Davis Jr.)/I Like To
Lead When I Dance (Sammy Davis Jr.)/ Bang Bang
Charlotte Couldn't Charleston (Chorus)/Give Praise Give
Praise Give Praise (Chorus)/Don't Be A Do-Badder
(with Messrs. Crosby, Martin & Davis)

TWELVE SONGS OF CHRISTMAS/FS 2022   1964
(With Bing Crosby, conducted by Fred Waring) White
Christmas (Fred Waring)/It's Christmas Time Again
(Bing Crosby)/Go Tell It On The Mountain (with Bing

Crosby)/An Old-Fashioned Christmas/When Angels
Sang Of Peace (Fred Waring)/The Little Drummer
Boy/I Heard The Bells On Christmas Day/Do You
Hear What I Hear (Fred Waring)/The Secret Of
Christmas (Bing Crosby)/The Twelve Days Of
Christmas (Fred Waring)/Christmas Candles (Bing
Crosby)/We Wish You The Merriest (with Bing
Crosby)

OL' BLUE EYES IS BACK/FS 2155   1973
(Arranged by Don Costa and Gordon Jenkins,
conducted by Gordon Jenkins) You Will Be My
Music/You're So Right/Winners/Nobody Wins/Send In
The Clowns/Dream Away/Let Me Try Again/There
Used To Be A Ballpark/Noah

SOME NICE THINGS I'VE MISSED/FS 2195   1973-74
(Arranged by Don Costa and Gordon Jenkins) You
Turned My World Around/Sweet Caroline/The
Summer Knows/I'm Gonna Make It All The Way/Tie
A Yellow Ribbon Round The Ole Oak Tree/Satisfy Me
One More Time/If/You Are The Sunshine Of My Life/
What Are You Doing The Rest Of Your Life/Bad Bad
Leroy Brown

SINATRA — THE MAIN EVENT/FS 2207   1974
(In concert with Woody Herman and the Young
Thundering Herd) The Lady Is A Tramp/I Get A Kick
Out Of You/Let Me Try Again/Autumn In New
York/I've Got You Under My Skin/Bad Bad Leroy
Brown/Angel Eyes/You Are The Sunshine Of My Life/
The House I Live In/My Kind Of Town/My Way

I SING THE SONGS/W 5409   1969-76
Empty Tables/The Saddest Thing Of All/A Baby Just
Like You/Christmas Mem'ries/The Only Couple On
The Floor/I Believe I'm Gonna Love You/Anytime/
The Hurt Doesn't Go Away/I Sing The Songs/Shadow
Of The Moon

More Reprise Releases

American Releases

A Man And His Music Part 2/R 5004; Frank Sinatra
Songbook Volume 1/FS 5230; The Frank Sinatra
Songbook Volume 2/2FS 5267

British Releases

Frank/K 64016; Sinatra-Basie/K 44192; Sinatra With
Count Basie/VS 144; With Count Basie/K 34005;
Twelve Songs Of Christmas/R 2022; White Christmas/
K 34013; The Summit/R 5031; The Sinatra Collection/
K 44145; The Reprise Years/K 94003 (4 record set);
Best of Ol' Blue Eyes/K 54042; Portrait Of Sinatra/K
64039

ACKNOWLEDGEMENTS

A book which covers the life of so talented a man necessarily involves the help and co-operation of many individuals and organizations. I am particularly indebted to Lindsay Anderson, Stan Britt, Robin Mayes, Fred Dellar, Arthur Cantor and Gay Haines, who all in various ways helped with the original research of the book; to Beryl Overbury and Dr John Ridgway for their specialist knowledge; Edward Sharp of the Sinatra Music Society for his help, interest and co-operation; and Diana Matias for typing the manuscript. I would also like to thank Gillian Hartnoll and the staff of the British Film Institute library for their help in supplying research material. Passages quoted from *Sinatra* by Robin Douglas-Home and *Sinatra* by Antony Scaduto are reproduced by kind permission of Michael Joseph Limited; from *Sinatra* by Arnold Shaw and *Bogie* by Joe Hyams by kind permission of W.H. Allen Limited.

I would like to thank the following agencies and organizations for the use of photographs from their archives: the National Film Archive, Associated Press, the Bettmann Archive, Camera Press, Keystone Press Agency, Popperfoto, Radio Times Hulton Picture Library, Rex Features, and especially, Stan Britt, Edward Sharp and Dezo Hoffman; and the record and film companies responsible for the release of Frank Sinatra's movies and music: Capitol, Columbia/CBS and Reprise; Columbia Pictures, Warner Brothers, Universal Pictures, United Artists Films, 20th Century Fox, MGM Films, Paramount Films, Embassy Pictures and RKO Pictures. Photographs from the Bettmann Archive are on pages: 26, 28, 29, 30, 35, 37, 47, 58, 75 and 76. It has not been possible in all cases to trace the copyright sources and my publishers would be glad to hear from any such unacknowledged copyright holders.

Finally, I would like to express my gratitude to Nicky Hayden and Ann Geaney for editorial work on the text and photographs; to Chris Lower for designing the book and to Jennie Smith for putting it into practice. I should especially like to thank my publishers Sandra Wake and Terry Porter for their constant help and encouragement, Keith Hutton of Lloyd's Bank for his appreciation of the writer's predicament, and my wife and daughters for their patience and understanding.

John Howlett

BIBLIOGRAPHY

Books on Frank Sinatra
Sinatra: A Biography by Arnold Shaw
Sinatra by Robin Douglas-Home
Sinatra by Antony Scaduto
Sinatra: An Unauthorised Biography by Earl Wilson
The Films of Frank Sinatra by Gene Ringgold
  and Clifford McCarty
The Sinatrafile Part 1 by John Ridgway
The Sinatrafile Part 2 by John Ridgway

Books of general interest
Marilyn by Norman Mailer
The Moon's A Balloon by David Niven
Ava by Charles Higham
Bogie by Joe Hyams
The Hollywood Musical by John Russell-Taylor